Edward Hewitt is a barrister at 5 Stone Buildings in Lincoln's Inn. He has a private client practice with a particular emphasis on inheritance and trust disputes. He is frequently asked to advise on the correct construction of wills and trust instruments. He has also acted in some of the leading recent cases involving the construction and rectification of wills and trust instruments, some of which have included ancillary professional negligence proceedings against the relevant draftsman.

A Practical Guide to the Construction and Rectification of Wills and Trust Instruments

Second Edition

A Practical Guide to the Construction and Rectification of Wills and Trust Instruments

Second Edition

Edward Hewitt, LL.B., B.C.L.
Barrister of Lincoln's Inn

Law Brief Publishing

Published 2023 by Law Brief Publishing, an imprint of Law Brief Publishing Ltd
30 The Parks
Minehead
Somerset
TA24 8BT

www.lawbriefpublishing.com

Paperback: 978-1-916698-26-0

For my wonderful parents, without whom

nothing would have been possible.

CONTENTS

CHAPTER ONE

INTRODUCTION

1.1 The problem

Construction and rectification problems in wills and other trust instruments[1] come in many different shapes and sizes. When considering a provision in a will or other trust instrument which is unclear and/or can be interpreted in different ways, the PRs or trustees, beneficiaries and other interested parties may ask themselves: what did the testator or settlor mean? Alternatively, a provision may be clear on its face, but the particular surrounding circumstances may lead interested parties to ask themselves: is that really what the testator or settlor meant? These sorts of questions are often a good indication that the provision in question may give rise to a construction or a rectification problem.

1.2 Structure of this book: distinction between wills and other trust instruments

Many trusts are created by will. These are usually – and unsurprisingly – referred to as 'will trusts'. A will can therefore itself be a trust instrument. However, there are some important differences between the rules governing the construction and rectification of wills on the one hand, and those governing the construction and rectification of other trust instruments (typically trust deeds by which a settlor settles property on trust during his lifetime) on the other. As a result, this book distinguishes between wills (whether or not they create any will trusts), which are considered in chapters 2 and 3, and other trust instruments (i.e. any

1 Other fertile ground for these problems are contracts and patents. In particular, contractual construction and rectification are huge subjects in their own right, which are beyond the scope of this book.

instrument which creates a trust except a will), which are considered in chapters 4 and 5.

In order to avoid a large amount of unwieldy cross-referencing, each of those four chapters has been written as self-standing. Because there is some similarity and overlap between the topics, this has resulted in some inevitable repetition across the chapters. However, that seemed to be a price worth paying to achieve what it is hoped are four chapters which are clearer and more straightforward to consult.

1.3 A bit of history

As this is intended to be a practical guide, and this particular section is not at all practical, it has been kept short. However, it has been included because, as with most legal doctrines, some knowledge of history is likely to help better understand how we have got to the current position, and why.

Wills and certain other trust instruments have a long history of being documents which are required by law to be in writing. Section 9 of the Wills Act 1837 has required wills to be "*in writing*" (save for some limited exceptions) for nearly 200 years, but the requirement can be traced back a further 300 years to the Statute of Wills of 1540. Similarly, sections 52 and 53 of the Law of Property Act 1925 impose some familiar writing requirements, the origin of which dates back to the Statute of Frauds of 1677. As a result, the courts have had to grapple with problematic drafting in wills and trust instruments for centuries. Unsurprisingly, the case law on the subject is enormous.

For the practitioner, one of the important points to emerge from history is a shift in the courts' approach to construction from what can be described as a strict literalist approach to a more purposive approach. A large amount of judicial and academic ink has been devoted to this topic,[2]

2 For more in-depth treatment of this interesting and difficult topic, see e.g. *Theobald on Wills*, 19th ed., chapter 18; *Williams on Wills*, 11th ed., chapter 50; *Lewin on Trusts*, 20th ed., chapter 7; Kessler, *Drafting Trusts*

which continues to be controversial. It will only be considered briefly – and thus no doubt overly-simplistically – here.

The shift can be illustrated by contrasting the following two quotes, the first from 1833, the second from 2014:

> *In expounding a will, the Court is to ascertain, not what the testator actually intended, as contradistinguished from what his words express, but what is the meaning of the words he has used. I consider it doubtful what the testator actually meant should be done. But I have no doubt as to the meaning of the words used by him.*[3]
>
> *19. When interpreting a contract, the court is concerned to find the intention of the party or parties, and it does this by identifying the meaning of the relevant words, (a) in the light of (i) the natural and ordinary meaning of those words, (ii) the overall purpose of the document, (iii) any other provisions of the document, (iv) the facts known or assumed by the parties at the time that the document was executed, and (v) common sense, but (b) ignoring subjective evidence of any party's intentions.*
>
> *20. When it comes to interpreting wills, it seems to me that the approach should be the same. Whether the document in question is a commercial contract or a will, the aim is to identify the intention of the party or parties to the document by interpreting the words used in their documentary, factual and commercial context.*[4]

The more strict literalist approach had generated several rules of construction which compelled judges to interpret particular words in a particular way, irrespective of context and no matter how absurd the

---

and Will Trusts, 14th ed., chapter 4; Kerridge, *Parry and Kerridge: The Law of Succession*, 13th ed., chapter 10.

3 *Doe v Gwillim* (1833) 5 B & Ad 122 *per* Parke J.

4 *Marley v Rawlings* [2015] AC 129 *per* Lord Neuberger.

result.

A landmark moment in the shift away from this approach was the House of Lords decision in *Perrin v Morgan*[5] in January 1943. Emily Morgan died in 1939 leaving a home-made will by which she gifted some cottages, and then included the following provision: "*all moneys of which I die possessed of shall be shared by my nephews and nieces now living*". The issue was whether the word "*moneys*" included the testatrix's investments, which represented the bulk of her estate.

At first instance, Farwell J followed a well-established rule of construction dating back to 1725[6] that, unless the context allowed a wider construction, "*money*" included only cash or currency in a testator's possession or due to him (such as sums on current or deposit account at a bank). As the context did not allow a wider construction on the facts, a partial intestacy arose in relation to the investments.

The Court of Appeal felt it had no option but to uphold Farwell J's decision because of previous binding authority.[7] It did so reluctantly, describing the rule as "*a blot on our jurisprudence*" and commenting that it had been "*said more than once by judges, members of the profession and laymen, that it defeats the intention of the testatrix*".

The House of Lords unanimously allowed the appeal. Although the result was unanimous, the different members of the Committee reached it in different ways. Perhaps the most colourful speech was that of Lord Atkin, who in his inimitable style held:

> "*The result of your Lordships' decision will be to relieve judges in the future from the thraldom, often I think self-imposed, of judgments in other cases believed to constrain them to give a meaning to wills which they know to be contrary to the testator's intention. [...] I anticipate*

5 [1943] AC 399.

6 *In re Shelmer* (1725) Gilb 200.

7 [1942] Ch 345.

> *with satisfaction that henceforth the group of ghosts of dissatisfied testators who, according to a late Chancery judge, wait on the other bank of the Styx to receive the judicial personages who have misconstrued their wills, may be considerably diminished. It will be a relief to the whole legal profession that at last what the Master of the Rolls rightly called a blot on our jurisprudence has been removed.*"[8]

Although this shift has not been linear,[9] in general terms it can be said that the courts have tried to free themselves somewhat from the shackles of the 'strict literalist' approach and nowadays can adopt a fairly liberal and flexible approach to construction (where the circumstances allow it). This more liberal approach has also had an impact on the development of the doctrine of rectification, as discussed in the next section.

Another important historical point in relation to the rectification of wills is that prior to the enactment of the Administration of Justice Act 1982, it seems the courts had no power to rectify a will. Therefore this jurisdiction, and the case law which explores its limits, is still relatively young.

1.4 Relationship between construction and rectification

It is now tolerably clear that the courts will generally approach a drafting problem by deciding its correct construction first, and only then moving on to consider whether the document should be rectified (if that issue arises at all).[10]

---

8 [1943] AC 399 at 415.

9 For a notable example of literalism prevailing in the Court of Appeal nearly 20 years after *Perrin v Morgan*, see *Re Rowland* [1963] Ch 1. The decision led to a large amount of correspondence, most of it critical, in *The Times*: see Albery, *Coincidence and the Construction of Wills*, (1963) 26 MLR 353.

10 See e.g. *Parkinson v Fawson* [2009] EWHC 1953 (Ch) at [5], *Burnard v Burnard* [2014] EWHC 340 (Ch) at [61]-[66], *Slattery v Jagger* [2015] EWHC 3976 (Ch) at [56], *Reading v Reading* [2015] EWHC 946 (Ch)

In relation to wills, this follows from the 3-stage approach to rectification identified in *Re Segelman*:[11]

> *The subsection [viz. section 20(1) of the Administration of Justice Act 1982] requires the court to examine three questions. First, what were the testator's intentions with regard to the dispositions in respect of which rectification is sought. Secondly, whether the will is so expressed that it fails to carry out those intentions. Thirdly, whether the will is expressed as it is in consequence of either (a) a clerical error or (b) a failure on the part of someone to whom the testator has given instructions in connection with his will to understand those instructions.*

The second question requires the court to construe the will. Only then will the court be able to determine whether there is a mismatch between the testator's intentions (i.e. the answer to the first question) and the effect of the will when properly construed (i.e. the answer to the second question).

There is authority for the proposition that the same approach applies in relation to other trust instruments.[12] In *Kevern v Ayers*[13] the court refused to rectify a deed of variation where the parties had asked it not to determine its construction first because that issue was to be determined by the tax tribunal. The court described the approach as "*unreal*"[14] and indicated that the separation between construction and rectification was "*essentially artificial*".[15]

---

at [40]. See also *Jump v Lister* [2016] EWHC 2160 (Ch), where only a will construction claim was advanced.

11 [1996] Ch 171. This is considered in more detail in chapter 3.

12 See e.g. *Millar v Millar* [2018] EWHC 1926 (Ch) at [16].

13 [2014] EWHC 165 (Ch).

14 [2014] EWHC 165 (Ch) at [12].

15 [2014] EWHC 165 (Ch) at [11].

However, in cases involving instruments other than wills, the court may be asked to decide whether to rectify the instrument without deciding its construction first.[16] This tends to happen where the rectification claim is considered to be very strong on the merits. If the circumstances justify it, this approach has the advantage of avoiding the "*mental gymnastics that are required to ensure the evidence of subjective intent [which is admissible in relation to a rectification claim] is disregarded when dealing with the issue of construction*".[17]

Although the approach of (usually) determining construction first and then rectification appears well settled as a matter of authority, it is right to point out that its correctness has been questioned by some academics.[18]

1.5 Miscellaneous

References to the male singular are used for ease and to avoid a repetitive overuse of "he or she" and "his or her". Personal representatives are referred to as "PRs". In chapters 2 and 3, references to PRs should be read as references to "PRs or trustees, as the case may be" (unless the context requires otherwise).

Unless otherwise stated, all references to the Chancery Guide are to the July 2022 edition as updated in October 2022. I have attempted to state the law as at 31 May 2023.

---

16 See e.g. *Re Hampel Discretionary Trust* [2012] EWHC 2395 (Ch), *Merchant Navy Officers Pension Fund Trustees v Watkins* [2013] EWHC 4741 (Ch) and *Re Chas A Blatchford & Sons Ltd Group Pension Scheme* [2019] EWHC 2743 (Ch).

17 *A v D* [2017] EWHC 2222 (Ch) at [30]. In *Re Chas A Blatchford & Sons Ltd Group Pension Scheme* [2019] EWHC 2743 (Ch) Chief Master Marsh described construction and rectification as "*two separate and conflicting exercises*" (at [18]).

18 See Kerridge, *Parry and Kerridge: The Law of Succession*, 13th ed., at 10-02.

In the conventional way, the responsibility for any error or omission – as well as for any offence my examples might cause to opera purists – is solely mine.

CHAPTER TWO

CONSTRUCTION OF WILLS

2.1 The law

Entire books have been written on the construction of wills,[19] and a large part of both *Theobald on Wills*[20] and *Williams on Wills*[21] is devoted to the construction of particular clauses, phrases and words in wills. It is beyond the scope of this short guide to attempt to consider this large subject in a similar level of detail. Instead, what follows is a summary of the key principles which apply to the construction of wills generally. For a more in-depth analysis of these principles and for guidance on how particular words and expressions have been construed in previous cases, reference should be made to the works mentioned above.

In *Marley v Rawlings*[22] the Supreme Court explained the modern approach to the construction of wills in a passage which is worth citing in full:

> *19. When interpreting a contract, the court is concerned to find the intention of the party or parties, and it does this by identifying the meaning of the relevant words, (a) in the light of (i) the natural and ordinary meaning of those words, (ii) the overall purpose of the document, (iii) any other provisions of the document, (iv) the facts known or assumed by the parties at the time that the document was*

19 See e.g. Kerridge, *Hawkins on the Construction of Wills*, 5th ed.

20 *Theobald on Wills*, 19th ed., Section D, chapters 17 to 36.

21 *Williams on Wills*, 11th ed., volume 1, Parts J to M.

22 [2014] UKSC 2.

executed, and (v) common sense, but (b) ignoring subjective evidence of any party's intentions. [...]

20. When it comes to interpreting wills, it seems to me that the approach should be the same. Whether the document in question is a commercial contract or a will, the aim is to identify the intention of the party or parties to the document by interpreting the words used in their documentary, factual and commercial context. [...]

23. [...] the well known suggestion of James LJ in Boyes v Cook (1880) 14 Ch D 53, 56, that, when interpreting a will, the court should "place [itself] in [the testator's] arm-chair", is consistent with the approach of interpretation by reference to the factual context.

24. However, there is now a highly relevant statutory provision relating to the interpretation of wills, namely section 21 of the 1982 Act ("section 21"). Section 21 is headed "Interpretation of wills—general rules as to evidence", and is in the following terms:

> *"(1) This section applies to a will— (a) in so far as any part of it is meaningless; (b) in so far as the language used in any part of it is ambiguous on the face of it; (c) in so far as evidence, other than evidence of the testator's intention, shows that the language used in any part of it is ambiguous in the light of surrounding circumstances.*
>
> *"(2) In so far as this section applies to a will extrinsic evidence, including evidence of the testator's intention, may be admitted to assist in its interpretation."*

25. In my view, section 21(1) confirms that a will should be interpreted in the same way as a contract, a notice or a patent, namely as summarised in para 19 above. In particular, section 21(1)(c) shows that "evidence" is admissible when construing a will, and that that includes the "surrounding circumstances". However, section 21(2) goes rather further. It indicates that, if one or more of the three requirements

> *set out in section 21(1) is satisfied, then direct evidence of the testator's intention is admissible, in order to interpret the will in question.*
>
> *26. Accordingly, as I see it, save where section 21(1) applies, a will is to be interpreted in the same way as any other document, but, in addition, in relation to a will, or a provision in a will, to which section 21(1) applies, it is possible to assist its interpretation by reference to evidence of the testator's actual intention (eg by reference to what he told the drafter of the will, or another person, or by what was in any notes he made or earlier drafts of the will which he may have approved or caused to be prepared).*

This authoritative statement has been followed in several subsequent first instance decisions.[23]

It is suggested that the court's approach can be broken down into three

---

23 See e.g. *Burnard v Burnard* [2014] EWHC 340 (Ch), *Re Huntley* [2014] EWHC 547 (Ch), *Re Freud* [2014] EWHC 2577 (Ch), *Reading v Reading* [2015] EWHC 946 (Ch), *Re Harte* [2015] EWHC 2351 (Ch), *Guthrie v Morel* [2015] EWHC 3172 (Ch), *Slattery v Jagger* [2015] EWHC 3976 (Ch), *Royal Society v Robinson* [2015] EWHC 3442 (Ch), *Jump v Lister* [2016] EWHC 2160 (Ch), *Re Aspinall* [2017] EWHC 454 (Ch), *Hives v Machin* [2017] EWHC 1414 (Ch), *Re Bathurst* [2018] EWHC 21 (Ch), *Re Wippell* [2018] EWHC 730 (Ch), *Tish v Olley* [2018] EWHC 1069 (Ch), *MacIntyre v Oliver* [2018] EWHC 3094 (Ch), *Jeffreys v Scruton* [2020] EWHC 536 (Ch), *Phoenix v Phoenix* [2020] EWHC 1409 (Ch), *Wales v Dixon* [2020] EWHC 1979 (Ch), *Knipe v British Racing Drivers' Motor Sport Charity* [2020] EWHC 3295 (Ch), *Burns v Bean* [2021] EWHC 838 (Ch), *Re Thomas* [2021] EWHC 937 (Ch), *Re Nodes* [2021] EWHC 1057 (Ch), *Almond v Goff* [2021] EWHC 1703 (Ch), *Equiom (Isle of Man) Ltd v Velarde* [2021] EWHC 1528 (Ch), *Sangha v Sangha* [2021] EWHC 1599 (Ch) (overturned on appeal: [2022] EWHC 2157 (Ch)), *Royal Commonwealth Society for the Blind v Beasant* [2021] EWHC 2315 (Ch), *Re Townsend* [2021] EWHC 3079 (Ch), *Re Bracey* [2022] EWHC 359 (Ch) and *Re McKay* [2023] EWHC 642 (Ch).

stages:[24]

(a) At the first stage, the court will identify the meaning of the relevant words in the light of: (i) the natural and ordinary meaning of those words, (ii) the overall purpose of the will, (iii) any other provisions of the will, (iv) the facts known or assumed by the testator at the time the will was executed, and (v) common sense.[25] In doing so, at this first stage the court cannot take into account any extrinsic evidence of the testator's subjective intention.[26] In the case of a professionally prepared will, the most common type of such evidence will be the draftsman's attendance note of the meeting(s) at which the testator gave instructions. As the judge pointed out in *Re Freud*,[27] "*To lay people involved in a single piece of litigation, this may seem surprising. Suppose a testator gives clear and unequivocal instructions in writing as to what he wants to achieve by his will, his solicitor sends him a draft will with a covering letter explaining how the solicitor has sought to reflect those intentions in the draft will, and the testator signs the will and returns it to the solicitor with a letter saying that he is happy that his intentions have been achieved? Some might think all that a good aid to interpretation*". There is some apparently conflicting case law on whether the testator's previous wills are part of the (admissible) 'factual matrix' or are (inadmissible) evidence of his subjective intention.[28] Evidence

---

24 See e.g. *Reading v Reading* [2015] EWHC 946 (Ch) at [40]-[49]. In *Re Bracey* [2022] EWHC 359 (Ch), the court treated the second and third stages as one (i.e. the second stage), and treated rectification as the third stage: see [17]-[22].

25 *Marley v Rawlings* [2014] UKSC 2 at [19] (cited in the text above).

26 See e.g. *Burns v Bean* [2021] EWHC 838 (Ch) at [24]-[25] and *Re Bracey* [2022] EWHC 359 (Ch) at [18].

27 [2014] EWHC 2577 (Ch) at [15].

28 In *Wales v Dixon* [2020] EWHC 1979 (Ch), Master Teverson held that the testator and his wife's prior wills "*are part of the surrounding circumstances and background facts known to the [testator]*" and rejected the submission that they were "*inadmissible as being evidence of the Deceased's*

subsequent to the making of the will is not part of the surrounding circumstances and is therefore inadmissible.[29]

(b) At the second stage, the court will consider whether any of the three gateways in section 21 of the Administration of Justice Act 1982 ("AJA") is engaged. Those three gateways are:

  (i) any part of the will is meaningless (section 21(1)(a) AJA);

  (ii) the language used in any part of the will is ambiguous on the face of it (section 21(1)(b) AJA);[30]

  (iii) evidence, other than evidence of the testator's intention, shows that the language used in any part of the will is ambiguous in the light of surrounding circumstances (section 21(1)(c) AJA).

It is important to note that section 21(1)(c) AJA in particular makes it clear that at this second stage the court is still not permitted to take into account any extrinsic evidence of the testator's subjective intention; only if the court decides that one of the gateways is open will such evidence become admissible.

(c) If at the second stage the court concludes that one of the section 21 gateways is engaged, then at this third stage the court may take into account "*extrinsic evidence, including evidence as to the testator's*

---

intention" (at [23]). On the other hand, in *Burns v Bean* [2021] EWHC 838 (Ch), Master Clark held that the testatrix's "*intentions as manifested in her [two previous] will*" were inadmissible "*insofar as it is advances as evidence of her subjective intention in making [the will in question]*" (at [42]).

29 *Wales v Dixon* [2020] EWHC 1079 (Ch) at [31].

30 As to the meaning of "ambiguous", the court in *Jeffreys v Scruton* [2020] EWHC 536 (Ch) explained at [18]: "*The language is ambiguous if it can reasonably be interpreted in more than one way or the words used can reasonably be given more than one meaning.*"

intention" to "*assist in [the] interpretation*" of the will. As indicated above, in the case of a professionally prepared will, this will typically be in the form of the attendance note of the draftsman which records the testator's instructions, and perhaps any other contemporaneous document which records the testator's intentions.[31] Taking that evidence into account may reinforce the construction the court had already reached at the first stage,[32] or may lead to a different one. On the other hand, if none of the section 21 gateways is engaged, then there will be no third stage and instead the court will construe the will in the accordance with the conclusion it had reached at the first stage.

Although each case inevitably turns on its own particular facts, some of the decisions which have followed *Marley v Rawlings* illustrate the flexibility of the court's approach to construction (where the circumstances allow it). For example:

(a) In *Reading v Reading*[33] a reference to "*issue of my mine*" was construed as including the testator's step-children,[34] even though the court observed that "*the ordinary and natural meaning of the word "issue" does not in its ordinary and natural meaning include*

---

31 In *Marley v Rawlings* [2014] UKSC 2 at [26] (cited in the text above) Lord Neuberger indicated that evidence of the testator's intentions could for example be evidence of "*what he told the drafter of the will, or another person, or [...] what was in any notes he made or earlier drafts of the will which he may have approved or caused to be prepared*".

32 As happened e.g. in *Reading v Reading* [2015] EWHC 946 (Ch) (see [49]) and *Royal Society v Robinson* [2015] EWHC 3442 (Ch), in which the judge commented that if extrinsic evidence had not been admissible under section 21 AJA he "*would then have found it much more difficult to conclude with the same confidence that I have that the proper construction of the Will would be that which I have adopted*" (at [35]).

33 [2015] EWHC 946 (Ch).

34 [2015] EWHC 946 (Ch) at [47].

stepchildren".[35]

(b) In *Slattery v Jagger*[36] the court read the words "*to my Wife*" into a specific devise of a property from which they had accidentally been omitted by a process of construction.[37]

(c) In *Royal Society v Robinson*[38] a reference to "*the United Kingdom*" was construed as including the Channel Islands and the Isle of Man,[39] even though the court observed that "*There is no doubt that the technical meaning of "United Kingdom" would not include Jersey in the Channel Islands or the Isle of Man*".[40]

However, it must be borne in mind that this flexibility has limits. For example, in *Jeffreys v Scruton*,[41] after referring to *Marley v Rawlings*, the court pointed out that "*in the absence of rectification, the courts cannot re-write a will. It "...is not the function of a court of construction to improve upon or perfect testamentary dispositions. The function of the court is to give effect to the dispositions actually made as appearing expressly or by necessary implication from the language of the will applied to the surrounding circumstances of the case",* Re Bailey [1951] Ch 407 *at 421 (Jenkins LJ). This is achieved by interpreting the words used in their proper context so as to give effect to a testatrix's apparent intention rather than by speculating about her intention. The testatrix's intention must be collected from the whole will and effect should generally be given to every word. Consistently with the guidance in Williams on Wills (10th edn) at Para 50.7, legal words should generally be construed according to their legal or technical meaning,*

35 [2015] EWHC 946 (Ch) at [41].

36 [2015] EWHC 3976 (Ch).

37 [2015] EWHC 3976 (Ch) at [93].

38 [2015] EWHC 3442 (Ch).

39 [2015] EWHC 3442 (Ch) at [34].

40 [2015] EWHC 3442 (Ch) at [26].

41 [2020] EWHC 536 (Ch).

particularly where the will has been prepared by a lawyer".

In *Re Hand*[42] the court accepted that human rights considerations can be relevant to the construction of a will. The reference in a 1946 will to "*children*" *prima facie* had to be construed as excluding adopted children as a result of the Adoption of Children Act 1926, which treated adopted children as children of their natural, rather than their adoptive, parents for succession purposes. Although that position had been reversed in 1950, it had been preserved in relation to existing dispositions. However, the court concluded that it was required by the Human Rights Act 1998 to read down the relevant preserving legislation,[43] and to construe "*children*" as including two adopted children so as not to breach their human rights.[44]The full impact of this decision is yet to be explored.[45]

It is also worth bearing in mind that several provisions of the Wills Act 1837 contain important statutory rules of construction. Those which are engaged most frequently are:

(a) section 18A, which provides that where after a will is made the testator's marriage is terminated by dissolution or annulment, the will is to be construed as if the testator's former spouse had died on the date of the dissolution or annulment, unless a contrary intention appears;

---

42 [2017] EWHC 533 (Ch).

43 Paragraph 6(1) of Schedule 2 to the Adoption Act 1976.

44 The relevant human rights were the right to respect for private and family life, protected by article 8 of the European Convention on Human Rights, and the right not to be discriminated against on the on the ground of "*birth or other status*", protected by article 14.

45 See e.g. *PQ v RS* [2019] EWHC 1643 (Ch), in which Chief Master Marsh expressed no view as to whether *Re Hand* had been correctly decided (at [24]). See also *Re JC Druce Settlement* [2019] EWHC 3701 (Ch) and *Goodrich v AB* [2022] EWHC 81 (Ch), in which *Re Hand* was followed.

(b) section 18C, which contains equivalent provisions in relation to the dissolution or annulment of a civil partnership;

(c) section 24, which provides that a will must be construed to "*speak and take effect as if it had been executed immediately before the death of the testator*", unless a contrary intention appears;

(d) section 33, which may prevent a gift to a child or children of the testator from lapsing where such child or children have predeceased the testator leaving issue, unless a contrary intention appears.[46]

Questions of construction are governed by the system of law intended by the testator, which is presumed to be the law of his domicile at the time when the will is made, unless a contrary intention appears from the will.[47]

2.2 Practice and procedure

2.2.1 Who is affected?

The first question PRs should ask themselves when faced with a construction problem is: who is affected by it?

The reason for this is that construction problems have a right answer – and one, or possibly several, wrong ones. Therefore PRs should not try to decide themselves what they think the answer is and then act on that basis. If they do and if they proceed on the basis of an answer which later turns out to be the wrong one, they can be personally liable for *devastavit* (i.e. for having administered and/or distributed the estate incorrectly).

It follows that the main concern for PRs faced with a construction problem is to ensure that before they take any step based on a particular construction they protect themselves from potential personal liability for

46 Section 33 and the existence of a contrary intention were considered in *Hives v Machin* [2017] EWHC 1414 (Ch) and *Burns v Bean* [2021] EWHC 838 (Ch).

47 See e.g. *Clarke-Sullivan v Clarke-Sullivan* [2021] EWHC 4 (Ch) at [37].

devastavit. They can do this by obtaining either the binding consent of all affected beneficiaries or authorisation from the court. To get to that position, the PRs will first have to establish who the affected beneficiaries are.

Needless to say, the answer to this will depend on the particular circumstances, and can vary widely. In simple terms, the way to go about ascertaining the affected beneficiaries is to consider the different possible constructions (which may be two or more) and then consider who would benefit under each possible construction, as illustrated by the following examples.

Example 1

Violetta's will gives her country estate to "*my husband Alfredo*", and the residue of her estate to the British Thoracic Society. At her death Violetta has been in a cohabiting relationship with Alfredo for 15 years, but the couple never married.

There are two possible constructions: either the gift to Alfredo takes effect or it does not. The affected beneficiaries are therefore Alfredo and the British Thoracic Society.

Example 2

Siegmund dies leaving a will which includes the following specific gift: "*I give my prized sword Nothung to my son absolutely free of tax*". The residuary estate is left to Siegmund's wife Sieglinde. Siegmund was survived by two sons: Siegfried, who was the child of Siegmund's marriage to Sieglinde; and Trevor, who was born from an extra-marital affair Siegmund had with a babysitter.

There are four possible constructions:

(a) the gift takes effect and passes Nothung to Siegfried;

(b) the gift takes effect and passes Nothung to Trevor;

(c) the gift takes effect and passes Nothung to both Siegfried and Trevor; or

(d) the gift fails and Nothung falls into residue and passes to Sieglinde.

The affected beneficiaries are therefore:

(a) Siegfried;

(b) Trevor; and

(c) Sieglinde.

Example 3

By his will, Buoso left his entire estate to "*those inhabitants of Fucecchio who were kind to me during my lifetime, if more than one in equal shares absolutely*".

There are two possible constructions:

(a) the gift takes effect and passes the estate to the inhabitants of Fucecchio who were kind to Buoso during his lifetime; or

(b) the gift fails and an intestacy arises.

The affected beneficiaries are therefore:

(a) the inhabitants of Fucecchio who were kind to Buoso during his lifetime; and

(b) Buoso's intestacy beneficiaries.

If the construction problem affects the amount of tax payable, some thought should be given to whether it is also necessary to involve HMRC.

The corollary to the above is that PRs should bear in mind that they have no personal interest in how the construction problem is resolved between the affected beneficiaries. It is not for the PRs to try to second guess what the testator might have intended, nor to form a view as to which of the affected beneficiaries is more 'worthy' or 'deserving'. The PRs should remain neutral and impartial, and simply do what they are told, either by a unanimous binding agreement reached by all of the affected beneficiaries, or by the court.[48]

2.2.2 Can the problem be resolved by agreement?

In principle, a construction problem can be resolved by the unanimous agreement of all of the beneficiaries affected by it. Therefore, once the PRs have identified all of the affected beneficiaries, the next question they should ask themselves is: can the problem be resolved by agreement?

Suppose that in Example 1 above the British Thoracic Society agrees that Violetta's country estate should pass to Alfredo. They are the only two parties affected by the uncertainty.[49] If they are able to agree what should happen, then provided Alfredo is a capacitous adult, they can resolve the construction problem between themselves without having to go to court. The PRs' only concern will be to ensure that the agreement is properly documented so that they cannot later be criticised by the British Thoracic Society or Alfredo for acting in accordance with it.

Resolving the problem by agreement is usually significantly cheaper and quicker than asking the court to do so. As indicated above, if the construction problem affects the amount of tax payable, some thought should be given to whether it is also necessary to obtain the agreement of HMRC. Typical examples are cases in which the problem concerns whether property passes to an IHT-exempt beneficiary (such as a

48 See e.g. *Re Aspinall* [2017] EWHC 454 (Ch), in which the executors as claimants brought the proceedings and then let the rival beneficiaries (who had been joined as defendants) advance the two construction arguments (see [11]); and *Wales v Dixon* [2020] EWHC 1979 (Ch), in which the PRs adopted the same neutral stance and the court dispensed with their attendance at the disposal hearing (see [4]).

49 This assumes the estate is sufficiently solvent for there to be residue.

surviving spouse or charity). HMRC's involvement will generally not be required if an agreement is reached and implemented by an instrument which is executed within two years of the testator's death, because in such cases it should be possible for the affected beneficiaries to determine the tax consequences.[50] However, if an agreement is only reached or implemented more than two years after the testator's death and affects (or purports to affect) the amount of tax payable, HMRC's agreement is likely to be required.

Suppose that in Example 2 above, Siegmund, Trevor and Sieglinde agree that Nothung should pass as part of residue to Sieglinde. As Sieglinde is the surviving spouse and thus an IHT-exempt beneficiary, whereas Siegmund and Trevor are sons and are not, this could affect the amount of IHT payable. It may therefore be necessary to involve HMRC.

In practice, construction problems are generally only resolved by agreement in the most straightforward cases. Two reasons can be identified for this. First, beneficiaries often have different views about what the testator did or did not intend, and are therefore simply unable to reach an agreement. Secondly, to avoid exposing themselves to potential personal liability to disappointed beneficiaries, PRs must obtain the binding consent of all of the beneficiaries who are affected by the construction problem. This will not be possible if the construction problem affects beneficiaries who are minors, unborn, lack capacity and/or cannot be found. As those types of beneficiaries are unable to give the PRs their binding consent, in cases in which they are affected, the court's intervention is likely to be necessary.

A useful way to explore whether the construction problem can be resolved by agreement is for the PRs, who are often the first to spot the problem, to obtain advice from counsel on the construction problem and then share that advice with all affected beneficiaries and canvass their views. If

50 By availing themselves of the 'reading back' mechanisms in section 142 of the Inheritance Tax Act 1984 and/or section 62 of the Taxation of Chargeable Gains Act 1992.

the will incorporates clause 12.3 of the STEP Standard Provisions (2nd edition), the PRs should consider obtaining the advice of counsel of "*at least five years' standing*" if they want to rely on the protection from liability afforded by that clause.[51]

This process should help both the PRs and all the affected beneficiaries to understand their respective positions, which in turn should inform all involved whether there is any hope of the construction problem being resolved by agreement and, if so, how this might be achieved. Depending on the circumstances, the affected beneficiaries may wish to try to reach an agreement by, for example, negotiating in correspondence, at a round-table meeting or at a mediation.

As indicated above, PRs should bear in mind that they have no personal interest in how the construction problem is resolved between the affected beneficiaries. Their focus should be to ensure:

(a) that they obtain the binding consent of all affected beneficiaries so

---

51 Clause 12.3 and the following two clauses provide:

12.3 A Trustee shall not be liable for acting in accordance with the advice of counsel, of at least five years' standing, with respect to the Trust. The Trustees may in particular conduct legal proceedings in accordance with such advice without obtaining a court order. A Trustee may recover from the Trust Fund any expenses where he has acted in accordance with such advice.

12.4 Clause 12.3 does not apply:

12.4.1 in relation to a Trustee who knows or has reasonable cause to suspect that the advice was given in ignorance of material facts;

12.4.2 if proceedings are pending to obtain the decision of the court on the matter;

12.4.3 in relation to a Trustee who has a personal interest in the subject matter of the advice; or

12.4.4 in relation to a Trustee who has committed a breach of trust relating to the subject matter of the advice.

12.5 Clause 12.3 does not prejudice any right of any Person to follow property or income into the hands of any Person, other than a purchaser, who may have received it.

they are protected from potential personal liability for *devastavit* (i.e. for having distributed to the wrong person); and

(b) that the agreement is one which the PRs can in fact implement. For example, the PRs should consider whether the agreement has tax consequences and, if so, how these should be addressed.

However, if all affected beneficiaries manage to reach a binding agreement which the PRs can implement, it is not for the PRs to 'approve' or 'disapprove' of it in any moral or ethical sense, e.g. on the basis that they think the testator would or would not have liked it. It also follows from this that PRs are generally not required to actively participate in any negotiations between the affected beneficiaries; indeed, PRs should ensure they do not incur unnecessary costs by doing so.

In cases in which professional negligence proceedings against the draftsman have also been threatened or are on foot, it may be sensible to try to compromise those proceedings at the same time.

There are two further tools which can help achieve a pragmatic solution without the court's intervention in a suitable case. The first is the possibility of the PRs agreeing to distribute on a particular basis provided the recipient beneficiaries in return provide the PRs with suitable indemnities, possibly backed by security. Such indemnities would be designed to protect the PRs against the risk that they may be personally liable to disappointed beneficiaries if the basis on which they have distributed subsequently turns out to be wrong. The second is the possibility of obtaining insurance to provide the PRs with that same protection.

Whether either of these tools is a useful one will depend on all of the particular surrounding circumstances. As a rather crude rule of thumb, it is suggested that the greater the financial value of the construction problem, the less likely these tools are to provide a practical solution. This is because the greater the amount of money that turns on the construction problem, the greater the potential liability of the PRs, and thus the more nervous both the beneficiaries and any insurance company will be in providing PRs with adequate protection. Further, in high value cases there is less of a risk of the estate being significantly depleted by the costs involved in making a court application, which might also point towards such an application being the better option.

2.2.3 Professional negligence

If the will was professionally prepared, it may be possible to argue that the construction problem amounts to professional negligence by the draftsman. If so, a professional negligence claim against the draftsman is usually threatened, and sometimes issued, before a construction claim is brought.

Depending on the circumstances, if both the professional negligence claim and the construction claim have merit, the draftsman's insurers might agree to fund the construction claim, particularly if the costs involved in doing so are likely to be lower than their potential exposure in the event the professional negligence claim is successful.[52]

2.2.4 Court intervention: section 48 of the Administration of Justice Act 1985

A construction problem will usually be incapable of resolution by agreement without the court's intervention for one of two reasons (and sometimes both):

(a) all affected beneficiaries cannot reach an agreement; or

(b) all adult capacitous affected beneficiaries have reached an agreement, but the problem also affects beneficiaries who are minors, unborn, lack capacity and/or cannot be found.

Section 48 of the Administration of Justice Act 1985 ("AJA") contains a

52 See e.g. the will rectification case of *Re Bimson* [2010] EWHC 3679 (Ch) at [23].

mechanism which can be useful in the latter situation (but not the former). The section provides:

> ***48.— Power of High Court to authorise action to be taken in reliance on counsel's opinion.***
>
> *(1) Where—*
>
> *(a) any question of construction has arisen out of the terms of a will or a trust; and*
>
> *(b) an opinion in writing given by a person who has a 10 year High Court qualification, within the meaning of section 71 of the Courts and Legal Services Act 1990, has been obtained on that question by the personal representatives or trustees under the will or trust,*
>
> *the High Court may, on the application of the personal representatives or trustees and without hearing argument, make an order authorising those persons to take such steps in reliance on the said opinion as are specified in the order.*
>
> *(2) The High Court shall not make an order under subsection (1) if it appears to the court that a dispute exists which would make it inappropriate for the court to make the order without hearing argument.*

There are two important points to note in relation to this mechanism. First, the procedure cannot be used where "*a dispute exists which would make it inappropriate for the court to make the order without hearing argument*" (section 48(2) AJA). That will generally be the case where two or more affected beneficiaries are actively advancing two or more competing constructions, both of which are "*reasonably tenable*"[53].

53 Paragraph 25.58 of the Chancery Guide. The paragraph, which is set out in full below, provides that the court may order a party who disagreed with the opinion when having "*no reasonably tenable argument [to the] contrary*" to pay "*all or part of any costs thrown away*".

However, it may also be the case where two conflicting opinions have been obtained from two different counsel as to the correct construction and the court feels it cannot resolve the conflict without hearing argument, as in *Greenwold v Pike*.[54]

Secondly, it is important to understand the nature of an order made under section 48 AJA and distinguish it from an order made at the conclusion of a contested construction claim (which is considered in the next section). An order made under section 48 AJA permits the PRs to proceed in accordance with counsel's opinion, and protects them from personal liability for *devastavit* if counsel's opinion later turns out to be wrong. However, it does not require the court to determine the construction problem itself, nor therefore to decide whether counsel's opinion is correct. It is therefore an order which is akin to a *Re Benjamin*[55] order (which authorises PRs to proceed on the footing that certain facts which cannot be established with certainty are correct).[56]

The significance of this is that an order made under section 48 AJA therefore leaves open the possibility that an affected beneficiary may subsequently[57] bring a contested construction claim and the court may at that stage determine that the opinion from counsel (in accordance with which the PRs have proceeded) is wrong. If this were to happen, the PRs will be protected from personal liability for *devastavit* because they have acted as authorised by the court's order (viz. in accordance with counsel's opinion). However, it would be open to the disappointed beneficiary to try to recover from the recipient beneficiaries any property which was distributed to them in accordance with the construction which the court has subsequently determined is wrong (subject to any applicable defences,

---

54 [2007] EWHC 2202 (Ch).

55 [1902] 1 Ch 723.

56 The classic example is an order authorising PRs to distribute the estate on the footing that a beneficiary who cannot be found predeceased the testator (which were the circumstances in *Re Benjamin* itself).

57 E.g. after he has attained majority.

such as laches and limitation).[58]

The question whether the mechanism provided by section 48 AJA should be used despite the fact that it carries this risk is generally answered by weighing up that risk against the costs saving in not having a fully contested construction claim. The mechanism provided by section 48 AJA is likely to be attractive if the estate is small and the capacitous adult beneficiaries are therefore keen to ensure that it is not depleted by a fully contested construction claim and/or the circumstances suggest that the risk of any beneficiary subsequently bringing a challenge is small or negligible. On the other hand, if the estate is large and/or it is thought that there is a serious risk that a beneficiary may subsequently bring a challenge, it may be worth incurring the extra cost of having a fully contested construction claim so as to have the construction problem resolved once and for all. For relatively rare examples of reported decisions in which the High Court made an order under section 48 AJA, see *Re Duffy*[59] and *Clarke-Sullivan v Clarke-Sullivan*.[60]

The CPR contain some procedural rules which apply to a claim for an order under section 48 AJA. Such a claim must be made in the High Court[61] and must be brought in the Chancery Division,[62] i.e. what has now become the Property, Trusts and Probate List (ChD) of the Business and Property Courts. It must be brought by the PRs or trustees[63] and can

58 The leading authority on this difficult topic remains the House of Lords decision in *Ministry of Health v Simpson* [1951] AC 251. In relation to the limitation period applicable to this sort of claim, see *Davies v Sharples* [2006] EWHC 362 (Ch).

59 [2013] EWHC 2395 (Ch).

60 [2021] EWHC 4 (Ch).

61 This is required by section 48(1) AJA itself, which confers jurisdiction to make the relevant order on the High Court.

62 CPR rule 64.1(3).

63 This is required by section 48(1) AJA itself, which refers to "*the application of the personal representatives or trustees*".

be brought either in the Rolls Building in London or in one of the District Registries (Birmingham, Bristol, Cardiff, Leeds, Liverpool, Manchester and Newcastle-upon-Tyne).[64]

Rule 64.3 CPR requires such a claim to be made by way of a CPR Part 8 claim form.[65] Paragraph 5 of CPR Practice Direction 64A provides:

> *A Part 8 claim form for an application by trustees*[66] *under section 48 of the Administration of Justice Act 1985 (power of High Court to authorise action to be taken in reliance on legal opinion) may be issued without naming a defendant, under rule 8.2A. No separate application for permission under rule 8.2A need be made.*[67]

Chapter 25 of the Chancery Guide provides the following detailed procedural guidance, which helpfully lists the topics which need to be addressed in the witness statement filed in support of the claim:[68]

> ***Applications under section 48 of the Administration of Justice Act 1985***
>
> *25.49 The jurisdiction conferred on the High Court by section 48 of the Administration of Justice Act 1985 to authorise action based on a*

64 Paragraph 1.3 of the Chancery Guide. Appendix C to the Chancery Guide ('Chancery Business outside the Rolls Building') contains helpful information regarding Chancery business outside London, including contact details of the various District Registries.

65 CPR rule 64.3 applies to claims under section 48 AJA as a result of CPR rule 64.2(a).

66 CPR rule 64.1(2) makes it clear that "*where appropriate, references to trustees include executors and administrators*".

67 This is confirmed by paragraph 13.37(e) of the Chancery Guide. Consistently with this, CPR rule 64.4 expressly states that its provisions (which govern who should be a party to a claim to which Section I of CPR Part 64 applies) do not apply to a claim under section 48 AJA.

68 This derives (with necessary modifications) from *Practice Direction (Chancery: Construction Summons)* [1987] 1 WLR 251.

written legal opinion about an issue of construction of a trust document may be invoked by trustees where such a question has arisen out of the terms of a trust.

25.50 Whilst the jurisdiction is particularly well suited to construction issues arising in relation to a trust of modest value where a conventional inter partes application would be prohibitively expensive, it may be (and has been) successfully invoked in other cases. It is intended to be used in clear cases only.

25.51 Applications under section 48 of the Administration of Justice Act 1985 should be made by Part 8 claim form (PD 64A 5).

25.52 The claim should be supported by a witness statement to which are exhibited: (a) copies of all relevant documents; (b) instructions to a person with a 10-year High Court qualification within the meaning of the Courts and Legal Services Act 1990 (the 'qualified person'); (c) the qualified person's opinion; and (d) draft terms of the desired order.

25.53 The application is for an order to authorise the trustees to act on the basis of a legal opinion, which may deal with construction issues; it should not seek a decision of the court itself on the construction of any instrument.

25.54 The court may consider that, as a matter of discretion, it would be preferable to have the issue finally and bindingly resolved at a substantive hearing, as opposed to its merely being made the subject of directions to the trustees. This is more likely where conflicting opinions have been expressed by different counsel advising the trustees: see Greenwold v Pike [2007] EWHC 2202 (Ch).

25.55 The witness statement (or exhibits thereto) should state: (a) the reason for the application; (b) the names of all persons who are, or may be, affected by the order sought; (c) all surrounding circumstances admissible and relevant in construing the document; (d) the date of qualification of the qualified person and his or her experience in the construction of trust documents; (e) the approximate value of the fund or property in question; (f) whether it is known to the applicant that a dispute exists and, if so, details of such dispute; and (g) what steps are proposed to be taken in reliance on the opinion.

25.56 The Master will consider the claim, and, if necessary, direct service of notices under CPR 19.8A[69] *or request further information. It is important that the evidence explains how those potentially affected have been identified, and what steps have been taken to consult them on the order sought. If the court is satisfied that the order sought is appropriate, it will be made without a hearing and sent to the claimant.*

25.57 If following service of notices under rule 19.8A[70] *any acknowledgment of service is received, the claimant must apply to the Master (on notice to the parties who have so acknowledged service) for directions. The Master will ordinarily direct that the case proceeds as a Part 8 claim.*

25.58 If on the hearing of the claim the court is of the opinion that any party who entered an acknowledgment of service has no reasonably tenable argument contrary to the qualified person's opinion, in the exercise of the court's discretion it may order such party to pay all or part of any costs thrown away.

Because applications pursuant to section 48 AJA are only suitable in non-contentious cases (as explained above), the incidence of the costs of the proceedings is also likely to be agreed in advance between the PRs and the adult capacitous affected beneficiaries. The usual agreement is likely to be that the costs of the proceedings will be borne by the estate as an administration expense. As the only active parties will be the PRs and the application must be uncontested (because the procedure is otherwise

69 With effect from 6th April 2023, what used to be CPR rule 19.8A became rule 19.13: see rules 1(1) and 12(14) of the Civil Procedure (Amendment) Rules 2023 (SI 2023/105).

70 Ibid.

unsuitable), the costs should be relatively modest.

2.2.5 Court intervention: construction claim in the Chancery Division

If the affected beneficiaries cannot reach an agreement and the mechanism provided by section 48 AJA cannot be used or is considered undesirable,[71] the solution will be to ask the court to resolve the construction problem by way of a construction claim.

Starting the claim

A claim asking the court to resolve a construction problem is a claim "*for the court to determine [a] question arising in (i) the administration of the estate of a deceased person; or (ii) the execution of a trust*" within CPR rule 64.2(a). Indeed, it is highly likely to be one of the types of claims which are listed in paragraph 1(1) of CPR Practice Direction 64A as examples of claims which may be made under CPR rule 64.2(a), viz.:

> *(1) a claim for the determination of any of the following questions –*
>
> *(a) any question as to who is included in any class of persons having –*
>
> *(i) a claim against the estate of a deceased person;*
>
> *(ii) a beneficial interest in the estate of such a person; or*
>
> *(iii) a beneficial interest in any property subject to a trust;*
>
> *(b) any question as to the rights or interests of any person claiming –*
>
> *(i) to be a creditor of the estate of a deceased person;*

71 E.g. because it is desirable to resolve the construction problem once and for all.

(ii) to be entitled under a will or on the intestacy of a deceased person; or

(iii) to be beneficially entitled under a trust;

As a result, Section I of CPR Part 64 applies to such a claim, which in turn means the claim must be made by issuing a CPR Part 8 claim form.[72]

The claim is started by filing a CPR Part 8 claim form and accompanying evidence (considered below). Particulars of claim are not required.[73] Claims brought by CPR Part 8 are automatically allocated to the multi-track.[74]

Claim form N208 must be used.[75] CPR rule 8.2 provides that the claim form must state:

(a) that CPR Part 8 applies;

(b) the question which the claimant wants the court to decide, or the remedy which the claimant is seeking and the legal basis for the claim to that remedy;

(c) if the claim is being made under an enactment, what that enactment is;

(d) if the claimant is claiming in a representative capacity, what that capacity is; and

(e) if the defendant is sued in a representative capacity, what that capacity is.

---

72 CPR rule 64.3. See also paragraph 13.2(a) of the Chancery Guide.

73 CPR rule 8.9(a), which disapplies CPR Part 16; see also paragraph 13.14 of the Chancery Guide.

74 CPR rule 8.9(c); see also paragraph 13.14 of the Chancery Guide.

75 Paragraph 13.6 of the Chancery Guide.

Although in some cases rectification will not be relevant, claims for construction and rectification are often brought in the alternative.[76] A construction problem may also arise in the context of another dispute, such as a claim pursuant to the Inheritance (Provision for Family and Dependants) Act 1975.[77] In these sorts of circumstances, the procedural rules governing any other claim must also be borne in mind. Where the construction problem is one of several aspects in dispute, it may be worth considering whether the court should be asked to deal with any aspect as a preliminary issue.[78]

Parties

Determining who should be made a party to a construction claim often requires some careful thought. In general, it is useful to bear in mind that:

(a) the court will expect someone to argue in favour of each of the various possible constructions (which may be two or more);

(b) it is generally desirable to take steps to ensure that everyone affected by the construction problem will be bound by the court's order;

(c) the PRs should generally remain neutral in their capacity as PRs and not argue in favour of one of the possible constructions;[79] and

76 See e.g. *Burnard v Burnard* [2014] EWHC 340 (Ch), *Reading v Reading* [2015] EWHC 946 (Ch), *Re Harte* [2015] EWHC 2351 (Ch), *Guthrie v Morel* [2015] EWHC 3172 (Ch), *Slattery v Jagger* [2015] EWHC 3976 (Ch), *Royal Society v Robinson* [2015] EWHC 3442 (Ch) and *Re Nodes* [2021] EWHC 1057 (Ch).

77 See e.g. *Burnard v Burnard* [2014] EWHC 340 (Ch) and *Tish v Olley* [2018] EWHC 1069 (Ch).

78 As in *Burnard v Burnard* [2014] EWHC 340 (Ch) (see [7]) and *Tish v Olley* [2018] EWHC 1069 (Ch) (see [1]).

79 See e.g. *Re Aspinall* [2017] EWHC 454 (Ch), in which the executors as claimants brought the proceedings and then let the rival beneficiaries (who had been joined as defendants) advance the two construction

(d) if the construction problem affects the amount of tax payable, it may be necessary to notify, and perhaps even join, HMRC.

As a starting point, CPR rule 64.4(1) provides the following rules in relation to who the parties should be:

> *(1) In a claim to which this Section applies, other than an application under section 48 of the Administration of Justice Act 1985 –*
>
> *(a) all the trustees*[80] *must be parties;*
>
> *(b) if the claim is made by trustees, any of them who does not consent to being a claimant must be made a defendant; and*
>
> *(c) the claimant may make parties to the claim any persons with an interest in or claim against the estate, or an interest under the trust, who it is appropriate to make parties having regard to the nature of the order sought.*

The claim can generally be brought either by the PRs, or by one or more of the beneficiaries.

All PRs must be parties (CPR rule 64.4(1)(a) and (b) above), which is unsurprising given that they need to be bound by the order. What may be less clear is how to ensure that all affected beneficiaries are joined or are otherwise bound by the court's order.

In cases involving a limited number of affected beneficiaries, the answer may be fairly straightforward. The simplest example is where there are two possible constructions and the affected beneficiaries are capacitous

---

arguments (see [11]); and *Wales v Dixon* [2020] EWHC 1979 (Ch), in which the PRs adopted the same neutral stance and the court dispensed with their attendance at the disposal hearing (see [4]).

80 CPR rule 64.1(2) makes it clear that in Part 64 and its accompanying Practice Directions "*where appropriate, references to trustees include executors and administrators*".

adults, as in Example 1 above (assuming Alfredo is a capacitous adult). In such cases, either the PRs bring the claim and join the affected beneficiaries as defendants,[81] or one of the affected beneficiaries can bring the claim and join the PRs and the other affected beneficiaries as defendants.[82] In either case, the PRs should generally adopt a neutral stance and let the two affected beneficiaries advance the two alternative construction arguments.[83] Exceptionally, the particular circumstances may mean that it is convenient for the PRs to advance one of the construction arguments; if so, they should ensure that they do so without jeopardising their neutrality.[84]

Where one or more of the affected beneficiaries is a minor or lacks capacity and is to be a party to the claim, that beneficiary will need a litigation friend (unless, in the case of a minor, the court makes an order permitting the child to conduct proceedings without a litigation friend).[85] CPR Part 21 contains detailed guidance on the procedure for the appointment of a litigation friend.

On the other hand, the position may be more complicated where the construction problem affects a large number of beneficiaries (e.g. large classes) and/or where some of the affected beneficiaries are minors, unborn, lack capacity and/or cannot be found. In Example 3 above, the class of intestacy beneficiaries may be large and/or its members difficult to trace, and it may be difficult to ascertain all members of the other class. In these sorts of cases, there is likely to be a tension between on the one hand ensuring that everyone who has an interest is properly represented

---

81 As e.g. in *Re Aspinall* [2017] EWHC 454 (Ch) (see [11]).

82 As e.g. in *Guthrie v Morel* [2015] EWHC 3172 (Ch) (see [4]).

83 See e.g. *Re Aspinall* [2017] EWHC 454 (Ch) at [11] and *Wales v Dixon* [2020] EWHC 1979 (Ch) at [4].

84 See e.g. *Re Wippell* [2018] EWHC 730 (Ch) at [8] and *Jeffreys v Scruton* [2020] EWHC 536 (Ch) at [4]; and the trust case of *PTNZ v AS* [2020] EWHC 3114 (Ch) at [8] and [86].

85 CPR rule 21.2.

and has an opportunity to be heard, and on the other trying to avoid depleting the estate or trust by incurring significant costs tracing and communicating with large classes of beneficiaries.

How the balance should be struck will inevitably depend on the circumstances of the particular case. In complicated cases, the provisions of CPR rule 19.9[86] and/or 19.13[87] can be of considerable assistance.[88] These govern respectively the appointment of a party to represent the interests of others and the service of proceedings and/or orders on non-parties so as to bind them. (The ability to issue a CPR Part 8 claim form without naming a defendant pursuant to CPR rule 8.2A can be useful where a claim is brought pursuant to section 48 AJA.[89] However, it is difficult to envisage a situation in which a construction claim will be issued without naming at least one defendant.)[90]

86 With effect from 6th April 2023, what used to be CPR rule 19.7 became rule 19.9: see rules 1(1) and 12(10) of the Civil Procedure (Amendment) Rules 2023 (SI 2023/105).

87 With effect from 6th April 2023, what used to be CPR rule 19.8A became rule 19.13: see rules 1(1) and 12(14) of the Civil Procedure (Amendment) Rules 2023 (SI 2023/105).

88 The relevance of these rules to claims concerning estates and trusts is highlighted by paragraphs 25.10 to 25.14 of the Chancery Guide, considered below. Note that CPR rule 19.8, which is entitled "*Representative parties with same interest*", does not apply to claims "*about (a) the estate of a deceased person, (b) property subject to a trust, or (c) the meaning of a document, including a statute*": see CPR rules 19.8(5) and 19.9(1). (CPR rule 19.8 used to be CPR rule 19.6 until it was renumbered with effect from 6th April 2023: see rules 1(1) and 12(9) of the Civil Procedure (Amendment) Rules 2023 (SI 2023/105)).

89 See 2.2.4 above.

90 Permission to issue the claim without naming a defendant was given in *Re Harte* [2015] EWHC 2351 (Ch). However, the claimant executors were then directed to take reasonable steps to trace the testatrix's statutory next of kin and to serve notices pursuant to CPR rule 19.8A (now CPR rule 19.13) on various people and charities (see [2]-[4]).

CPR rule 19.9(2) provides:

> *The court may make an order appointing a person to represent any other person or persons in the claim where the person or persons to be represented –*
>
> *(a) are unborn;*
>
> *(b) cannot be found;*
>
> *(c) cannot easily be ascertained; or*
>
> *(d) are a class of persons who have the same interest in a claim and –*
>
> > *(i) one or more members of that class are within sub-paragraphs (a), (b) or (c); or*
> >
> > *(ii) to appoint a representative would further the overriding objective.*

This caters for several different scenarios:

(a) is self-explanatory;

(b) covers situations in which it is clear who the affected beneficiary is, but (reasonable) attempts to find him have proved unsuccessful;

(c) covers situations in which it is not clear who the affected beneficiary is, nor can this be easily clarified;

(d) covers two alternative situations where a class of persons has the same interest in the claim:

- (i) is self-explanatory;
- (ii) is potentially wide and flexible. It can be used, for example, where there is a large class of affected beneficiaries scattered around the world, all of whom

> have the same interest, and it would further the overriding objective to appoint one of them to represent the whole class (e.g. by reducing procedural delay and costs) – ideally one who can be served within the jurisdiction.[91]

CPR rule 19.9(3) provides that an application for a representation order under CPR rule 19.9(2) may be made "*by any person who seeks to be appointed under the order or any party to the claim*", and may be made "*at any time before or after the claim has started*". CPR rule 19.9(4) provides that the application notice for such an order must be served on:

> *(a) all parties to the claim, if the claim has started;*
>
> *(b) the person sought to be appointed, if that person is not the applicant or a party to the claim; and*
>
> *(c) any other person as directed by the court.*

It is important to note that where the court has made a representation order under CPR rule 19.9, the court's approval is required to settle the claim.[92] This is to safeguard the position of the represented parties and to ensure their representative does not enter into a compromise which is disadvantageous to them: CPR rule 19.9(6) gives the court jurisdiction to approve a settlement "*where it is satisfied that the settlement is for the benefit of all represented persons*".

In relation to CPR rule 19.9, the Chancery Guide explains: "*Where the claim relates to the internal affairs of the trust or estate it may be appropriate for a representation order to be made so that the interests of all classes of beneficiaries are represented and protected but they are also all bound by the*

91 For an example, see the trust case of *Public Trustee v Harrison* [2018] EWHC 166 (Ch) at [8].

92 CPR rule 19.9(5).

decision."[93]

CPR rule 19.13 provides:

Power to make judgements binding on non-parties

(1) This rule applies to any claim relating to –

(a) the estate of a deceased person;

(b) property subject to a trust; or

(c) the sale of any property.

(2) The court may at any time direct that notice of –

(a) the claim; or

(b) any judgment or order given in the claim,

be served on any person who is not a party but who is or may be affected by it.

(3) An application under this rule –

(a) may be made without notice; and

(b) must be supported by written evidence which includes the reasons why the person to be served should be bound by the judgment in the claim.

(4) Unless the court orders otherwise –

93 Paragraph 25.11 of the Chancery Guide. (The paragraph refers to "*CPR 19.7*", which was the old numbering of the rule before it was renumbered rule 19.9 with effect from 6th April 2023: see rules 1(1) and 12(10) of the Civil Procedure (Amendment) Rules 2023 (SI 2023/105))).

(a) a notice of a claim or of a judgment or order under this rule must be –

(i) in the form required by the practice direction;

(ii) issued by the court; and

(iii) accompanied by a form of acknowledgment of service with any necessary modifications;

(b) a notice of a claim must also be accompanied by –

(i) a copy of the claim form; and

(ii) such other statements of case, witness statements or affidavits as the court may direct; and

(c) a notice of a judgment or order must also be accompanied by a copy of the judgment or order.

(5) If a person served with notice of a claim files an acknowledgment of service of the notice within 14 days they will become a party to the claim.

(6) If a person served with notice of a claim does not acknowledge service of the notice they will be bound by any judgment given in the claim as if they were a party.

(7) If, after service of a notice of a claim on a person, the claim form is amended so as substantially to alter the relief claimed, the court may direct that a judgment shall not bind that person unless a further notice, together with a copy of the amended claim form, is served on them.

(8) Any person served with a notice of a judgment or order under this rule –

(a) shall be bound by the judgment or order as if they had been a party to the claim; but

(b) may, provided they acknowledge service –

(i) within 28 days after the notice is served on them, apply to the court to set aside or vary the judgment or order; and

(ii) take part in any proceedings relating to the judgment or order.

(9) The following rules of Part 10 (acknowledgment of service) apply –

(a) rule 10.4; and

(b) rule 10.5, subject to the modification that references to the defendant are to be read as references to the person served with the notice.

(10) A notice under this rule is issued on the date entered on the notice by the court.

The procedure in CPR rule 19.13 can be useful to bind interested beneficiaries who do not want to take an active role in the proceedings, such as the adult children of an 'active' interested beneficiary who are content to simply support their parent's position. However, it suggests that it is unlikely to be a good idea to press on with the proceedings and to then try to rely on CPR rule 19.13 to serve a judgment or order on an interested beneficiary who it is thought will want to actively have a say. In such cases there is a risk that such a beneficiary will then apply to set aside the judgment or order (pursuant to CPR rule 19.13(8)(b)) to, in effect, re-open the case to advance his argument, and this could significantly increase the overall costs. In this sort of situation it is likely to be preferable to ensure that such a beneficiary is able to actively participate from the outset.

It should be borne in mind that the issue of representation is likely to be considered by the court at the first directions hearing, at which creative and pragmatic solutions can be considered with the Master, particularly in complex cases.[94]

Limitation

No limitation period applies to construction claims. However, a time limit or limitation period may be relevant if the dispute involves one or more other claims to which a time limit or limitation period does apply, such as a claim pursuant to the Inheritance (Provision for Family and Dependants) Act 1975 or a professional negligence claim, and/or if the intention is to ask the court to rectify the will.[95]

Which court

The County Court appears to have jurisdiction to determine a construction problem if the value of the estate or trust fund does not exceed £350,000.[96] However, in practice most construction claims are

94 See e.g. *Re Harte* [2015] EWHC 2351 (Ch), in which the PRs were initially given permission to issue the construction and rectification claims without naming a defendant (pursuant to CPR rule 8.2A), and were then given directions as to the steps they should take to ascertain the intestacy beneficiaries (including by advertisement) and as to the parties to whom they should give notice of the proceedings pursuant to CPR rule 19.8A (now CPR rule 19.13) (see [3]-[4]); and the trust case of *Womble Bond Dickinson (Trust Corp) Ltd v No Named Defendant* [2022] EWHC 43 (Ch), in which the trustees of an employee benefit trust were given permission to issue the construction claim without naming a defendant, and the court directed their solicitors to instruct a separate counsel to advance the opposing arguments effectively as Advocate to the Court, given that there was no individual who could obviously be appointed to represent all of the beneficiaries: see [6].

95 In relation to which see chapter 3.

96 Section 23 of the County Courts Act 1984 and article 3 of the County Court Jurisdiction Order 2014 (SI 2014/503). This assumes that the construction claim in question is a type of "*proceedings for the administration of the estate of a deceased person*" or "*proceedings for the*

issued in the High Court, where they must be brought in the Chancery Division,[97] i.e. what has now become the Property, Trusts and Probate List (ChD) of the Business and Property Courts. If it is to be issued in the High Court, a construction claim can be issued either in the Rolls Building in London or in one of the District Registries (Birmingham, Bristol, Cardiff, Leeds, Liverpool, Manchester and Newcastle-upon-Tyne).[98]

Evidence

The claimant must file the evidence on which he intends to rely when his claim form is issued[99] (unless the claimant only intends to rely on the evidence contained in the claim form itself, which it is suggested is unlikely to be the case in construction claims). This will generally be in the form of one or more witness statements. CPR Practice Direction 57AC, which applies to "*trial witness statements*"[100] in the Business and Property Courts, does not apply to proceedings under CPR Part 64, unless the court orders otherwise.[101] The claimant's evidence must be

execution of any trust" within section 23(a) or (b) respectively.

97 CPR rule 64.1(3). See also section 61 and paragraphs 1(c) and 1(d) of Schedule 1 to the Senior Courts Act 1981.

98 Paragraph 1.3 of the Chancery Guide. Appendix C to the Chancery Guide ('Chancery Business outside the Rolls Building') contains helpful information regarding Chancery business outside London, including contact details of the various District Registries.

99 CPR rule 8.5(1); see also paragraph 13.10 of the Chancery Guide.

100 Defined by paragraph 1.2 of CPR Practice Direction 57AC as "*a witness statement that is served pursuant to an order made under rule 32.4(2), or pursuant to rule 8.5 or an order made under rule 8.6(1)(b), or that is prepared for the trial of an unfair prejudice petition or a contributory's just and equitable winding up petition, including supplemental or reply witness statements where allowed by the court*".

101 Paragraph 1.3(8) of CPR Practice Direction 57AC.

served on the defendant with the claim form.[102]

The contents of the witness statement(s) will of course depend on the circumstances of the particular case, and on whether the claimant is a neutral PR who is simply explaining the construction problem to the court, or an interested beneficiary who is advancing a particular construction. In general terms, the topics which one should consider covering in the evidence filed in support of the claim are likely to be:

(a) the claimant's role and the capacity in which he brings the claim;

(b) the factual background;

(c) the construction problem;

(d) how the will was prepared;

(e) if it is contended that section 21 AJA is engaged, extrinsic evidence of the testator's intention (e.g. the will file);

(f) the position of the other interested parties;

(g) the approximate value of the estate or fund in issue.[103]

If the will was professionally prepared, some thought should be given as to whether evidence should be obtained from the draftsman responsible for preparing it (if available) and, if so, as to who should call the draftsman as a witness.[104]

It should be borne in mind that the CPR requires witness statements to be in the witness's own words[105] and that construction problems are

---

102 CPR rule 8.5(2).

103 Paragraph 25.4 of the Chancery Guide.

104 See e.g. *Re McKay* [2023] EWHC 642 (Ch) at [39]-[40].

105 Paragraph 18.1 of CPR Practice Direction 32; see also paragraph 8.1 of the Chancery Guide.

usually issues of law rather than fact. The temptation to include in a witness statement extensive legal submissions and references to case law should generally be resisted, particularly in witness statements of lay witnesses; these are properly a matter for skeleton arguments and submissions.

Prospective (or pre-emptive) costs orders

In some construction cases it may be appropriate to consider at an early stage of the proceedings whether a mechanism should be put in place for the costs of one or more of the parties to be paid out of the estate or trust fund in any event irrespective of the outcome.[106] This can be either by way of a contractual agreement by the PRs or by a so-called prospective (or pre-emptive) costs order by the court. This issue tends to arise primarily in pension cases, where an individual pension scheme member may be made a party to complex litigation as representative of other scheme members, and it may be unfair for him to have to bear his costs personally at least until the conclusion of the litigation, which can create a cash flow problem.[107] However, the issue is unlikely to arise in claims concerning the correct construction of a will.

Where the issue does arise, the eight sub-paragraphs of paragraph 6 of CPR Practice Direction 64A contain some detailed guidance about prospective costs orders, as do paragraphs 25.30 to 25.32 of the Chancery Guide. A model form of prospective costs order is appended to CPR Practice Direction 64A.

---

106 The costs orders which are likely to be made at the conclusion of the proceedings are considered at "Costs" below.

107 The principles governing the making of a prospective costs order have been considered in a line of pensions cases which includes *McDonald v Horn* [1995] 1 All ER 961 and *IBM United Kingdom Pensions Trust Ltd v Metcalfe* [2012] EWHC 125 (Ch).

Costs management

CPR rule 3.12 makes it clear that costs management does not apply to CPR Part 8 claims unless the court orders that it should pursuant to CPR rule 3.12(1A).[108] Paragraph 5(e) of CPR Practice Direction 3D provides that an order for costs management may be "*particularly appropriate*" in "*any Part 8 or other claims or applications involving a substantial dispute of fact and/or likely to require oral evidence and/or extensive disclosure*". The Chancery Guide also provides that: "*It is the court's experience that it is often helpful for costs budgets to be exchanged in cases in the ChD B&PCs London even if costs budgeting would not otherwise apply. Parties should consider exchanging costs budgets and/or opting into costs management even in cases which are outside the costs management regime. If the parties agree that a costs management order should be made, a consent order should be lodged in advance of the CMC including proposed directions for costs management*".[109]

A party seeking an order that costs management should apply to the proceedings should "*give notice to the other parties and the court well in advance of the directions hearing, and explain, preferably in a witness statement, why such an order is sought*".[110]

In will construction claims an obligation to file and serve a costs budget may be imposed by paragraph 5 of CPR Practice Direction 3E.[111] Significantly, the obligation applies early on in the proceedings when the party files his evidence (as explained below).

Section II of Practice Direction 3E is entitled '*Costs Capping in Relation to Trust Funds*'; paragraph 5 is the Section's only paragraph. It

108 In relation to which see also paragraph 2 of CPR Practice Direction 3D. This is reiterated by paragraph 13.30 of the Chancery Guide.

109 Paragraph 6.31 of the Chancery Guide.

110 Paragraph 13.31 of the Chancery Guide.

111 Paragraph 25.15 of the Chancery Guide draws attention to this.

supplements CPR rules 3.19 to 3.21 and paragraphs 1 to 4 of Practice Direction 3E,[112] which govern costs capping orders generally. Paragraph 5.1 makes it clear that references in it to "*trust fund*" includes the estate of a deceased person. The provisions of the paragraph are designed to "*enable the parties to consider whether to apply for, and the court to consider whether to make of its own initiative, a costs capping order in relation to proceedings relating to trust funds*".[113]

The obligation to file and serve a costs budget is imposed by paragraphs 5.4 and 5.5, which provide:

> *5.4 Any party to such proceedings who intends to apply for an order for the payment of costs out of the trust fund must file and serve on all other parties written notice of that intention together with a budget of the costs likely to be incurred by that party.*
>
> *5.5 The documents mentioned in paragraph 5.4 must be filed and served –*
>
> *[...]*
>
> *(b) in a Part 8 claim, with the evidence (or, if a defendant does not intend to serve and file evidence, with the acknowledgement of service).*

Finally, paragraph 5.6 provides that when the proceedings first come before the court for directions, the court may make a costs capping order of its own initiative, whether or not any party has applied for such an order.

In most construction claims, all parties will seek an order that their costs of the proceedings be paid out of the estate or trust fund[114] – or at least will "*intend*" to apply for such an order when the proceedings are started

112 Paragraph 5.3 of CPR Practice Direction 3E.

113 Paragraph 5.2 of CPR Practice Direction 3E.

114 See further under "Costs" below.

and/or when the relevant party files his evidence. This appears to trigger the obligation (imposed by paragraph 5.4) to file and serve on all other parties both "*written notice of that intention*" and a budget "*of the costs likely to be incurred by that party*".

On the other hand, costs capping orders are rare in will construction claims, and anecdotal evidence suggests that this provision is rarely (if ever) complied with or enforced in practice in such claims. It is also unclear what the sanction for non-compliance is (if any). However, the provision is there, and practitioners ought to be aware of it, at least unless and until it is amended by the Civil Procedure Rule Committee.

<u>Service</u>

The usual rules for service contained in the CPR – mostly in CPR Part 6 – apply to claims for the construction of a will. If it is necessary to seek the court's permission to serve the claim form out of the jurisdiction pursuant to CPR rule 6.36, the grounds listed in paragraph 3.1 of CPR Practice Direction 6B which are likely to be relevant are grounds (11) to (13):

> *Claims about property within the jurisdiction*
>
> *(11) The subject matter of the claim relates wholly or principally to property within the jurisdiction, provided that nothing under this paragraph shall render justiciable the title to or the right to possession of immovable property outside England and Wales.*
>
> *Claims about trusts etc.*
>
> *(12) A claim is made in respect of a trust which is created [...] by a written instrument [...] and which is governed by the law of England and Wales.*
>
> *(12A) A claim is made in respect of a trust which is created [...] by a written instrument [...] and which provides that jurisdiction in respect*

of such a claim shall be conferred upon the courts of England and Wales.

(12B) A claim is made in respect of a trust which is created [...] by a written instrument [...] and which expressly or impliedly designates England and Wales as the principal place of administration.

(12C) A claim is made in respect of a trust created in the jurisdiction.

(12D) A claim is made for a declaration that no trust has arisen where, if the trust was found to have arisen, it would comply with one of the conditions set out in paragraph (12), (12A), (12B) or (12C).

[...]

(13) A claim is made for any remedy which might be obtained in proceedings for the administration of the estate of a person who died domiciled within the jurisdiction or whose estate includes assets within the jurisdiction.

Responding to the claim

A defendant who wishes to respond to the claim must file an acknowledgment of service in the relevant practice form (viz. form N210) not more than 14 days after service of the claim form on him.[115] At the same time he must also serve his acknowledgment of service on the claimant and on any other party.[116] If he fails to do so, the defendant may attend the hearing of the claim but may not take part in the hearing unless the court gives permission.[117] As the Chancery Guide makes clear,

115 CPR rule 8.3(1); see also paragraph 13.8 of the Chancery Guide. Note that different (longer) periods apply if the proceedings have been served on the defendant out of the jurisdiction: see CPR rules 8.3(3) and 10.3(2).

116 CPR rule 8.3(1).

117 CPR rule 8.4(2).

these are "*serious consequences*".[118]

The defendant must indicate in his acknowledgment of service whether he contests the claim, and if he seeks a different remedy from that set out in the claim form, what that remedy is.[119] There is no need to file a defence, as CPR Part 15 does not apply to claims brought pursuant to CPR Part 8.[120]

Defendants who acknowledge service but do not intend to file any evidence should notify the court in writing when they file their acknowledgment of service that they do not intend to file evidence. This "*enables the court to know what each defendant's intention is when it considers the file and avoids delay*".[121]

CPR rule 8.8(1) provides that where a defendant "*contends that the CPR Part 8 procedure should not be used because there is (a) a substantial dispute of fact and (b) the use of the Part 8 procedure is not required or permitted by a rule or practice direction, he must state his reasons when he files his acknowledgment of service*". This is unlikely to apply in construction claims, as such claims tend not to involve substantial disputes of fact, and in any event must be started by issuing a Part 8 claim form as a result of CPR rule 64.3. However, in cases in which the dispute does involve a dispute of fact, it may be appropriate for directions to be given for the claim to proceed as, in effect, a hybrid claim, as explained below.[122]

A defendant who wishes to rely on written evidence must file it when he files his acknowledgment of service,[123] and must at the same time serve a

---

118 Paragraph 13.8 of the Chancery Guide.

119 CPR rule 8.3(2).

120 CPR rule 8.9(a); see also paragraph 13.10 of the Chancery Guide.

121 Paragraph 13.15 of the Chancery Guide.

122 See "Directions hearing" below.

123 CPR rule 8.5(3); see also paragraph 13.10 of the Chancery Guide.

copy of his evidence on the other parties.[124] The defendant may not rely on any written evidence which has not been served in accordance with these rules at the hearing of the claim unless the court gives permission.[125]

As the time limit for the defendant to file and serve his evidence is quite short (viz. 14 days from service of the claim on him), CPR rule 8.5(9) allows the parties to "*agree in writing on an extension of time of not more than 14 days for serving and filing evidence from the defendant*". Such an agreement must be filed at court with the acknowledgment of service.[126] The Chancery Guide recognises that it is "*not unusual for an extension of time to be agreed between the parties for the service of evidence*".[127]

If a defendant requires more time to file his evidence, he should apply to the court for an extension of time by way of an application pursuant to CPR Part 23.[128] If the parties are in agreement that such an extension should be granted, the application should be made by filing a consent order.[129] If there is no agreement, an application "*should be made to a Master using the urgent applications procedure set out in paragraphs 15.11 to 15.14 [of the Chancery Guide] but does not need to be certified as urgent business. When issuing the application the applicant should add 'Urgent Application EOT' to the comment box on CE-File to assist the court staff to process the application promptly*".[130] The Chancery Guide indicates that "*[i]n substantial matters the court will normally be willing to grant a reasonable extension*".[131]

124 CPR rule 8.5(4).

125 CPR rule 8.6(1).

126 CPR rule 8.5(10).

127 Paragraph 13.11 of the Chancery Guide.

128 CPR rule 8.5(8).

129 As to which, see paragraphs 16.36 to 16.41 of the Chancery Guide.

130 Paragraph 15.28 of the Chancery Guide.

131 Paragraph 13.11 of the Chancery Guide.

As for the claimant's evidence, the contents of any witness statement(s) adduced by a defendant will of course depend on the circumstances of the particular case. In general terms, the topics one should consider covering are likely to be the same as those to be covered by the claimant in his evidence (discussed above). An aspect which can give rise to conflicting factual evidence is the extrinsic evidence of the testator's intention (which may be relevant if section 21 AJA is engaged). This might be the case, for example, where that evidence consists of conversations the testator had with different people at different times about his will, which are inconsistent with one another;[132] or where the draftsman gives evidence as to the testator's intentions which conflicts with that given by the testator's family members, friends and/or business associates.[133]

Default and summary judgment

It is not possible to obtain judgment in default in a claim commenced by pursuant to CPR Part 8[134] or a claim which seeks declaratory relief.[135] Construction claims are usually both.

If the claim is unopposed and is brought by way of CPR Part 8 proceedings, it will generally be unnecessary to apply for summary

132 See e.g. *Hives v Machin* [2017] EWHC 1414 (Ch), in which the judge heard and analysed conflicting oral evidence as to the testatrix's intentions, but ultimately concluded that section 21 AJA was not engaged and such evidence was therefore inadmissible (see in particular [39] to [59]).

133 See e.g. *Re Nodes* [2021] EWHC 1057 (Ch), where the evidence as to the testator's intentions given by the draftsman conflicted with that given by the testator's widow and his long-term business associate.

134 CPR rules 8.1(5) and 12.2(b); see also paragraphs 5.9 and 13.14 of the Chancery Guide.

135 Paragraph 5.7 of the Chancery Guide provides: "*Declaratory relief and relief by way of rectification will not be granted without evidence and will not ordinarily be appropriate for resolution by way of default judgment.*"

judgment, and the claimant can instead ask the court to list the claim for a disposal hearing, as Chief Master Marsh explained in *Sovereign Trustees Ltd v Lewis*:[136]

> "*Part 8 claims are markedly different to Part 7 claims. Although there is no bar to issuing a Part 24 application [i.e. an application for summary judgment] in a Part 8 claim, it will rarely be necessary for the claimant to do so where it is seeking judgment on the whole of the claim. In part this is because the second limb of CPR 24.2 will normally have no application because there will be no 'trial' as such. Part 8 claims are normally resolved at a 'disposal hearing'. This is made clear by paragraph 8.1 of Practice Direction 8A which states:*
>
> *'8.1 The court may on the hearing date –*
>
> *(i) proceed to hear the case and dispose of the claim;*
>
> *(ii) give case management directions.'*
>
> *It follows that in most Part 8 claims, where the relief sought is unopposed, or cannot realistically be opposed, it will suffice for the claimant to ask the court to fix a disposal hearing at which the court may determine whether or not the relief sought by the claimant should be granted.*"[137]

---

136 [2016] EWHC 2593 (Ch) at [3]. However, see also *Guthrie v Morel* [2015] EWHC 3172 (Ch), where summary judgment was granted in a contested will construction claim.

137 Although paragraph 8.1 of CPR Practice Direction 8A has since been repealed, it is suggested that the reasoning remains valid.

Claimant's evidence in reply

If the claimant wishes to rely on further written evidence in reply to the defendant's evidence, he must file it within 14 days of service of the defendant's evidence on him,[138] and he must also serve a copy of it on the other parties "*within the same time limit*".[139] In the same way as a defendant, a claimant may not rely on any written evidence which has not been served in accordance with these rules at the hearing of the claim unless the court gives permission.[140]

As that time limit is also quite short, CPR rule 8.5(9) allows the parties to "*agree in writing on an extension of time [...] of not more than 28 days for serving and filing evidence in reply*". Such an agreement must be filed at court "*with 48 hours of the agreement*".[141] As indicated above, the Chancery Guide recognises that it is "*not unusual for an extension of time to be agreed between the parties for the service of evidence*".[142]

If a claimant requires more time to file his evidence in reply to the defendant's, he too should apply to the court for an extension of time by way of an application pursuant to CPR Part 23.[143] The guidance considered above in the context of the defendant's evidence applies equally to applications for extensions of time by claimants in relation to their evidence in reply. In particular, it should be noted that the Chancery Guide indicates that "*[i]n substantial matters the court will normally be willing to grant a reasonable extension*".[144]

---

138 CPR rule 8.5(5).

139 CPR rule 8.5(6).

140 CPR rule 8.6(1).

141 CPR rule 8.5(10).

142 Paragraph 13.11 of the Chancery Guide.

143 CPR rule 8.5(8).

144 Paragraph 13.11 of the Chancery Guide.

Directions hearing

Claims issued under the Part 8 procedure are treated as having been allocated to the multi-track and CPR Part 26 ('*Case Management – Preliminary Stage*') does not apply.[145] No directions questionnaires are required.[146]

The court file will generally be considered by the assigned Master[147] after the time for acknowledgment of service has expired, or, if the time for serving the defendant's evidence has been extended, after the expiry of that period. If a defendant has not acknowledged service, the assigned Master will typically make an order in the form of CH44.[148] This is an order which directs a defendant who intends to contest the claim to file and serve an acknowledgment of service and evidence by a specified date, failing which he shall not be entitled to rely on any evidence at the disposal hearing unless the court gives permission.[149]

If 21 days after the expiry of any extended period for service of evidence no notice of a directions hearing has been received, the claimant should contact the court by letter filed on CE-File together, if appropriate, with a draft order substantially in form CH44, requesting either a directions or disposal hearing. The letter should provide dates to avoid, and a realistic time estimate for both the hearing and any pre-reading.[150]

At that stage the Master will consider whether the claim and decide:

145 CPR rule 8.9(c); see also paragraph 13.14 of the Chancery Guide.

146 Paragraph 13.14 of the Chancery Guide.

147 Or District Judge of the High Court if the claim is in one of the District Registries.

148 Paragraph 13.15 of the Chancery Guide.

149 A specimen CH44 order is available on the Government website: https://www.gov.uk/government/publications/form-ch44-order-for-disposal-hearing (accessed 31st May 2023).

150 Paragraph 13.16 of the Chancery Guide.

(a) Whether the claim may be capable of being dealt with 'on paper', i.e. on the papers without a hearing.[151] The Chancery Guide makes it clear that "*[d]isposal without a hearing is exceptional*"[152] and indicates that if the claimant considers that a hearing is not required, and the defendant has filed an acknowledgment of service saying the claim will not be defended, the claimant may ask the court to consider whether the claim may be dealt with on paper.[153] Examples provided by the Chancery Guide are: "*some Norwich Pharmacal applications, some claims for relief where the court has directed that the claim need not name a defendant, and some unopposed applications for relief such as applications for a vesting order*";[154] and in the trusts context, a claim "*for approval of a sale, purchase, compromise or other transaction by a trustee, provided the claim is able to satisfy the court that there is no conflict of interest or prejudice to beneficiaries*".[155] It is suggested that a construction claim is unlikely to be dealt with in this way.

(b) If not, whether directions may be given without a hearing. The Chancery Guide explains: "*In most Part 8 claims, the Master will either make an order for directions at the point of initial review or direct that a hearing is fixed. If directions are given at that stage they will usually give notice of a disposal hearing and give directions concerning further evidence to be filed. The court will give notice of the hearing to all the parties, and the notice or order will specify to whom the notice has been sent*".[156]

(c) Whether the claim is likely to be referred to a different level of judge

151 Paragraph 13.18(a) of the Chancery Guide.

152 Paragraph 13.18(a)(i) of the Chancery Guide.

153 Ibid.

154 Paragraph 13.18(a)(ii) of the Chancery Guide.

155 Paragraph 25.9 of the Chancery Guide.

156 Paragraph 13.18(b) of the Chancery Guide.

for disposal.[157]

A directions hearing with a time estimate of half a day or less (and no more than 90 minutes pre-reading) will take place remotely unless the court orders otherwise.[158] It is suggested that this is likely to be the case in most construction claims. If a party considers that the directions hearing should take place using a format other than the default format, they should CE-File and serve on the other parties a letter setting out their alternative proposal, together with brief reasons, within 7 days of receipt of the Notice of Hearing.[159] Appendix Z to the Chancery Guide contains helpful guidance on the preparation and conduct of remote or hybrid hearings.

The Chancery Guide explains that at a directions hearing, "*the court will generally wish to establish whether:*

(a) the court has all the evidence it will need (including expert evidence)

(b) the claim is ready for a disposal hearing;

(c) any witnesses will need to attend the final hearing for cross-examination, in which case the court will give directions with a view to fixing the period during which the case will be heard;

(d) the disposal hearing should be dealt with by a Master or by a [High Court Judge], Section 9 Judge or Deputy [High Court Judge]."[160]

It is suggested that in a construction claim, the court is likely to consider

157 Paragraph 13.18(c) of the Chancery Guide.

158 Paragraph 13.19 of the Chancery Guide.

159 Ibid.

160 paragraph 13.20 of the Chancery Guide.

the following at a directions hearing:

(a) Evidence, including whether directions should be given for the filing of any further evidence (in addition to the evidence which will already have been filed by that point) and whether any witnesses should be required to attend to give oral evidence and be cross-examined at the disposal hearing.[161] In general, the CPR Part 8 procedure is designed for claims which do not involve substantial disputes of fact, and the starting point in CPR Part 8 claims seems to be that there should be no oral evidence at the disposal hearing unless the court orders otherwise.[162] However, as indicated above, an aspect which can give rise to conflicting factual evidence is the extrinsic evidence of the testator's intention, which may be relevant if section 21 AJA is engaged.[163] This might be the case, for example, where that evidence consists of conversations the testator had with different people at different times about his will, which are inconsistent with one another; or where the draftsman's evidence as to the testator's intentions conflicts with that given by the testator's family members, friends and/or business associates. In cases in which this sort of factual conflict arises, directions may be given for witnesses to attend the disposal hearing to give oral evidence and be cross-examined.[164] The Chancery Guide points

161 CPR rule 8.6(2) provides "*The court may require or permit a party to give oral evidence at the hearing*" and CPR rule 8.6(3) provides "*The court may give directions requiring the attendance for cross-examination of a witness who has given written evidence*".

162 See paragraph 13.13 of the Chancery Guide: "*Part 8 claims will generally be disposed of on written evidence without cross-examination. The witness statements together with the claim form should be sufficient in most cases to define the issues*".

163 This can be contrasted with claims for the construction of other trust instruments, where such evidence is inadmissible.

164 See e.g. *Hives v Machin* [2017] EWHC 1414 (Ch), in which the judge heard and considered conflicting oral evidence as to the testatrix's intentions, but ultimately concluded that section 21 AJA was not

out that: "*Part 8 is flexible and the court can adopt a hybrid procedure under which limited factual disputes requiring oral evidence or disclosure can be accommodated within Part 8 proceedings – see Vitpol Building Service v Samen [2008] EWHC 2283 (TCC) (paragraph 18)*".[165]

(b) Representation of the parties, such as whether any litigation friend needs to be appointed and/or whether any representation order should be made and/or notice given pursuant to CPR rule 19.13 (as to which, see Parties above).

(c) Directions in relation to the disposal hearing, such as directions about when and how the disposal hearing should be listed, its time estimate, and the level of judge required.

   (i) As regards listing, if there is to be no oral evidence at the disposal hearing, then "*a trial will be listed before the relevant level of judge as directed by a Master*".[166] However, if oral evidence is required at the disposal hearing, then the listing of the trial will involve a two-stage procedure.[167] First, a trial window, usually of 3 months, will be specified during which the trial is to take place. Then the parties should provide the court with an agreed list of dates to avoid, and the court will then proceed to fix a date for the start of the trial.[168]

---

engaged and that such evidence was therefore inadmissible (see in particular [39] to [59]); and *Re Nodes* [2021] EWHC 1057 (Ch), where the court rejected the evidence as to the testator's intentions given by the draftsman, and preferred that given by the testator's widow.

165 Paragraph 13.28 of the Chancery Guide.

166 Paragraph 12.24 of the Chancery Guide.

167 See paragraphs 12.16 to 12.23 of the Chancery Guide.

168 Paragraph 12.17 of the Chancery Guide.

(ii) As regards time estimate, this is likely to depend in particular on the number and complexity of the construction arguments which are being advanced, and on whether extrinsic evidence is admissible pursuant to section 21 AJA and, if so, whether that evidence consists of live oral evidence from witnesses who will be cross-examined.

(iii) As regards level of judge, CPR rule 2.4 provides that in proceedings in the High Court, any act which may be performed by the court may be performed "*by any judge, Master, Registrar in Bankruptcy or District Judge*".[169] Section II of CPR Practice Direction 2B does not impose any restriction on the jurisdiction of Masters or District Judges in relation to construction claims. On the contrary, the Chancery Guide provides: "*Most claims relating to trusts, estates and charities will be disposed of by a Master. The master will only release a claim to be heard by a High Court Judge if, exceptionally, the claim is of particularly high value, complexity, or legal novelty*".[170]

(d) 'Housekeeping' directions to prepare the case for the disposal hearing, such as directions relating to the hearing bundle,[171] skeleton arguments,[172] and other documents such as dramatis

169 Note the reference to 'District Judge' here is to a District Judge of the High Court (who is broadly the equivalent in the District Registries of a Master in London), not to a District Judge of the County Court.

170 Paragraph 25.2 of the Chancery Guide.

171 Detailed rules in relation to hearing bundles are contained in paragraph 27 of CPR Practice Direction 32 and are supplemented by the guidance contained in Chapter 12 of, and Appendix X to, the Chancery Guide.

172 In relation to which see paragraphs 12.49 to 12.51 of, and Appendix Y to, the Chancery Guide.

personae, chronologies, lists of issues,[173] reading lists[174] and bundles of authorities.[175] As regards the latter, it is important to bear in mind that the court is being asked to construe the particular will in question (or one of its provisions) in the circumstances in which it was made, and is therefore unlikely to be assisted by the citation of numerous authorities which have construed similar provisions in different wills made in different circumstances. The Privy Council made this clear in *Sammut v Manzi*:[176]

> *There were placed before their Lordships no less than 17 decided cases, some of which involved decisions on wording that bore some similarity with that used in the present case. Little assistance in construing a will is likely to be gained by consideration of how other judges have interpreted similar wording in other cases. Counsel rightly recognised that the starting point must be to look at the natural meaning of the wording of the will to be construed without reference to other decisions or to prima facie principles of construction.*

(e) Whether the court should make a costs capping order of its own initiative pursuant to CPR rules 3.19 to 3.21. These are rare in practice in construction claims.

173 In relation to which see paragraphs 12.52 to 12.55 of the Chancery Guide.

174 In relation to which see paragraph 12.56 to 12.58 of the Chancery Guide.

175 In relation to which see paragraph 12.59 to 12.61 of the Chancery Guide.

176 [2009] 1 WLR 1834 at [3]-[4].

Disclosure

(a) The disclosure process in the Business and Property Courts was substantially overhauled with the coming into effect of CPR Practice Direction 57AD on 1st October 2022.[177] However, the Practice Direction does not apply to claims proceeding under CPR Part 8 "*unless the court orders otherwise*".[178]

(b) Given the disclosure obligations already imposed by CPR Part 8, it is suggested that orders for extended disclosure pursuant to CPR Practice Direction 57AD are likely to be rare in construction claims. Some support for this can be found in paragraph 13.25 of the Chancery Guide: "*PD 57AD does not apply to Part 8 claims when issued, and it is rare for an order for disclosure to be made in a Part 8 claim. However, if any form of disclosure is ordered the court will adopt such parts of PD 57AD as are appropriate (and CPR 31 does not apply)*".

Disposal hearing

At the disposal hearing, the court will hear the competing construction arguments, which may be two or, sometimes, more.

Disposal hearings in construction claims are generally listed in public, i.e. in a court which is open to members of the public.[179] Whilst it may be possible in some cases to persuade a court to list the claim in private pursuant to CPR rule 39.2(3),[180] or to impose some other less extensive

177 This followed a pilot introduced with effect from 1st January 2019 by what was CPR Practice Direction 51U.

178 Paragraph 1.4(7) of CPR Practice Direction 57AD.

179 Under the general rule in CPR rule 39.2(1).

180 CPR rule 39.2 requires the court to sit in private if it is satisfied (i) that "*it is necessary to sit in private to secure the proper administration of justice*" and (ii) that one or more of the 7 sub-rules of CPR rule 39.2(3) is engaged. Of those sub-rules, those which may be engaged in a

reporting restriction, a party seeking such an order is likely to have to show compelling reasons why the court should depart from the principle of open justice.[181]

Judgment

The Master or judge will decide how, when and where to deliver judgment. Judgment may be delivered orally immediately at the conclusion of the hearing (a so-called '*ex tempore*' judgment),[182] or may be reserved. A reserved judgment may be delivered orally at a later date or, more commonly, may be circulated in written draft to the parties and then formally handed down at a subsequent date.

---

construction claim are likely to be (c), (d) and (g), viz.:

(c) *[the hearing] involves confidential information (including information relating to personal financial matters) and publicity would damage that confidentiality;*

(d) *a private hearing is necessary to protect the interests of any child or protected party; [...]*

(g) *the court considers [a hearing in private] to be necessary, in the interests of justice.*"

On the other hand, sub-rule (f) is unlikely to be engaged where the correct construction is in dispute, as that sub-rule is engaged in relation to hearings involving "*uncontentious matters arising in the administration of trusts or in the administration of a deceased person's estate*" (emphasis added).

181 See in this regard the Court of Appeal's guidance in *MN v OP* [2019] EWCA Civ 679 regarding privacy and reporting restrictions in the context of applications pursuant to the Variation of Trusts Act 1958, which was subsequently applied by Chief Master Marsh in a case involving the construction of a trust deed: *MN v OP* [2019] EWHC 1643 (Ch) (although the same letters were used to anonymise the parties in both cases, the two cases were unrelated).

182 See e.g. *Slattery v Jagger* [2015] EWHC 3976 (Ch) and *Jump v Lister* [2016] EWHC 2160 (Ch).

Costs

In *Re Buckton*,[183] Kekewich J identified the following two classes of cases in which he considered it appropriate to order that all parties' costs be paid out of the estate or trust (instead of following the general rule, now contained in CPR rule 44.2(2)(a), that the unsuccessful party will be ordered to pay the costs of the successful party):

> *In a large proportion of the summonses adjourned into Court for argument the applicants are trustees of a will or settlement who ask the Court to construe the instrument of trust for their guidance, and in order to ascertain the interests of the beneficiaries, or else ask to have some question determined which has arisen in the administration of the trusts. In cases of this character I regard the costs of all parties as necessarily incurred for the benefit of the estate, and direct them to be taxed as between solicitor and client and paid out of the estate. It is, of course, possible that trustees may come to the Court without due cause. A question of construction or of administration may be too clear for argument, or it may be the duty of trustees to inform a claimant that they must administer their trust on the footing that his claim is unfounded, and leave him to take whatever course he thinks fit. But, although I have thought it necessary sometimes to caution timid trustees against making applications which might with propriety be avoided, I act on the principle that trustees are entitled to the fullest possible protection which the Court can give them, and that I must give them credit for not applying to the Court except under advice which, though it may appear to me unsound, must not be readily treated as unwise. I cannot remember any case in which I have refused to deal with the costs of an application by trustees in the manner above mentioned.*
>
> *There is a second class of cases differing in form, but not in substance, from the first. In these cases it is admitted on all hands, or it is apparent from the proceedings, that although the application is made, not by trustees (who are respondents), but by some of the beneficiaries, yet it is*

183 [1907] 2 Ch 406.

> *made by reason of some difficulty of construction, or administration, which would have justified an application by the trustees, and it is not made by them only because, for some reason or other, a different course has been deemed more convenient. To cases of this class I extend the operation of the same rule as is observed in cases of the first class. The application is necessary for the administration of the trust, and the costs of all parties are necessarily incurred for the benefit of the estate regarded as a whole.*

Construction claims generally fall in either the first or the second class of cases identified in *Re Buckton* (depending on whether the claim is brought by the PRs or a beneficiary). As a result, the general starting point is that the costs of all of the parties will be payable out of the estate or trust.[184]

Costs are however ultimately in the discretion of the court,[185] and the court may therefore decide to depart from that starting point and make a different costs order. It may decide to do so, for example, if it considers that the unreasonable conduct of one of the parties has materially increased costs unnecessarily,[186] or that the construction problem was not in fact a problem at all because one of the possible constructions was unarguable.[187]

---

184 In *Wales v Dixon* [2020] EWHC 1979 (Ch) the court encouraged the parties to agree such an order, indicating that it would be prepared to carry out a summary assessment if the costs could not be agreed: see [35].

185 Section 51(1) of the Senior Courts Act 1981.

186 See *Harrison-Mills v Public Trustee* [2019] EWCA Civ 966 at [66].

187 In *Re Buckton* [1907] 2 Ch 406 Kekewich J acknowledged the possibility that trustees "*may come to the Court without due cause*". However, his subsequent comments suggest that cases in which PRs or trustees will be deprived of their costs as a result will be rare: "*although I have thought it necessary sometimes to caution timid trustees against making applications which might with propriety be avoided, I act on the principle that trustees are entitled to the fullest possible protection which the Court can give them, and that I must give them credit for not applying to the Court except under*

In general terms, in deciding costs the court will try to ensure that the costs are in fact borne by the negligent draftsman and/or (in a contested case) by the party who has lost, and not by the successful party. In deciding precisely how this should be achieved, the court will have to take into account all of the circumstances, including the parties' respective interests under the will and who would in fact bear the costs if the costs are ordered to be paid out of the estate.[188] As indicated at 2.2.3 above, in cases involving professional negligence, the draftsman's insurers may have agreed in advance to pay the costs of the construction claim.[189] Alternatively, it may be possible to seek a non-party costs order against the firm responsible for the negligent drafting.[190]

Order

In construction claims the order which gives effect to the judgment will generally consist of two parts:

(a) a declaration by which the court formally declares the correct meaning of the will, or of one or more of its provisions; and

(b) an order directing the PRs or trustees to administer and distribute the estate or trust in question in accordance with the declaration.

CPR Practice Direction 40E contains guidance in relation to reserved

---

advice which, though it may appear to me unsound, must not be readily treated as unwise." See also *Harrison-Mills v Public Trustee* [2019] EWCA Civ 966 at [59].

188 See e.g. *Marley v Rawlings (costs)* [2014] UKSC 51 and *Slattery v Jagger* [2015] EWHC 3976 (Ch) at [103]-[112].

189 See e.g. *Slattery v Jagger* [2015] EWHC 3976 (Ch) at [103]-[112] (which involved both a construction and a rectification claim).

190 See CPR rule 46.2. Such an order was sought e.g. in *Royal Commonwealth Society for the Blind v Beasant* [2021] EWHC 352 (Ch) at [19]-[48] (the costs order was not considered on appeal: [2022] EWHC 1319 (Ch) at [35]).

judgments. Paragraphs 16.8 to 16.22 of the Chancery Guide contain guidance in relation to the drafting, filing and sealing of orders following a hearing; paragraph 16.23 contains an example form of order.

Appeals

A party who is dissatisfied with the court's decision must obtain the court's permission in order to appeal it.[191] The court will only grant permission to appeal if it considers that the appeal would have a real prospect of success, or that there is some other compelling reason for the appeal to be heard.[192]

Although this is not strictly required, it is generally sensible for a party who wishes to appeal to first seek permission from the lower court.[193] This is usually done when judgment is delivered or handed down and consequential issues, such as the terms of the order giving effect to the judgment and costs, are decided.[194]

If the lower court refuses permission, or if permission was not sought from it, permission must be sought from the appeal court by filing an Appellant's Notice.[195] Unless the court orders otherwise, the time limit for doing so is "*21 days after the date of the decision of the lower court*".[196] That is a relatively short time limit, which cannot be extended by agreement between the parties,[197] and it must be borne in mind that the period starts to run from the date of the decision of the lower court and not, if later, the date on which consequential matters are decided or the

191 CPR rule 52.3(1).

192 CPR rule 52.6(1).

193 Pursuant to CPR rule 52.3(2)(a); see e.g. *In re T (A Child)* [2002] EWCA Civ 1736 at [12]-[13].

194 See paragraph 12.91 of the Chancery Guide.

195 CPR rules 52.3(2)(b) and 52.12(1).

196 CPR rule 52.12(2)(b).

197 CPR rule 52.15(2).

date on which the order giving effect to the decision is approved and sealed.[198] If – as is quite common – the lower court's judgment is circulated to the parties in draft and then formally handed down in the absence of the parties, and a hearing to decide consequential matter is arranged at a later date, the lower court should be asked to direct[199] that the 21-day period will only start to run from the date of the later hearing, rather than from the date on which judgment was handed down.[200]

Compromise

In some cases it may be possible to compromise a construction claim after proceedings have been issued.[201] The mechanism by which the compromise should be implemented will inevitably depend on its terms and on the particular circumstances of the case. In most cases, the following will have to be considered:

(a) Whether the compromise has any tax implications and, if so, whether it is desirable to implement it by way of a deed of variation which can be 'read back' for IHT and/or CGT purposes.[202]

(b) Whether a declaration by the court as to the correct construction of the will, or of one or more of its provisions, is required or desirable, and if so whether the court can be asked to make it by consent without hearing full argument in accordance with the

198 See e.g. *Sayers v Clarke Walker (A Firm)* [2002] EWCA Civ 645 at [8]-[9] and *Owusu v Jackson* [2002] EWCA Civ 877 at [24]-[27].

199 Pursuant to CPR 52.12(2)(a).

200 See e.g. *Jackson v Marina Homes Ltd* [2007] EWCA Civ 1404 at [8]. This is envisaged by paragraph 12.91 of the Chancery Guide.

201 The circumstances in which it may be possible to resolve a construction issue without the need for court proceedings are considered at 2.2.2 above.

202 See section 142 of the Inheritance Tax Act 1984 and section 62 of the Taxation of Chargeable Gains Act 1992.

principles in *Hayim v Couch*,[203] *Pavilion Property Trustees Ltd v Permira Advisers LLP*[204] and *Singh v Singh*.[205] It should be borne in mind that this jurisdiction tends to be exercised sparingly.

(c) Whether the court's approval of the compromise is required, which will be the case where one or more of the parties is a minor,[206] an adult who lacks capacity to conduct litigation[207] and/or a party who has been appointed to represent others pursuant to CPR rule 19.9.[208]

Paragraphs 16.36 to 16.41 of the Chancery Guide contain guidance in relation to consent orders.

---

203 [2009] EWHC 1040 (Ch) at [12]-[18].

204 [2014] EWHC 145 (Ch) at [9]-[10].

205 [2014] EWHC 2762 (Ch) at [5]-[9].

206 CPR rule 21.10.

207 *Ibid.*

208 CPR rule 19.9(5).

CHAPTER THREE

RECTIFICATION OF WILLS

3.1 The law

Until 1982 there was limited scope to correct the wording of a will which appeared to contain an error, or to insert words which appeared to have been accidentally omitted from a will.[209] However, that position was changed by the enactment of section 20 of the Administration of Justice Act 1982 ("AJA"). Section 20(1) AJA grants the court a statutory jurisdiction to rectify wills.[210] It provides:

> *(1) If a court is satisfied that a will is so expressed that it fails to carry out the testator's intentions, in consequence—*
>
> *(a) of a clerical error; or*
>
> *(b) of a failure to understand his instructions,*
>
> *it may order that the will shall be rectified so as to carry out his intentions.*

---

209 Before 1982, a mechanism which could help cure drafting errors was the court's power to omit certain words from probate on the basis that the testator did not know or approve them (although this jurisdiction did not allow the court to add words to a will). For a recent example, see *Mundil-Williams v Williams* [2021] EWHC 586 (Ch), in which no rectification claim had been brought and in which some of the pre-1982 authorities were considered and discussed (at [71]-[75]).

210 The jurisdiction also extends to codicils: see e.g. *Barrett v Hamond* [2020] EWHC 3585 (Ch).

In certain circumstances, this statutory jurisdiction gives the Court power to rectify a will made abroad: see e.g. *Kelly v Brennan*,[211] in which the (English) court rectified a will made in Ireland by an English-domiciled testator.

In *Re Segleman*,[212] Chadwick J (as he then was) explained that the court will approach a claim for a rectification of a will in three stages:

> *The subsection requires the court to examine three questions. First, what were the testator's intentions with regard to the dispositions in respect of which rectification is sought. Secondly, whether the will is so expressed that it fails to carry out those intentions. Thirdly, whether the will is expressed as it is in consequence of either (a) a clerical error or (b) a failure on the part of someone to whom the testator has given instructions in connection with his will to understand those instructions.*

The judge also made it clear that in order to answer the first of those questions, the court must admit extrinsic evidence of the testator's intentions with regard to the relevant dispositions.

Several cases involving claims for the rectification of wills have emphasised that the court will require cogent evidence before being persuaded that the will does indeed need rectifying, given that the court is being asked to correct a document made by a person who cannot himself give evidence as to his intentions. For example, in *Re Segelman*[213] itself Chadwick J (as he then was) pointed out: "*although the standard of proof required in a claim for rectification made under section 20(1) of the Act of 1982 is that the court should be satisfied on the balance of probability, the probability that a will which a testator has executed in circumstances of some formality reflects his intentions is usually of such weight that convincing*

211 [2020] EWHC 245 (Ch).

212 [1996] Ch 171.

213 *Ibid.*

evidence to the contrary is necessary". Norris J cited this passage in *Sprackling v Sprackling*[214] and commented:[215] "*This emphasises that speculation is no basis upon which to interfere with a formal expression of testamentary intentions. One must be confident that the will as expressed does not record the instructions given because of error or misunderstanding, "confident" in the sense of being satisfied on the balance of probabilities by evidence of a quality commensurate with the inherent probabilities of the case itself.*" Similarly, in *Goodman v Goodman*[216] Evans-Lombe J accepted the submission that the court's conclusion is "*to be arrived at on the balance of probabilities but bearing in mind a strong bias in favour of the conclusion that a duly executed will evidences the intention of the testator*".[217]

In *Marley v Rawlings*[218] the Supreme Court explained: "*As a general proposition, there may be force in the point that the greater the extent of the correction sought, the steeper the task for a claimant who is seeking rectification. However, I can see no reason in principle why a wholesale correction should be ruled out as a permissible exercise of the court's power to rectify, as a matter of principle. On the contrary: to impose such a restriction on the power of rectification would be unprincipled — and it would also lead to uncertainty*".[219]

It is generally relatively straightforward to determine whether an error in a will is the result of a failure to understand the testator's instructions (for the purposes of section 20(1)(b) AJA).[220]

---

214 [2008] EWHC 2696 (Ch).

215 [2008] EWHC 2696 (Ch) at [15].

216 [2006] EWHC 1757 (Ch).

217 [2006] EWHC 1757 (Ch) at [18]. See also paragraphs 18.18 and 18.19 of the Chancery Guide.

218 [2014] UKSC 2.

219 [2014] UKSC 2 at [53].

220 For some examples, see *Lilly v Pegram* [2002] EWHC 2817 (Ch), *Foster-Orr v Colliss* [2005] EWHC 2600 (Ch), *Goodman v Goodman* [2006]

On the other hand, the expression "*clerical error*" (contained in section 20(1)(a) AJA) has proved more controversial. It is now clear that the expression should be given a wide rather than a narrow meaning.[221] One of the reasons for this is that section 20 AJA is one of the provisions of the AJA "*aimed at making the law on wills more flexible and rendering it easier to validate or "save" a will than previously*"[222] (the others being sections 17, 18, 19 and 21 AJA). The expression "*is not one with a precise or well-established, let alone a technical, meaning*".[223] Lord Neuberger identified the expression's wider meaning as "*a mistake arising out of office work of a relatively routine nature, such as preparing, filing, sending, organising the execution of, a document (save, possibly, to the extent that the activity involves some special expertise).*"[224] The omission of an entire clause from a will can be a clerical error.[225]

Importantly, a line of authorities makes it clear that rectification will not be available in cases in which the draftsman has correctly understood the testator's intentions and has then considered how to give effect to them, but has (advertently) chosen inapposite words.[226] These cases fall outside of the scope of section 20 AJA altogether: the error is not a "*clerical error*" (within section 20(1)(a) AJA), and there is also no failure to understand instructions (within section 20(1)(b) AJA). Rather, the error is one which might be described as a conscious drafting error, and thus falls outside the scope of the statutory jurisdiction to rectify contained in section 20

EWHC 1757 (Ch) and *Royal Society v Robinson* [2015] EWHC 3442 (Ch).

221 *Marley v Rawlings* [2014] UKSC 2 at [76].

222 *Marley v Rawlings* [2014] UKSC 2 at [79].

223 *Marley v Rawlings* [2014] UKSC 2 at [75].

224 *Ibid.*

225 *Wordingham v Royal Exchange Trust Co Ltd* [1992] Ch 412.

226 *Kell v Jones* [2013] WTLR 507, *Reading v Reading* [2015] EWHC 946 (Ch). In *Bracey v Curley* [2022] EWHC 359 (Ch) the Court expressed "*some doubts*" about the correctness of *Reading v Reading* on this point (at [86]).

AJA. In these sorts of situations, the only possible recourse may be to pursue professional negligence proceedings against the draftsman.

Section 20(2) AJA contains an important statutory time limit which applies to rectification claims: "*An application for an order under this section shall not, except with the permission of the court, be made after the end of the period of six months from the date on which representation with respect to the estate of the deceased is first taken out.*"[227]

The statute itself contains no guidance on how the court should decide whether to grant the claimant permission to bring a rectification claim more than 6 months from the date on which representation was first taken out. In *Chittock v Stevens*[228] the court held that the approach to be adopted is similar to that adopted when deciding whether to grant a claimant permission to bring a claim pursuant to the Inheritance (Provision for Family and Dependants) Act 1975 ("1975 Act") more than 6 months after representation in respect of the estate was first taken out. In summary, the court will approach an application for permission by considering the following factors:[229]

(1) The court's discretion is unfettered but must be exercised judicially in accordance with what is right and proper.

---

227 Sections 20(4) and (5) AJA provide that certain types of limited grants of representations are to be left out of account in calculating the 6-month period prescribed by section 20(2) AJA.

228 [2000] WTLR 643.

229 The leading authorities in the jurisprudence concerning Inheritance (Provision for Family and Dependants) Act 1975 claims are *Re Salmon* [1981] Ch 167, *Re Dennis* [1981] 2 All ER 140, *Berger v Berger* [2013] EWCA Civ 1305 (where the seven factors are referred to at [44]), *Cowan v Foreman* [2019] EWCA Civ 1336 (where the seven factors are referred to at [32]) and *Begum v Ahmed* [2019] EWCA Civ 1794. The summary contained in *Berger v Berger* was cited and applied in *Kelly v Brennan* [2020] EWHC 245 (Ch) at [32].

(2) The onus is on the applicant to show sufficient grounds for the granting of permission to apply out of time.

(3) The court must consider whether the Applicant has acted promptly and the circumstances in which he applied for an extension of time after the expiry of the time limit.

(4) Were negotiations begun within the time limit?

(5) Has the estate been distributed before the claim was notified to the defendants?

(6) Would dismissal of the claim leave the applicant without recourse to other remedies?

(7) Looking at the position as it is now, has the applicant an arguable rectification claim if the claim is allowed to proceed?

However, both *Chittock v Stevens* itself and the more recent decision in *Kelly v Brennan* emphasise that when considering an application for permission to bring a rectification claim out of time, the Court must bear in mind that rectification claims are different in nature from claims brought pursuant to the 1975 Act: "*To simply align the guidelines from applications under section 4 of the 1975 Act to applications to extend time under section 20(2) of the 1982 Act is to disregard the fundamentally different nature of these claims. The former can effectively drive a coach and horses through testamentary intention whereas the latter seeks to find the true testamentary intention and give effect to it by rectifying the will. Whilst noting that section 20(3) of the 1982 Act is analogous to section 20 of the 1975 Act I do consider that section 20 of the 1982 Act is and should be more flexible than the 1975 Act.*"

In *Fielden v Christie-Miller*[230] the court suggested that it might have been prepared to grant the claimant permission to bring a rectification claim

230 [2015] EWHC 2940 (Ch) at [45].

over 15 years after representation in respect of the estate was first taken out had the claim been more meritorious.

Section 20(3) AJA provides PRs with protection against personal liability for having distributed the estate after the end of the period of six months from the date on which representation was first taken out, on the ground that they ought to have taken into account the possibility that the court might grant permission to bring a late rectification claim. However, the subsection does not affect the ability to recover any distribution from the recipient if the will is rectified.

In cases involving professionally prepared wills in which professional negligence proceedings are likely to be relevant, regard must also be had to the limitation period which applies to those proceedings.

3.2 Practice and procedure

3.2.1 Who is affected?

The first question PRs should ask themselves when faced with a rectification problem is: who is affected by it?

The main concern for PRs faced with a possible rectification problem is to ensure that before they take any step based on a particular provision of the will, they protect themselves from potential personal liability for *devastavit* (i.e. for having administered and/or distributed the estate incorrectly), which they can do by obtaining either the binding consent of all affected beneficiaries or authorisation from the court. To get to that position, the PRs will first have to establish who the affected beneficiaries are.

Needless to say, the answer to this will depend on the particular circumstances, and can vary widely. In simple terms, the way to go about ascertaining the affected beneficiaries is to consider the different possible outcomes depending on whether the will is or is not rectified (which may be two or more) and then consider who would benefit in each situation, as illustrated by the following examples.

Example 4

In 2005 Manrico made a professionally prepared will by which he appointed two partners in the firm of Di Luna & Co as his executors and trustees and gave a legacy of £500,000 to Azucena and the residue of his estate to Leonora. He subsequently fell out with his solicitors and in 2010 he instructed a different firm to prepare his last will. The will file indicates that he told his new solicitors that the only changes he wanted to make were to appoint his friend Ruiz as his executor and trustee in the place of the partners in Di Luna & Co, and to give Ruiz a legacy of £10,000. Manrico's last will includes that appointment and legacy and leaves the residuary estate to Leonora, but it omits the legacy of £500,000 to Azucena.

The issue is whether the 2010 will should be rectified to include the legacy of £500,000 to Azucena.

Assuming Manrico's estate is worth over £510,000 (and that Ruiz's legacy will therefore be paid in any event), the affected beneficiaries are Azucena and Leonora.

Example 5

By clause 5 of his will Tristan gave his castle, Kareol, to "*my trusted servant Brangäne who has been loyal to me for over 20 years*"; he then gave the residue of his estate to his wife Isolde.

In fact, Tristan's long-term loyal servant is Kurwenal, and Brangäne is Isolde's maid, whom Tristan had only known for 3 years when he made his will.

The issue is whether clause 5:

(a) takes effect as a gift to Brangäne;

(b) should be rectified by replacing "*Brangäne*" with "*Kurwenal*"; or

(c) fails, with the result that Kareol falls into residue and passes to Isolde.

The affected beneficiaries are therefore:

(a) Brangäne;

(b) Kurwenal; and

(c) Isolde.

Example 6

The will file relating to Simon Boccanegra's will indicates that his instructions to his solicitor were that he wished to leave his residuary estate to the people of Genoa. However, the gift of residue in his will reads: "*for the patricians of Genoa alive at the date of my death, if more than one in equal shares absolutely*".

The issue is whether the gift should be rectified by replacing the word "*patricians*" with "*people*".

The affected beneficiaries are therefore:

(a) the patricians of Genoa;

(b) the people of Genoa; and

(c) possibly Simon Boccanegra's intestacy beneficiaries who may argue that the gift is void for uncertainty and therefore gives rise to a partial intestacy.

If the rectification problem affects the amount of tax payable, some thought should be given to whether it is also necessary to involve HMRC.[231]

231 Paragraph 18.26 of the Chancery Guide provides: "*If there are fiscal*

The corollary to the above is that PRs should bear in mind that they have no personal interest in how the rectification problem is resolved between the affected beneficiaries. It is not for the PRs to try to second guess what the testator might have intended, nor to form a view as to which of the affected beneficiaries is more 'worthy' or 'deserving'. The PRs should remain neutral and impartial, and simply do what they are told, either by a unanimous binding agreement reached by all of the affected beneficiaries, or by the court.

3.2.2 Can the problem be resolved by agreement?

Some rectification problems can be resolved by the unanimous agreement of all of the beneficiaries affected by it. Therefore, once the PRs have identified all of the affected beneficiaries, the next question they should ask themselves is: can the problem be resolved by agreement?

Suppose that in Example 4 above, Azucena and Leonora agree that Azucena should receive a legacy of £500,000. Azucena and Leonora are the only two individuals affected by the uncertainty.[232] If they are both capacitous adults and agree what should happen, they can resolve the construction problem between themselves without having to go to court. The PRs' only concern will be to ensure that the agreement is properly documented so that they cannot later be criticised by Azucena or Leonora for acting in accordance with it.

Resolving the problem by agreement is usually significantly cheaper and quicker than asking the court to do so. As indicated above, if the rectification problem affects the amount of tax payable, some thought

consequences which will arise from the changes to the document, HMRC (or any appropriate foreign tax body or bodies) should be notified, preferably before the claim is issued, and invited to confirm whether they wish to be joined as a party to the claim in order to make representations. The evidence in support of the claim should include such notification, and the position of HMRC (or any appropriate foreign tax body or bodies)".

232 This assumes the estate is sufficiently solvent for there to be residue.

should be given to whether it is also necessary to obtain the agreement of HMRC. Typical examples are cases in which the problem concerns whether property passes to an IHT-exempt beneficiary (such as a surviving spouse or charity). HMRC's involvement will generally not be required if an agreement is reached and implemented by an instrument which is executed within two years of the testator's death, because in such cases it should be possible for the affected beneficiaries to determine the tax consequences.[233] However, if an agreement is only reached or implemented more than two years after the testator's death and affects (or purports to affect) the amount of tax payable, HMRC's agreement is likely to be required.

Suppose that in Example 5 above, Brangäne, Kurwenal and Isolde agree that Kareol should pass as part of residue to Isolde. As Isolde is the surviving spouse and thus an IHT-exempt beneficiary, whereas Brangäne and Kurwenal are not, this could affect the amount of IHT payable. It may therefore be necessary to involve HMRC.

In practice, rectification problems are generally only resolved by agreement in the most straightforward cases. Two reasons can be identified for this. First, beneficiaries often have different views about what the testator did or did not intend, and are therefore simply unable to reach an agreement. Secondly, to avoid exposing themselves to potential personal liability to disappointed beneficiaries, PRs must obtain the binding consent of all of the beneficiaries who are affected by the problem. This will not be possible if the problem affects beneficiaries who are minors, unborn, lack capacity and/or cannot be found. As those types of beneficiaries are unable to give the PRs their binding consent, in cases in which they are affected, the court's intervention will be necessary.

A useful way to explore whether the rectification problem can be resolved by agreement is for the PRs, who are often the first to spot the problem,

233 By availing themselves of the 'reading back' mechanisms in section 142 of the Inheritance Tax Act 1984 and/or section 62 of the Taxation of Chargeable Gains Act 1992.

to obtain advice from counsel on the rectification problem and then share that advice with all affected beneficiaries and canvass their views. If the will incorporates clause 12.3 of the STEP Standard Provisions (2nd edition), the PRs should consider obtaining the advice of counsel of "*at least five years' standing*" if they want to rely on the protection from liability afforded by that clause.[234]

This process should help both the PRs and all affected beneficiaries understand their respective positions, which in turn should inform all involved whether there is any hope of the rectification problem being resolved by agreement and, if so, how this might be achieved. Depending on the circumstances, the affected beneficiaries may wish to try to reach an agreement by, for example, negotiating in correspondence, at a round-table meeting or at a mediation.

As indicated above, PRs should bear in mind that they have no personal interest in how the rectification problem is resolved between the affected

---

234 Clause 12.3 and the following two clauses provide:

12.3 A Trustee shall not be liable for acting in accordance with the advice of counsel, of at least five years' standing, with respect to the Trust. The Trustees may in particular conduct legal proceedings in accordance with such advice without obtaining a court order. A Trustee may recover from the Trust Fund any expenses where he has acted in accordance with such advice.

12.4 Clause 12.3 does not apply:

12.4.1 in relation to a Trustee who knows or has reasonable cause to suspect that the advice was given in ignorance of material facts;

12.4.2 if proceedings are pending to obtain the decision of the court on the matter;

12.4.3 in relation to a Trustee who has a personal interest in the subject matter of the advice; or

12.4.4 in relation to a Trustee who has committed a breach of trust relating to the subject matter of the advice.

12.5 Clause 12.3 does not prejudice any right of any Person to follow property or income into the hands of any Person, other than a purchaser, who may have received it.

beneficiaries. The focus of the PRs should be to ensure:

(a) that they obtain the binding consent of all affected beneficiaries so they are protected from potential personal liability for *devastavit* (i.e. for having distributed to the wrong person); and

(b) that the agreement is one which the PRs can in fact implement. For example, the PRs should consider whether the agreement has tax consequences and, if so, how these should be addressed.

However, if all affected beneficiaries manage to reach a binding agreement which the PRs can implement, it is not for the PRs to 'approve' or 'disapprove' of it in any moral or ethical sense, e.g. on the basis that they think the testator would or would not have liked it. It also follows from this that PRs are generally not required to actively participate in any negotiations between the affected beneficiaries; indeed, PRs should ensure they do not incur unnecessary costs by doing so.

In cases in which professional negligence proceedings against the draftsman have also been threatened or are on foot, it may be sensible to try to compromise the professional negligence at the same time.

There are two further tools which can help achieve a pragmatic solution without the court's intervention in a suitable case. The first is the possibility of the PRs agreeing to distribute on a particular basis provided the recipient beneficiaries in return provide the PRs with suitable indemnities, possibly backed by security. Such indemnities would be designed to protect the PRs against the risk that they may be personally liable to disappointed beneficiaries if the basis of which they have distributed subsequently turns out to be wrong. The second is the possibility of obtaining insurance to provide the PRs with that same protection.

Whether either of these tools is a useful one will depend on all of the particular surrounding circumstances. As a rather crude rule of thumb, it is suggested that the greater the financial value of the rectification problem, the less likely these tools are to provide a practical solution. This is because the greater the amount of money that turns on the rectification problem, the greater the potential liability of the PRs, and thus the more nervous both the beneficiaries and any insurance company will be in providing PRs with adequate protection. Further, in high value cases there is less of a risk of the estate being significantly depleted by the costs involved in making a court application, which might also point towards such an application being the better option.

3.2.3 Professional negligence

If the will was professionally prepared, it may be possible for a disappointed beneficiary to argue that the rectification problem amounts to professional negligence by the draftsman and seek damages on the basis of *White v Jones*.[235] In these sorts of circumstances, the disappointed beneficiary is usually under a duty to mitigate his loss by seeking to rectify the will before pursuing professional negligence proceedings against the draftsman[236] (although if limitation is a concern, a limitation standstill may have to be agreed, or the professional negligence claim issued protectively and stayed).

Depending on the circumstances, if both the professional negligence claim and the rectification claim have merit, the draftsman's insurers might agree to fund the rectification claim, particularly if the costs

---

235 [1995] 2 AC 207.

236 See e.g. *Walker v Geo H Medlicott & Son* [1999] 1 WLR 727 and *Horsfall v Haywards* [1999] 1 FLR 1182. See also *Grattan v McNaughton* [2001] WTLR 1305 in which the claimant was criticised for pursuing the professional negligence claim first up to and including trial, and only once that claim had been dismissed, pursuing a rectification claim based on the same evidence which she had issued only 14 days before the trial of the professional negligence claim. Although no application to strike out the rectification claim on the grounds that it was an abuse of process was pursued, the judge indicated that he would have been "*provisionally very attracted to it*" as it could not be "*in the public interest to permit virtually the same issues in relation to the drafting of the will to be litigated twice*".

involved in doing so are likely to be lower than their potential exposure in the event the professional negligence claim is successful.[237]

3.2.4. Court intervention: rule 55 of the Non-Contentious Probate Rules 1987

In cases in which it is necessary to rectify a will and the proposed rectification is not opposed by those who might be prejudiced by it, it may be possible to apply to a district judge of the Principal Registry of the Family Division (in London) or a district probate registrar in one of the District Probate Registries to rectify the will pursuant to rule 55 of the Non-Contentious Probate Rules 1987 ("NCPR"). This procedure is likely to be cheaper and quicker than bringing a rectification claim in the Chancery Division[238] (considered below).

Rule 55 NCPR provides:

> *55.— Application for rectification of a will*
>
> *(1) An application for an order that a will be rectified by virtue of section 20(1) of the Administration of Justice Act 1982 may be made to a district judge or registrar, unless a probate action has been commenced.*
>
> *(2) The application shall be supported by an affidavit or witness statement, setting out the grounds of the application, together with such evidence as can be adduced as to the testator's intentions and as to whichever of the following matters as are in issue:–*
>
> *(a) in what respects the testator's intentions were not understood; or*
>
> *(b) the nature of any alleged clerical error.*

---

237 See e.g. *Re Bimson* [2010] EWHC 3679 (Ch) at [23].

238 i.e. what has now become the Property, Trusts and Probate List (ChD) of the Business and Property Courts.

> *(3) Unless otherwise directed, notice of the application shall be given to every person having an interest under the will whose interest might be prejudiced, or such other person who might be prejudiced by the rectification applied for and any comments in writing by any such person shall be exhibited to the affidavit or witness statement in support of the application.*
>
> *(4) If the district judge or registrar is satisfied that, subject to any direction to the contrary, notice has been given to every person mentioned in paragraph (3) above, and that the application is unopposed, he may order that the will be rectified accordingly.*

This procedure will not be appropriate where:

(a) a probate action has been commenced (rule 55(1) NCPR); or

(b) the application is opposed (rule 55(4) NCPR).

The first step is to give notice of the intended application to every person "*having an interest under the will whose interest might be prejudiced*", or such other person "*who might be prejudiced by the rectification applied for*" (rule 55(3) NCPR). This can be done by writing to the relevant person(s) explaining the problem, indicating that it is proposed to resolve the problem by asking the court to rectify the will, and asking the notified person to indicate whether they oppose the intended application for rectification. This first step is likely to be necessary in almost all cases, and will also help determine whether there is scope to resolve the rectification problem by agreement (as discussed above).

Although the position is not entirely clear, it is suggested that the requirement to notify imposed by rule 55(3) NCPR means that this procedure will not be appropriate where the affected beneficiaries who are to be notified include minors, unborns, individuals who lack capacity and/or individuals who cannot be found. In such cases an application for rectification should be made to the Chancery Division instead (considered at 3.2.5. below).

If none of the notified persons opposes the application, the next step will be to draft an affidavit or witness statement "*setting out the grounds of the application, together with such evidence as can be adduced as to the testator's intentions and as to [...] in what respects the testator's intentions were not understood or the nature of any alleged clerical error*". If the will was professionally prepared and the draftsman can be located and contacted, it is likely to be sensible for the draftsman to prepare such affidavit or witness statement, as he will be best placed to explain first-hand how the error occurred.

Once the affidavit or witness statement has been prepared in draft, it should be submitted to a district judge/probate registrar for settling before it is actually finalised (i.e. sworn or signed). This is a helpful way of ensuring that the affidavit or witness statement is in order before it is finalised and is well worth the small fee charged by the Probate Registry for the service (currently £4).[239]

The settled affidavit or witness statement should then be finalised (including by exhibiting any relevant documents). The finalised version can then be submitted to the Probate Registry. As the affidavit or witness statement itself seeks rectification, no separate application notice is required.

As explained above, the application should be made – i.e. the finalised affidavit or witness statement submitted to the Probate Registry – within 6 months of the date on which representation in respect of the estate was first taken out, failing which the claimant will require the court's permission. If the court's permission is required, the maker of the affidavit or witness statement should explain this in the evidence, which should include evidence which addresses the seven factors referred to above.

239 Article 2 of, and item 11 in the table in paragraph 1 of the Schedule to, the Non-Contentious Probate Fees Order 2004 (SI 2004/3120) (as amended).

If the district judge/probate registrar is satisfied that the will should be rectified, he may make an order to that effect. Where a will has been ordered to be rectified by virtue of section 20 AJA, an engrossment of the will in the form in which it is to be proved must be lodged at the Probate Registry.[240]

Because applications pursuant to rule 55 NCPR are only suitable in unopposed cases (as explained above), the incidence of the costs of the application is also likely to be agreed in advance. If the will was professionally drafted and the circumstances strongly suggest that the draftsman was responsible for the error, it is fairly common for the draftsman's insurers to agree to pay the costs of the rectification application, which are likely to be relatively modest if the application is unopposed and can be made pursuant to rule 55 NCPR.

3.2.5 Court intervention: rectification claims in the Chancery Division

Where the procedure provided by rule 55 NCPR cannot be used, for example because the rectification is opposed or because the affected beneficiaries include individuals who lack capacity, are minors and/or are unborn, the appropriate procedure will be to bring a rectification claim in the Chancery Division.[241]

Notifying HMRC

The Chancery Guide provides: "*If there are fiscal consequences which will arise from the changes to the document, HMRC (or any appropriate foreign tax body or bodies) should be notified, preferably before the claim is issued,*

240 Rule 11(2) NCPR.

241 Rectification cannot be obtained by way of an application pursuant to section 48 AJA (discussed in 2.2.4), no matter how strong the claim and/or clear the evidence: see *Greenwold v Pike* [2007] EWHC 2002 (Ch) at [5] and *Clarke-Sullivan v Clarke-Sullivan* [2021] EWHC at [25] and [62(3)].

and invited to confirm whether they wish to be joined as a party to the claim in order to make representations. The evidence in support of the claim should include such notification, and the position of HMRC (or any appropriate foreign tax body or bodies)".[242]

Starting the claim

In many cases rectification claims are brought by way of CPR Part 8 proceedings. This may be because the claim is not opposed by the beneficiaries who are capacitous adults, but it also affects beneficiaries who are minors, unborn, lack capacity and/or cannot be found, and/or it is necessary to obtain a court order granting rectification because the drafting problem has tax consequences.[243] This may also be done because the rectification claim is being brought together with one or more other claims – typically a construction claim[244] – which must be brought by way of a CPR Part 8 claim (see 2.2.5.). In this sort of situation, the procedural rules governing the other claim(s) must also be borne in mind. The Chancery Guide exhorts parties to a rectification claim to "*give careful consideration to whether the claim should be brought under the Part 7 or Part 8 procedure*".[245] It also indicates that where a rectification claim is brought by CPR Part 8 proceedings and there are therefore no particulars of claim, "*the claimant should [...] consider whether to prepare a document which summarises the claim to be provided to the court and the parties with the claim form*".[246]

Some thought should also be given as to whether the court should be

242 Paragraph 18.26 of the Chancery Guide.

243 See e.g. the trust instrument cases of *Racal Group Services Ltd v Ashmore* [1995] STC 1151 and *Allnutt v Wilding* [2007] EWCA Civ 412.

244 See e.g. *Reading v Reading* [2015] EWHC 946 (Ch), *Re Harte* [2015] EWHC 2351 (Ch) and *Guthrie v Morel* [2015] EWHC 3172 (Ch).

245 Paragraph 18.21 of the Chancery Guide.

246 Paragraph 18.22 of the Chancery Guide.

asked to deal with any aspects in dispute as a preliminary issue.[247]

On the other hand, if the rectification claim is brought on its own and is opposed, it is likely to involve a substantial dispute of fact, and it is therefore likely to be more appropriate for the claim to be brought as a CPR Part 7 claim rather than a CPR Part 8 claim.[248]

Parties

Determining who should be made a party to a rectification claim often requires some careful thought. In general, it is useful to bear in mind that:

(a) if the rectification problem is being resolved by way of a contested rectification claim, it should be clear that there are at least two opposing parties, and who they are; they will need to be joined;

(b) the court will want to ensure that everyone affected by the rectification problem has an opportunity to be heard;

(c) in a contentious situation, the PRs should generally remain neutral in their capacity as PRs and not advocate in favour or against rectification, and should instead let the opposing beneficiaries fight it out; and

(d) as indicated above, if the rectification problem affects the amount of tax payable, it may be necessary to notify, and perhaps even join, HMRC.[249]

CPR rule 57.12(2) requires every PR of the estate to be joined as a party

247 As in *Burnard v Burnard* [2014] EWHC 340 (Ch) (see [7]).

248 CPR rule 8.1(2). In *Kelly v Brennan* [2020] EWHC 245 (Ch) the claim was brought by CPR Part 8 (see [3]) despite the fact that rectification was the only relief sought and that the claim was opposed. However, the defendants' position appears to have evolved over time (see [5]-[7]) and there was perhaps no substantial dispute of fact.

249 See "Notifying HMRC" above.

to a rectification claim, which is unsurprising given that the PRs need to be bound by the order. What may be less clear is how to ensure that all affected beneficiaries are joined and are able to have their say.

In cases involving a limited number of affected beneficiaries, the answer may be fairly straightforward. The simplest example is where there are two possible outcomes and the only affected beneficiaries are capacitous adults, as in Example 4 above (assuming both Azucena and Leonora are capacitous adults). In such cases, it may be sensible for the PRs to leave it to the beneficiary who would benefit from the rectification to bring the claim, and to join both the PRs and the other affected beneficiaries as defendants. As the contest is in substance between the affected beneficiaries, the PRs should adopt a neutral stance and let the affected beneficiaries advance the two alternative arguments.

Where one or more of the affected beneficiaries is a minor or lacks capacity and is to be a party to the claim, that beneficiary will need a litigation friend (unless, in the case of a minor, the court makes an order permitting the child to conduct proceedings without a litigation friend).[250] CPR Part 21 contains detailed guidance on the procedure for the appointment of a litigation friend.

On the other hand, the position may be more complicated where the rectification problem affects a large number of beneficiaries (e.g. large classes) and/or where some of the affected beneficiaries are minors, unborn, lack capacity and/or cannot be found. In Example 6 above, the various classes may present several – and possibly all – of these problems. In these sorts of cases, there is likely to be a tension between on the one hand ensuring that everyone who has an interest is properly represented and has an opportunity to be heard, and on the other trying to avoid depleting the estate or trust by incurring significant costs tracing and communicating with large classes of beneficiaries.

How the balance should be struck will inevitably depend on the

250 CPR rule 21.2(1).

circumstances of the particular case. In complicated cases, the provisions of CPR rule 19.9[251] and/or 19.13[252] can be of considerable assistance.[253] These govern respectively the appointment of a party to represent the interests of others and the service of proceedings and/or orders on non-parties so as to bind them. In a suitable case, the ability to issue a CPR Part 8 claim form without naming a defendant pursuant to CPR rule 8.2A may also be useful.[254]

CPR rule 19.9(2) provides:

> *The court may make an order appointing a person to represent any other person or persons in the claim where the person or persons to be represented –*
>
> *(a) are unborn;*

---

251 With effect from 6th April 2023, what used to be CPR rule 19.7 became rule 19.9: see rules 1(1) and 12(10) of the Civil Procedure (Amendment) Rules 2023 (SI 2023/105).

252 With effect from 6th April 2023, what used to be CPR rule 19.8A became rule 19.13: see rules 1(1) and 12(14) of the Civil Procedure (Amendment) Rules 2023 (SI 2023/105).

253 The relevance of these rules to claims concerning estates and trusts is highlighted by paragraphs 25.10 to 25.14 of the Chancery Guide, considered below. Note that CPR rule 19.8, which is entitled "*Representative parties with same interest*", does not apply to claims "*about (a) the estate of a deceased person, (b) property subject to a trust, or (c) the meaning of a document, including a statute*": see CPR rules 19.8(5) and 19.9(1). (CPR rule 19.8 used to be CPR rule 19.6 until it was renumbered with effect from 6th April 2023: see rules 1(1) and 12(9) of the Civil Procedure (Amendment) Rules 2023 (SI 2023/105)).

254 Permission to issue the claim without naming a defendant was given in the will construction case of *Re Harte* [2015] EWHC 2351 (Ch). However, the claimant executors were then directed to take reasonable steps to trace the testatrix's statutory next of kin and to serve notices pursuant to CPR rule 19.8A (now CPR rule 19.13) on various people and charities (see [2]-[4]).

(b) cannot be found;

(c) cannot easily be ascertained; or

(d) are a class of persons who have the same interest in a claim and –

(i) one or more members of that class are within sub-paragraphs (a), (b) or (c); or

(ii) to appoint a representative would further the overriding objective.

This caters for several different scenarios:

(a) is self-explanatory;

(b) covers situations in which it is clear who the affected beneficiary is, but (reasonable) attempts to find him have proved unsuccessful;

(c) covers situations in which it is not clear who the affected beneficiary is, nor can this be easily clarified;

(d) covers two alternative situations where a class of persons has the same interest in the claim:

(i) is self-explanatory;

(ii) is potentially wide and flexible. It can be used, for example, where there is a large class of affected beneficiaries scattered around the world, all of whom have the same interest, and it would further the overriding objective to appoint one of them to represent the whole class (e.g. by reducing procedural delay and costs) – ideally one who can be served within the jurisdiction.[255]

---

255 For an example, see *Public Trustee v Harrison* [2018] EWHC 166 (Ch)

CPR rule 19.9(3) provides that an application for a representation order under CPR rule 19.9(2) may be made "*by any person who seeks to be appointed under the order or any party to the claim*", and may be made "*at any time before or after the claim has started*". CPR rule 19.9(4) provides that the application notice for such an order must be served on:

> *(a) all parties to the claim, if the claim has started;*
>
> *(b) the person sought to be appointed, if that person is not the applicant or a party to the claim; and*
>
> *(c) any other person as directed by the court.*

It is important to note that where the court has made a representation order under CPR rule 19.9, the court's approval is required to settle the claim.[256] This is to safeguard the position of the represented parties and to ensure their representative does not enter into a compromise which is disadvantageous to them: CPR rule 19.9(6) gives the court jurisdiction to approve a settlement "*where it is satisfied that the settlement is for the benefit of all represented persons*".

In relation to CPR rule 19.9, the Chancery Guide explains: "*Where the claim relates to the internal affairs of the trust or estate it may be appropriate for a representation order to be made so that the interests of all classes of beneficiaries are represented and protected but they are also all bound by the decision.*"[257]

CPR rule 19.13 provides:

---

at [8].

256 CPR rule 19.9(5).

257 Paragraph 25.11 of the Chancery Guide. (The paragraph refers to "*CPR 19.7*", which was the old numbering of the rule before it was renumbered rule 19.9 with effect from 6th April 2023: see rules 1(1) and 12(10) of the Civil Procedure (Amendment) Rules 2023 (SI 2023/105))).

Power to make judgements binding on non-parties

(1) This rule applies to any claim relating to –

(a) the estate of a deceased person;

(b) property subject to a trust; or

(c) the sale of any property.

(2) The court may at any time direct that notice of –

(a) the claim; or

(b) any judgment or order given in the claim,

be served on any person who is not a party but who is or may be affected by it.

(3) An application under this rule –

(a) may be made without notice; and

(b) must be supported by written evidence which includes the reasons why the person to be served should be bound by the judgment in the claim.

(4) Unless the court orders otherwise –

(a) a notice of a claim or of a judgment or order under this rule must be –

(i) in the form required by the practice direction;

(ii) issued by the court; and

(iii) accompanied by a form of acknowledgment of service with any necessary modifications;

(b) a notice of a claim must also be accompanied by –

(i) a copy of the claim form; and

(ii) such other statements of case, witness statements or affidavits as the court may direct; and

(c) a notice of a judgment or order must also be accompanied by a copy of the judgment or order.

(5) If a person served with notice of a claim files an acknowledgment of service of the notice within 14 days they will become a party to the claim.

(6) If a person served with notice of a claim does not acknowledge service of the notice they will be bound by any judgment given in the claim as if they were a party.

(7) If, after service of a notice of a claim on a person, the claim form is amended so as substantially to alter the relief claimed, the court may direct that a judgment shall not bind that person unless a further notice, together with a copy of the amended claim form, is served on them.

(8) Any person served with a notice of a judgment or order under this rule –

(a) shall be bound by the judgment or order as if they had been a party to the claim; but

(b) may, provided they acknowledge service –

(i) within 28 days after the notice is served on them, apply to the court to set aside or vary the judgment or order; and

(ii) take part in any proceedings relating to the judgment or order.

(9) The following rules of Part 10 (acknowledgment of service) apply –

(a) rule 10.4; and

(b) rule 10.5, subject to the modification that references to the defendant are to be read as references to the person served with the notice.

(10) A notice under this rule is issued on the date entered on the notice by the court.

The procedure in CPR rule 19.13 can be useful to bind interested beneficiaries who do not want to take an active role in the proceedings, such as the adult children of an 'active' interested beneficiary who are content to simply support their parent's position. However, it suggests that it is unlikely to be a good idea to press on with the proceedings and to then try to rely on CPR rule 19.13 to serve a judgment or order on an interested beneficiary who it is thought will want to actively have a say. In such cases there is a risk that such a beneficiary will then apply to set aside the judgment or order (pursuant to CPR rule 19.13(8)(b)) to, in effect, re-open the case to advance his argument, and this could significantly increase the overall costs. In this sort of situation it is likely to be preferable to ensure that such a beneficiary is able to actively participate from the outset.

It should be borne in mind that the issue of representation is likely to be considered by the court at the first directions hearing, at which creative and pragmatic solutions can be considered with the Master, particularly in complex cases.[258]

---

258 See e.g. *Re Harte* [2015] EWHC 2351 (Ch), in which the PRs were initially given permission to issue the construction and rectification claims without naming a defendant (pursuant to CPR rule 8.2A), and were then given directions as to the steps they should take to ascertain the intestacy beneficiaries (including by advertisement) and as to the

Limitation

If a rectification claim is brought within 6 months of the date on which representation in respect of the estate was first taken out, the court's permission is not required; otherwise, the claimant will have to obtain the court's permission. This is considered in more detail at 3.1 above.

Which court

The County Court appears to have jurisdiction to determine a claim for the rectification of a will if the value of the estate or trust fund does not exceed £350,000.[259] However, in practice rectification claims are invariably issued in the Chancery Division of the High Court,[260] i.e. what has now become the Property, Trusts and Probate List (ChD) of the Business and Property Courts. A rectification claim can be issued either in the Rolls Building in London or in one of the District Registries (Birmingham, Bristol, Cardiff, Leeds, Liverpool, Manchester and Newcastle-upon-Tyne).[261]

---

parties to whom they should give notice of the proceedings pursuant to CPR rule 19.8A (now CPR rule 19.13) (see [3]-[4]); and the trust case of *Womble Bond Dickinson (Trust Corp) Ltd v No Named Defendant* [2022] EWHC 43 (Ch), in which the trustees of an employee benefit trust were given permission to issue the construction claim without naming a defendant, and the court directed their solicitors to instruct a separate counsel to advance the opposing arguments effectively as Advocate to the Court, given that there was no individual who could obviously be appointed to represent all of the beneficiaries: see [6].

259 Section 23 of the County Courts Act 1984 and article 3 of the County Court Jurisdiction Order 2014 (SI 2014/503). This assumes that the rectification claim in question is a type of "*proceedings for relief against [...] mistake*" within section 23(g).

260 Section 61 and paragraph 1(g) of Schedule 1 to the Senior Courts Act 1981; see also paragraph 18.16 of the Chancery Guide.

261 Paragraph 1.3 of the Chancery Guide. Appendix C to the Chancery Guide ('Chancery Business outside the Rolls Building') contains helpful information regarding Chancery business outside London, including

Lodging the grant

If the claimant is the person to whom the grant was made in respect of the will of which rectification is sought, he must, unless the court orders otherwise, lodge the probate or letters of administration with the will annexed with the court when the claim form is issued.[262]

Evidence/Pleadings

A distinction needs to be drawn between rectification claims brought by way of a CPR Part 8 claim and those brought by way of a CPR Part 7 claim.[263]

CPR Part 8 claims: evidence

If the rectification claim is brought by way of a CPR Part 8 claim, the claimant must file the evidence on which he intends to rely when his claim form is issued[264] (unless the claimant only intends to rely on the evidence contained in the claim form itself, which it is suggested is unlikely to be the case in rectification claims). This will generally be in the form of one or more witness statements. CPR Practice Direction 57AC, which applies to "*trial witness statements*"[265] in the Business and Property Courts, does not apply to claims for the rectification of wills, unless the court orders otherwise.[266] The claimant's evidence must be

---

contact details of the various District Registries.

262 Paragraph 10.1 of CPR Practice Direction 57.

263 See "Starting the claim" above.

264 CPR rule 8.5(1); see also paragraph 13.10 of the Chancery Guide.

265 Defined by paragraph 1.2 of CPR Practice Direction 57AC as "*a witness statement that is served pursuant to an order made under rule 32.4(2), or pursuant to rule 8.5 or an order made under rule 8.6(1)(b), or that is prepared for the trial of an unfair prejudice petition or a contributory's just and equitable winding up petition, including supplemental or reply witness statements where allowed by the court*".

266 Paragraph 1.3(6) of CPR Practice Direction 57AC provides that the

served on the defendant with the claim form.[267]

The contents of the witness statement(s) will of course depend on the circumstances of the particular case. In general terms, the topics which one should consider covering in the evidence filed in support of the claim are likely to be:

(a) the claimant's role and the capacity in which he brings the claim;

(b) the factual background;

(c) the current drafting of the will and its construction;

(d) what the testator's intentions are alleged to have been;

(e) how the current drafting of the will fails to give effect to the testator's intentions, and whether this is due to a clerical error and/or a failure to understand the testator's instructions;

(f) how the court is being asked to rectify the will;[268]

(g) the position of the other interested parties;

Practice Direction does not apply to "*proceedings falling within CPR Part 57, which applies to [...] claims for the rectification of wills*", unless the court orders otherwise. Accordingly, it appears that the guidance in paragraph 18.28 of the Chancery Guide (which applies to the preparation of "*trial witness statements in a rectification claim*") does not apply to a claim for the rectification of a will.

267 CPR rule 8.5(2).

268 Paragraph 18.27 of the Chancery Guide encourages "*[c]laimants (and any parties agreeing or consenting to the claim) [...] to consider carefully the form of order sought in advance of issuing the claim*" and "*how the document in respect of which rectification is sought is intended to be treated (i.e. whether the order will be indorsed on the document to be rectified, and, if so, how)*". It also points out that the court "*is likely to wish to make the minimum possible changes in order to rectify the document in question*".

(h) the approximate value of the estate or fund in issue.[269]

If the will was professionally prepared, some thought should be given as to whether evidence should be obtained from the draftsman responsible for preparing it (if available) and, if so, as to who should call the draftsman as a witness.[270]

It should be borne in mind that the CPR requires witness statements to be in the witness's own words.[271] Furthermore, the temptation to include in a witness statement extensive legal submissions and references to case law should generally be resisted, particularly in witness statements of lay witnesses; these are properly a matter for skeleton arguments and submissions.

CPR Part 7 claims: particulars of claim and Initial Disclosure

If the rectification claim is brought by way of a CPR Part 7 claim,[272] the particulars of claim must either be contained in or served with the claim form, or be served on the defendant within 14 days after service of the claim form, subject to them being served no later than the latest time for serving the claim form.[273] The contents of the particulars of claim will of course depend on the circumstances of the particular case. In general terms, the topics which the party seeking rectification should consider covering in the particulars of claim are likely to be the same as those the claimant's evidence should over in CPR Part 8 claims, viz.:

(a) the claimant's role and the capacity in which he brings the claim;

269 Paragraph 25.4 of the Chancery Guide.

270 See e.g. *Re McKay* [2023] EWHC 642 (Ch) at [39]-[40].

271 Paragraph 18.1 of CPR Practice Direction 32; see also paragraph 8.1 of the Chancery Guide.

272 See "Starting the claim" above.

273 CPR rule 7.4.

(b) the factual background;

(c) the current drafting of the will and its construction;

(d) what the testator's intentions are alleged to have been;

(e) how the current drafting of the will fails to give effect to the testator's intentions, and whether this is due to a clerical error and/or a failure to understand the testator's instructions;

(f) how the court is being asked to rectify the will;[274]

(g) the position of the other interested parties;

(h) the approximate value of the estate or fund in issue.

As well as the rules in CPR rule 16.4 and CPR Practice Direction 16, the drafting guidelines contained in paragraphs 4.2 to 4.9 of the Chancery Guide apply to particulars of claim.

In claims proceeding under CPR Part 7,[275] paragraph 5.1 of CPR Practice Direction 57AD requires the claimant to provide at the same time as his statement of case "*an Initial Disclosure List of Documents that lists and is accompanied by copies of:*

> *(1) the key documents on which it has relied (expressly or otherwise) in support of the claims or defences advanced in its statement of case (and*

---

274 Paragraph 18.27 of the Chancery Guide encourages "*[c]laimants (and any parties agreeing or consenting to the claim) [...] to consider carefully the form of order sought in advance of issuing the claim*" and "*how the document in respect of which rectification is sought is intended to be treated (i.e. whether the order will be indorsed on the document to be rectified, and, if so, how)*". It also points out that the court "*is likely to wish to make the minimum possible changes in order to rectify the document in question*".

275 CPR Practice Direction 57AD does not apply to claims proceeding under CPR Part 8, unless otherwise ordered: see paragraph 1.4(7).

including the documents referred to in that statement of case); and

(2) the key documents that are necessary to enable the other parties to understand the claim or defence they have to meet.

Initial Disclosure is not required where a party concludes and states in writing, approaching the matter in good faith, that giving Initial Disclosure would involve it or any other party providing more than the larger of about 1,000 pages or 200 documents.[276] It is suggested that this threshold is unlikely to be met in most rectification claims, and Initial Disclosure is therefore likely to apply.

The parties can also agree in writing prior to the commencement of proceedings that Initial Disclosure should not apply; however, they should only do so with good reason, as the court may review the parties' reasons for disapplying Initial Disclosure at the first case management conference and may set aside such an agreement aside if it considers that Initial Disclosure "*is likely to provide significant benefits and the costs of providing Initial Disclosure are unlikely to be disproportionate to such benefits*".[277]

A party may also apply to the court for directions limiting or abrogating the obligation to provide Initial Disclosure, for example where complying with the obligation "*will incur disproportionate cost or be unduly complex*".[278] Again, it is suggested that this is unlikely to be the case in most will rectification claims.

<u>Prospective (or pre-emptive) costs orders</u>

In some rectification cases it may be appropriate to consider at an early stage of the proceedings whether a mechanism should be put in place for the costs of one or more of the parties to be paid out of the estate or trust

276 Paragraph 5.3(3) of CPR Practice Direction 57AD.

277 Paragraph 5.8 of CPR Practice Direction 51AD.

278 Paragraph 5.10 of CPR Practice Direction 57AD.

fund in any event irrespective of the outcome.[279] This can be either by way of a contractual agreement by the PRs or by a so-called prospective (or pre-emptive) costs order by the court. This issue tends to arise primarily in pension cases, where an individual pension scheme member may be made a party to complex litigation as representative of other scheme members, and it may be unfair for him to have to bear his costs personally at least until the conclusion of the litigation, which can create a cash flow problem.[280] However, the issue is unlikely to arise in claims concerning the rectification of a will.

Where the issue does arise, the eight sub-paragraphs of paragraph 6 of CPR Practice Direction 64A contain some detailed guidance about prospective costs orders, as do paragraphs 25.30 to 25.32 of the Chancery Guide. A model form of prospective costs order is appended to CPR Practice Direction 64A.

Costs management

CPR Part 8 claims

CPR rule 3.12 makes it clear that costs management does not apply to CPR Part 8 claims unless the court orders that it should pursuant to CPR rule 3.12(1A).[281] Paragraph 5(e) of CPR Practice Direction 3D provides that an order for costs management may be "*particularly appropriate*" in "*any Part 8 or other claims or applications involving a substantial dispute of fact and/or likely to require oral evidence and/or extensive disclosure*". The Chancery Guide also provides that: "*It is the court's experience that it is*

279 The costs orders which are likely to be made at the conclusion of the proceedings are considered at "Costs" below.

280 The principles governing the making of a prospective costs order have been considered in a line of pensions cases which includes *McDonald v Horn* [1995] 1 All ER 961 and *IBM United Kingdom Pensions Trust Ltd v Metcalfe* [2012] EWHC 125 (Ch).

281 In relation to which see also and paragraph 2 of CPR Practice Direction 3D. This is reiterated by paragraph 13.30 of the Chancery Guide.

often helpful for costs budgets to be exchanged in cases in the ChD B&PCs London even if costs budgeting would not otherwise apply. Parties should consider exchanging costs budgets and/or opting into costs management even in cases which are outside the costs management regime. If the parties agree that a costs management order should be made, a consent order should be lodged in advance of the CMC including proposed directions for costs management".[282]

A party seeking an order that costs management should apply to the proceedings should "*give notice to the other parties and the court well in advance of the directions hearing and explain, preferably in a witness statement, why such an order is sought*".[283]

CPR Part 7 claims

If a rectification claim is brought by way of CPR Part 7 proceedings, it is likely to be a multi-track claim and costs management is likely to apply to it, unless the court dispenses with costs management pursuant to CPR rule 3.12(e). It seems likely that the court will only do so if it is satisfied that the litigation can be conducted justly and at proportionate cost in accordance with the overriding objective without costs management.[284] Costs budgets and budget discussion reports will have to be filed and exchanged in accordance with the procedure contained in Section II of CPR Part 3.

Service

The usual rules for service contained in the CPR – mostly in CPR Part 6 – apply to claims for the rectification of a will. If it is necessary to seek the court's permission to serve the claim form out of the jurisdiction

282 Paragraph 6.31 of the Chancery Guide.

283 Paragraph 13.31 of the Chancery Guide.

284 This is the basis on which the court can decide (pursuant to CPR rule 3.15(2)) not to make a costs management order even where costs budgets have been filed.

pursuant to CPR rule 6.36, the relevant ground of those listed in paragraph 3.1 of CPR Practice Direction 6B is ground (14), which expressly refers to claims "*for the rectification of a will*".

Responding to the claim

CPR Part 8 claims: defendant's acknowledgment of service and evidence

A defendant who wishes to respond to the claim must file an acknowledgment of service in the relevant practice form (viz. form N210) not more than 14 days after service of the claim form on him.[285] At the same time he must also serve his acknowledgment of service on the claimant and on any other party.[286] If he fails to do so, the defendant may attend the hearing of the claim but may not take part in the hearing unless the court gives permission.[287] As the Chancery Guide makes clear, these are "*serious consequences*".[288]

The defendant must indicate in his acknowledgment of service whether he contests the claim, and if he seeks a different remedy from that set out in the claim form, what that remedy is.[289] There is no need to file a defence, as CPR Part 15 does not apply to claims brought pursuant to CPR Part 8.[290]

Defendants who acknowledge service but do not intend to file any evidence should notify the court in writing when they file their acknowledgment of service that they do not intend to file evidence. This

285 CPR rule 8.3(1); see also paragraph 13.8 of the Chancery Guide. Note that different (longer) periods apply if the proceedings have been served on the defendant out of the jurisdiction: see CPR rules 8.3(3) and 10.3(2).

286 CPR rule 8.3(1).

287 CPR rule 8.4(2).

288 Paragraph 13.8 of the Chancery Guide.

289 CPR rule 8.3(2).

290 CPR rule 8.9(a); see also paragraph 13.9 of the Chancery Guide.

"*enables the court to know what each defendant's intention is when it considers the file and avoids delay*".[291]

CPR rule 8.8(1) provides that where a defendant "*contends that the CPR Part 8 procedure should not be used because there is (a) a substantial dispute of fact and (b) the use of the Part 8 procedure is not required or permitted by a rule or practice direction, he must state his reasons when he files his acknowledgment of service*". In such cases, it may be appropriate for directions to be given for the claim to proceed as, in effect, a hybrid claim, as explained below.[292]

A defendant who wishes to rely on written evidence must file it when he files his acknowledgment of service,[293] and must at the same time serve a copy of his evidence on the other parties.[294] The defendant may not rely on any written evidence which has not been served in accordance with these rules at the hearing of the claim unless the court gives permission.[295]

As the time limit for the defendant to file and serve his evidence is quite short (viz. 14 days from service of the claim on him), CPR rule 8.5(9) allows the parties to "*agree in writing on an extension of time of not more than 14 days for serving and filing evidence from the defendant*". Such an agreement must be filed at court with the acknowledgment of service.[296] The Chancery Guide recognises that it is "*not unusual for an extension of time to be agreed between the parties for the service of evidence*".[297]

If a defendant requires more time to file his evidence, he should apply to the court for an extension of time by way of an application pursuant to

---

291 Paragraph 13.15 of the Chancery Guide.

292 See "<u>Directions hearing</u>" below.

293 CPR rule 8.5(3); see also paragraph 13.10 of the Chancery Guide.

294 CPR rule 8.5(4).

295 CPR rule 8.6(1).

296 CPR rule 8.5(10).

297 Paragraph 13.11 of the Chancery Guide.

CPR Part 23.[298] If the parties are in agreement that such an extension should be granted, the application should be made by filing a consent order.[299] If there is no agreement, an application "*should be made to a Master using the urgent applications procedure set out in paragraphs 15.11 to 15.14 [of the Chancery Guide] but does not need to be certified as urgent business. When issuing the application the applicant should add 'Urgent Application EOT' to the comment box on CE-File to assist the court staff to process the application promptly*".[300] The Chancery Guide indicates that "*[i]n substantial matters the court will normally be willing to grant a reasonable extension*".[301]

As for the claimant's evidence, the contents of any witness statement(s) adduced by a defendant will of course depend on the circumstances of the particular case. In general terms, the topics one should consider covering are likely to be the same as those to be covered by the claimant in his evidence (discussed above). An aspect which can give rise to conflicting factual evidence is the extrinsic evidence of the testator's intention. This might be the case, for example, where that evidence consists of conversations the testator had with different people at different times about his will, which are inconsistent with one another;[302] or where the draftsman gives evidence as to the testator's intentions which conflicts with that given by the testator's family members, friends and/or business associates.[303]

---

298 CPR rule 8.5(8).

299 As to which, see paragraphs 16.36 to 16.41 of the Chancery Guide.

300 Paragraph 15.28 of the Chancery Guide.

301 Paragraph 13.11 of the Chancery Guide.

302 See e.g. *Hives v Machin* [2017] EWHC 1414 (Ch), in which the judge heard and analysed conflicting oral evidence as to the testatrix's intentions, but ultimately concluded that section 21 AJA was not engaged and such evidence was therefore inadmissible (see in particular [39] to [59]).

303 See e.g. *Re Nodes* [2021] EWHC 1057 (Ch), where the evidence as to

If a defendant has the probate or letters of administration in his possession or under his control, he must, unless the court orders otherwise, lodge it in the relevant office within 14 days after the service of the claim form on him.[304]

CPR Part 7 claims: defendant's acknowledgement of service and defence

In most cases,[305] a defendant who wishes to defend a CPR Part 7 claim must either file a defence within 14 days of service of the particulars of claim on him,[306] or file an acknowledgment of service within in the same period[307] and then file a defence within 28 days of service of the particulars of claim.[308] A copy of the defence must also be served on the other parties.[309] The parties can agree to extend these time limits by up to 28 days;[310] if they do, the defendant must notify the court of the agreement in writing.[311]

At the same time as filing a defence, the defendant should consider whether he wishes or needs to bring a counterclaim. This is because the defendant can bring a counterclaim against the claimant by filing particulars of the counterclaim[312] without the court's permission if the

---

the testator's intentions given by the draftsman conflicted with that given by the testator's widow and his long-term business associate.

304 Paragraph 10.2 of CPR Practice Direction 57.

305 Special time limits apply, for example, where the proceedings are served on the defendant out of the jurisdiction: see e.g. CPR rules 10.3(2) and 15.4(2).

306 CPR rule 15.4(1)(a).

307 CPR rule 10.3(1).

308 CPR rule 15.4(1)(b).

309 CPR rule 15.6.

310 CPR rule 15.5(1).

311 CPR rule 15.5(2).

312 CPR rule 20.4(1).

counterclaim is filed at the same time as the defence;[313] however, the defendant will need the court's permission if the counterclaim is filed at any other time.[314] Whether it is necessary to bring a counterclaim will depend on the particular circumstances of the litigation and on the relief the defendant is seeking from the court. For example, if a defendant who is resisting a rectification claim is a beneficiary of a will which has already been admitted to probate and which does not cause any construction problems, it may be sufficient for him to simply file a defence denying that the claimant is entitled to the rectification he seeks (and thus impliedly asking the court to dismiss the claimant's rectification claim). On the other hand, if for example the defendant wishes to ask the court to rectify the will in a different way from that which the claimant is arguing for, and/or wishes to ask the court to determine the meaning of a particular provision of the will, then it may be necessary for him to both defend the claimant's rectification claim and bring a counterclaim.

As well as the rules in CPR rule 16.5 and CPR Practice Direction 16, the drafting guidelines contained in paragraphs 4.2 to 4.12 of the Chancery Guide apply to defences.

In claims proceeding under CPR Part 7,[315] paragraph 5.1 of CPR Practice Direction 57AD requires the defendant to provide at the same time as his statement of case 'Initial Disclosure'. This is considered in more detail above.[316]

If a defendant has the probate or letters of administration in his possession or under his control, he must, unless the court orders otherwise, lodge it in the relevant office within 14 days after the service

---

313 CPR rule 20.4(2)(a).

314 CPR rule 20.4(2)(b).

315 CPR Practice Direction 57AD does not apply to claims proceeding under CPR Part 8, unless otherwise ordered: see paragraph 1.4(7).

316 See "*CPR Part 7 claims: particulars of claim and Initial Disclosure*", under "Evidence/Pleadings" above.

of the claim form on him.[317]

Default and summary judgment

It is generally not possible to obtain judgment in default in a rectification claim. The Chancery Guide explains that: "*It is not the practice of the court to make an order for rectification by default or by consent or without a hearing save in exceptional cases. In all cases, even if unopposed, the court will not make an order without being satisfied that it is justified by the evidence. The court will therefore wish to scrutinise carefully the changes that are proposed and the reasons for them.*"[318]

On the other hand, it is generally possible to obtain summary judgment in a rectification claim in an appropriate case. This will usually be where the claim is opposed and is brought by CPR Part 7 proceedings, and the applicant is able to demonstrate that the claim or defence (as the case may be) has no real prospect of success and that there is no other compelling reason why the claim should be disposed of at a trial. However, if the claim is unopposed and is brought by way of CPR Part 8 proceedings, it will generally be unnecessary to apply for summary judgment, and the claimant can instead ask the court to list the claim for a disposal hearing, as Chief Master Marsh explained in *Sovereign Trustees Ltd v Lewis*:[319]

"*Part 8 claims are markedly different to Part 7 claims. Although there is no bar to issuing a Part 24 application [i.e. an application for summary*

317 Paragraph 10.2 of CPR Practice Direction 57.

318 Paragraphs 18.23 and 18.24 of the Chancery Guide; see also paragraph 5.7: "*Declaratory relief and relief by way of rectification will not be granted without evidence and will not ordinarily be appropriate for resolution by way of default judgment*".

319 [2016] EWHC 2593 (Ch) at [3]. See also paragraph 26.17 of the Chancery Guide in relation to uncontentious claims for the rectification of pension schemes. However, it should be noted that in *The Girls' Day School Trust v GDST Pension Trustees Ltd* [2016] EWHC 1254 (Ch) summary judgment was granted without a hearing in an unopposed claim for the rectification of a pension scheme.

judgment] in a Part 8 claim, it will rarely be necessary for the claimant to do so where it is seeking judgment on the whole of the claim. In part this is because the second limb of CPR 24.2 will normally have no application because there will be no 'trial' as such. Part 8 claims are normally resolved at a 'disposal hearing'. This is made clear by paragraph 8.1 of Practice Direction 8A which states:

> *'8.1 The court may on the hearing date –*
>
> *(i) proceed to hear the case and dispose of the claim;*
>
> *(ii) give case management directions.'*
>
> *It follows that in most Part 8 claims, where the relief sought is unopposed, or cannot realistically be opposed, it will suffice for the claimant to ask the court to fix a disposal hearing at which the court may determine whether or not the relief sought by the claimant should be granted."*

Claimant's reply

CPR Part 8 claims: claimant's evidence in reply

If the claimant wishes to rely on further written evidence in reply to the defendant's evidence, he must file it within 14 days of service of the defendant's evidence on him,[320] and he must also serve a copy of it on the other parties "*within the same time limit*".[321] In the same way as a defendant, a claimant may not rely on any written evidence which has not been served in accordance with these rules at the hearing of the claim unless the court gives permission.[322]

As that time limit is also quite short, CPR rule 8.5(9) allows the parties

320 CPR rule 8.5(5).

321 CPR rule 8.5(6).

322 CPR rule 8.6(1).

to "*agree in writing on an extension of time [...] of not more than 28 days for serving and filing evidence in reply*". Such an agreement must be filed at court "*with 48 hours of the agreement*".[323] As indicated above, the Chancery Guide recognises that it is "*not unusual for an extension of time to be agreed between the parties for the service of evidence*".[324]

If a claimant requires more time to file his evidence in reply to the defendant's, he too should apply to the court for an extension of time by way of an application pursuant to CPR Part 23.[325] The guidance considered above in the context of the defendant's evidence applies equally to applications for extensions of time by claimants in relation to their evidence in reply. In particular, it should be noted that the Chancery Guide indicates that "*[i]n substantial matters the court will normally be willing to grant a reasonable extension*".[326]

CPR Part 7 claims: claimant's reply

If the claimant wishes to file a reply, he must file it with his directions questionnaire.[327] The CPR requires the claimant to serve a reply on the other parties "*at the same time it is filed*".[328] However, the Chancery Guide encourages claimants to serve replies before filing directions questionnaires if possible to give the other parties an opportunity to consider the reply before they file their own directions questionnaires.[329]

As well as the rules in CPR rule 16.7 and CPR Practice Direction 16, the drafting guidelines contained in paragraphs 4.2 to 4.12 of the Chancery

323 CPR rule 8.5(10).

324 Paragraph 13.11 of the Chancery Guide.

325 CPR rule 8.5(8).

326 Paragraph 13.11 of the Chancery Guide.

327 CPR rule 15.8(a)(i).

328 CPR rule 15.8(a)(ii).

329 Paragraph 4.12 of the Chancery Guide.

Guide apply to replies.

Directions and case management

The Chancery Guide encourages parties in all rectification claims – whether proceeding under CPR Part 7 or Part 8 – to "*consider whether it may be of assistance to the court (and the parties) in addition to any witness evidence to seek a direction for a narrative chronology with key documents*".[330] It continues:

"*If such an order is made the parties should seek to identify and agree the key documents and a narrative chronology with reference where appropriate to those key documents. Where there is disagreement, the narrative chronology should set out each of the parties' positions making clear where there is a divergence between them on a particular issue. A bundle containing that narrative chronology and the key documents should be made available to the judge by any PTR and/or provided with skeleton arguments for trial or final hearing.*"[331]

CPR Part 8 claims

Claims issued under the Part 8 procedure are treated as having been allocated to the multi-track and CPR Part 26 ('*Case Management – Preliminary Stage*') does not apply.[332] No directions questionnaires are required.[333]

The court file will generally be considered by the assigned Master[334] after the time for acknowledgment of service has expired, or, if the time for serving the defendant's evidence has been extended, after the expiry of

330 Paragraph 18.29 of the Chancery Guide.

331 Ibid.

332 CPR rule 8.9(c); see also paragraph 13.14 of the Chancery Guide.

333 Paragraph 13.14 of the Chancery Guide.

334 Or District Judge of the High Court if the claim is in one of the District Registries.

that period. If a defendant has not acknowledged service, the assigned Master will typically make an order in the form of CH44.[335] This is an order which directs a defendant who intends to contest the claim to file and serve an acknowledgment of service and evidence by a specified date, failing which he shall not be entitled to rely on any evidence at the disposal hearing unless the court gives permission.[336]

If 21 days after the expiry of any extended period for service of evidence no notice of a directions hearing has been received, the claimant should contact the court by letter filed on CE-File together, if appropriate, with a draft order substantially in form CH44, requesting either a directions or disposal hearing. The letter should provide dates to avoid, and a realistic time estimate for both the hearing and any pre-reading.[337]

At that stage the Master will consider whether the claim and decide:

(a) Whether the claim may be capable of being dealt with 'on paper', i.e. on the papers without a hearing.[338] The Chancery Guide makes it clear that "*[i]t is not the practice of the court to make an order for rectification by default or by consent or without a hearing save in exceptional cases. In all cases, even if unopposed, the court will not make an order without being satisfied that it is justified by the evidence. The court will therefore wish to scrutinise carefully the changes that are proposed and the reasons for them.*"[339] It is suggested that in most (if not all) will rectification claims, a hearing will be

---

335 Paragraph 13.15 of the Chancery Guide.

336 A specimen CH44 order is available on the Government website: https://www.gov.uk/government/publications/form-ch44-order-for-disposal-hearing (accessed 31st May 2023).

337 Paragraph 13.16 of the Chancery Guide.

338 Paragraph 13.18(a) of the Chancery Guide.

339 Paragraphs 18.23 and 18.24 of the Chancery Guide; see also paragraph 5.7: "*Declaratory relief and relief by way of rectification will not be granted without evidence and will not ordinarily be appropriate for resolution by way of default judgment*".

required.

(b) If not, whether directions may be given without a hearing. The Chancery Guide explains: "*In most Part 8 claims, the Master will either make an order for directions at the point of initial review or direct that a hearing is fixed. If directions are given at that stage they will usually give notice of a disposal hearing and give directions concerning further evidence to be filed. The court will give notice of the hearing to all the parties, and the notice or order will specify to whom the notice has been sent*".[340]

(c) Whether the claim is likely to be referred to a different level of judge for disposal.[341] In this regard, the Chancery Guide makes it clear that "*[r]ectification claims will be case managed and determined by a Master save in exceptional cases. In particular, the Master will only refer to a HCJ a claim which is consented to or not opposed if it raises issues of particular complexity or difficulty.*"[342]

A directions hearing with a time estimate of half a day or less (and no more than 90 minutes pre-reading) will take place remotely unless the court orders otherwise.[343] It is suggested that this is likely to be the case in most rectification claims. If a party considers that the directions hearing should take place using a format other than the default format, they should CE-File and serve on the other parties a letter setting out their alternative proposal, together with brief reasons, within 7 days of receipt of the Notice of Hearing.[344] Appendix Z to the Chancery Guide contains helpful guidance on the preparation and conduct of remote or hybrid hearings.

340 Paragraph 13.18(b) of the Chancery Guide.

341 Paragraph 13.18(c) of the Chancery Guide.

342 Paragraph 18.20 of the Chancery Guide.

343 Paragraph 13.19 of the Chancery Guide.

344 Ibid.

The Chancery Guide explains that at a directions hearing, "*the court will generally wish to establish whether:*

(a) the court has all the evidence it will need (including expert evidence)

(b) the claim is ready for a disposal hearing;

(c) any witnesses will need to attend the final hearing for cross-examination, in which case the court will give directions with a view to fixing the period during which the case will be heard;

(d) the disposal hearing should be dealt with by a Master or by a [High Court Judge], Section 9 Judge or Deputy [High Court Judge]."[345]

It is suggested that in a rectification claim, the court is likely to consider the following at a directions hearing:

(a) Evidence, including whether directions should be given for the filing of any further evidence (in addition to the evidence which will already have been filed by that point) and whether any witnesses should be required to attend to give oral evidence and be cross-examined at the disposal hearing.[346] If a rectification claim is proceeding pursuant to CPR Part 8 because it is unopposed (at least by the affected beneficiaries who are capacitous adults), it is likely to be decided on written evidence only.[347] However, if it is opposed but is proceeding pursuant to CPR Part 8 because it has

345 paragraph 13.20 of the Chancery Guide.

346 CPR rule 8.6(2) provides "*The court may require or permit a party to give oral evidence at the hearing*" and CPR rule 8.6(3) provides "*The court may give directions requiring the attendance for cross-examination of a witness who has given written evidence*".

347 See paragraph 13.3 of the Chancery Guide: "*Part 8 claims will generally be disposed of on written evidence without cross-examination. The witness statements with the claim form should be sufficient in most cases to define the issues*".

been brought as an alternative to a construction claim, thought should be given as to whether to seek directions for witnesses (such as the draftsman, if the will was professionally prepared) to be required to attend to give oral evidence and be cross-examined at the disposal hearing.[348] The Chancery Guide provides: "*The evidence in support must establish the common or unilateral mistake on which the claim in rectification is based even where the parties consent to, or do not oppose, the claim. The court may direct that oral evidence be given even where all relevant parties consent (or do not oppose), with or without cross-examination. The court may also wish to hear argument on all relevant matters and may direct that arguments against the remedy are put, including if appropriate by directing that a party take such a role.*"[349] The Chancery Guide also points out that: "*Part 8 is flexible and the court can adopt a hybrid procedure under which limited factual disputes requiring oral evidence or disclosure can be accommodated within Part 8 proceedings – see Vitpol Building Service v Samen [2008] EWHC 2283 (TCC) (paragraph 18)*".[350]

(b) Representation of the parties, such as whether any litigation friend needs to be appointed and/or whether any representation order should be made and/or notice given pursuant to CPR rule 19.13 (as to which, see <u>Parties</u> above).

(c) Directions in relation to the disposal hearing, such as directions about when and how the disposal hearing should be listed, its time estimate, and the level of judge required.

 (i) As regards listing, if there is to be no oral evidence at the disposal hearing, then "*a trial will be listed before the*

348 See e.g. *Re McKay* [2023] EWHC 642 (Ch) at [39]-[40].

349 Paragraph 18.25 of the Chancery Guide.

350 Paragraph 13.28 of the Chancery Guide.

relevant level of judge as directed by a Master".[351] However, if oral evidence is required at the disposal hearing, then the listing of the trial will involve a two-stage procedure.[352] First, a trial window, usually of 3 months, will be specified during which the trial is to take place. Then the parties should provide the court with an agreed list of dates to avoid, and the court will then proceed to fix a date for the start of the trial.[353]

(ii) As regards time estimate, this is likely to depend in particular on the number and complexity of the rectification arguments which are being advanced, and on whether there is going to be live oral evidence from witnesses who will be cross-examined.

(iii) As regards level of judge, as indicated above, paragraph 18.20 of the Chancery Guide provides: "*[r]ectification claims will be case managed and determined by a Master save in exceptional cases. In particular, the Master will only refer to a HCJ a claim which is consented to or not opposed if it raises issues of particular complexity or difficulty*". However, for claims proceeding in a District Registry, it should be noted that paragraph 7B.2(e) of CPR Practice Direction 2B provides that a District Judge in a District Registry may not make an order for rectification without the consent of the Supervising Judge for the region in which the District Judge is sitting, or their nominee.

(d) 'Housekeeping' directions to prepare the case for the disposal hearing, such as directions relating to the hearing bundle,[354]

351 Paragraph 12.24 of the Chancery Guide.

352 See paragraphs 12.16 to 12.23 of the Chancery Guide.

353 Paragraph 12.17 of the Chancery Guide.

354 Detailed rules in relation to hearing bundles are contained in paragraph

skeleton arguments,[355] and other documents such as dramatis personae, chronologies, lists of issues,[356] reading lists[357] and bundles of authorities.[358]

CPR Part 7 claims: costs and case management conference

The Chancery Guide provides that all cases "*appropriately issued in the ChD B&PCs London will be automatically allocated to the multi-track*".[359] Once defences have been filed, the court will send the parties a Notice of Proposed Allocation (form N149C) confirming the allocation to multi-track and providing a date for the filing of Directions Questionnaires ("DQs") (form N181).[360] If any defendant fails to file a defence, this may not happen automatically. Therefore if a Notice of Proposed Allocation has not been received within 21 days of the last deadline for filing a defence, the claimant should contact the court by letter filed on CE-file to request such a Notice.[361]

The parties will then have to file and serve DQs and attempt to agree directions by the date specified in the Notice of Proposed Allocation. Parties can extend the deadline for one or more periods of up to 28 days. To do so, they must file a consent order, which must be approved by the

---

27 of CPR Practice Direction 32 and are supplemented by the guidance contained in Chapter 12 of, and Appendix X to, the Chancery Guide.

355 In relation to which see paragraphs 12.49 to 12.51 of, and Appendix Y to, the Chancery Guide.

356 In relation to which see paragraphs 12.52 to 12.55 of the Chancery Guide.

357 In relation to which see paragraph 12.56 to 12.58 of the Chancery Guide.

358 In relation to which see paragraph 12.59 to 12.61 of the Chancery Guide.

359 Paragraph 6.4 of the Chancery Guide.

360 *Ibid.*

361 Paragraph 6.5 of the Chancery Guide.

court.[362]

On receipt of the DQs, the court will list a case management conference ("CMC") or a costs and case management conference ("CCMC") with a time estimate of 1½ hours plus 1 hour pre-reading, unless the parties provide a different agreed time estimate.[363]

After the DQs are filed and before the first CMC/CCMC, if any of the following issues are raised in the DQs or in any letter accompanying them, the Master will review the DQs and draft directions and may make and order in respect of such issues in advance of the CMC/CCMC:[364]

(a) Whether the claim should remain in the ChD B&PCs London.

(b) Whether a listing of more than 1½ hours is required for a CCMC or CMC.

(c) The appropriate hearing format for the CMC / CCMC.

(d) Whether cost management applies (if the parties disagree about that: see paragraphs 6.28 and 6.29 of the Chancery Guide) and whether or not a costs management order is required.

(e) (If requested) whether there should be a stay of proceedings, or a continuation of an existing stay.

(f) (If requested) whether the claim should be docketed (see Chapter 3 and paragraph 6.25 of the Chancery Guide for further guidance).

A CMC/CCMC with a time estimate of half a day or less (and no more than 90 minutes pre-reading) will take place remotely unless the court

362 Paragraph 6.6 of the Chancery Guide.

363 Paragraphs 6.8 and 6.44 of the Chancery Guide.

364 Paragraphs 6.41 and 6.42 of the Chancery Guide.

orders otherwise.[365] It is suggested that this is likely to be the case in most rectification claims. Appendix Z to the Chancery Guide contains helpful guidance on the preparation and conduct of remote or hybrid hearings.

At the CMC/CCMC, the issues which the court is likely to consider are the same as those which would be considered at a directions hearing if the claim were proceeding as a CPR Part 8 claim (discussed above). However, the sequence of events is likely to be different: in CPR Part 8 claims, by the time the case reaches a directions hearing, witness statements will have already been filed and exchanged, and the relevant documents which the parties wish to rely on will usually have already been disclosed (generally as exhibits to the witness statements). On the other hand, in CPR Part 7 claims, directions for disclosure and witness statements are generally given at the CCMC.

Disclosure

In general terms, in contested will rectification claims which involve a professionally prepared will, the key documentary evidence – and often the only documentary evidence – is usually the will file. Will files are rarely particularly extensive, usually running into the dozens of pages (sometimes into the hundreds, but very rarely into the thousands). As a result, there is normally little difficulty or cost in the file being disclosed in its entirety, usually when the rectification problem is being investigated (and thus before any proceedings are issued).

Where a will file relates to more than one client – which is not uncommon for example where both members of a couple have made wills at the same time using the same solicitor – it may be necessary to redact privileged information relating to the other client (unless that client waives privilege).

In addition to the will file, it may be useful to consider whether there could be any other documentary evidence of the testator's intentions, for

365 Paragraph 6.44 of the Chancery Guide.

example in any diary or other notes he may have kept (including electronic notes such as draft emails or notes made on a computer or a mobile phone or a tablet). Often testators do not discuss what they might consider to be their private personal affairs with friends or even family, but another source of documentary evidence of the testator's intentions could be any correspondence in which these were discussed, including both formal correspondence, such as letters and emails, and more informal communications, such as text messages, WhatsApp messages or other forms of electronic communication.

CPR Part 8 claims

The disclosure process in the Business and Property Courts was substantially overhauled with the coming into effect of CPR Practice Direction 57AD on 1st October 2022.[366] However, the Practice Direction does not apply to claims proceeding under CPR Part 8 "*unless the court orders otherwise*".[367]

Given the disclosure obligations already imposed by CPR Part 8, it is suggested that orders for extended disclosure pursuant to CPR Practice Direction 57AD are likely to be rare in rectification claims proceeding under CPR Part 8. Some support for this can be found in paragraph 13.25 of the Chancery Guide: "*PD 57AD does not apply to Part 8 claims when issued, and it is rare for an order for disclosure to be made in a Part 8 claim. However, if any form of disclosure is ordered the court will adopt such parts of PD 57AD as are appropriate (and CPR 31 does not apply)*".

CPR Part 7 claims

As indicated above, the disclosure process in the Business and Property Courts was substantially overhauled with the coming into effect of CPR

---

366 This followed a pilot introduced with effect from 1st January 2019 by what was CPR Practice Direction 51U.

367 Paragraph 1.4(7) of CPR Practice Direction 57AD.

Practice Direction 57AD on 1st October 2022.[368]

The provisions of Practice Direction 57AD are detailed. In summary, it is suggested that the following points are likely to be particularly relevant in rectification claims.

(a) The Practice Direction imposes a duty to "*to take reasonable steps to preserve documents [...] that may be relevant to any issue in the proceedings*".[369] This duty applies to:

- "*[a] person who knows that it is or may become a party to proceedings that have been commenced or who knows that it may become a party to proceedings that may be commenced*";[370] and

- "*[l]egal representatives who have the conduct of litigation on behalf of a party to proceedings that have been commenced, or who are instructed with a view to the conduct of litigation where their client knows it may become a party to proceedings that have been or may be commenced*".[371]

The duty to preserve documents applies to "*documents which might otherwise be deleted or destroyed in accordance with a document retention policy or in the ordinary course of business*"[372] and "*[p]reservation includes, in suitable cases, making copies of sources and documents and storing them.*"[373] Legal representatives are also under

368 This followed a pilot introduced with effect from 1st January 2019 by what was CPR Practice Direction 51U.

369 Paragraph 3.1(1) and 3.2(1) of CPR Practice Direction 51AD.

370 Paragraph 3.1 of CPR Practice Direction 51AD.

371 Paragraph 3.2 of CPR Practice Direction 51AD.

372 Paragraph 4.1 of CPR Practice Direction 51AD; see also paragraph 4.2 and 4.3.

373 Paragraph 4.1 of CPR Practice Direction 51AD.

a duty to notify their client of the duty to preserve documents "*within a reasonable period of being instructed*"[374] and to obtain written confirmation from the client that any document deletion or destruction processes have been suspended for the duration of the proceedings in accordance with paragraphs 4.2 and 4.3 of CPR Practice Direction 51AD.

(b) The Practice Direction creates a new concept of 'Initial Disclosure', which imposes disclosure obligations at the time a party files his statement of case – and thus before any directions for disclosure are given by the court. This is discussed above.[375]

(c) Once proceedings have commenced, the parties are under a duty "*to disclose, regardless of any order for disclosure made, known adverse documents, unless they are privileged*"[376] in accordance with the provisions of the pilot. 'Known adverse documents' are "*documents (other than privileged documents) that a party is actually aware (without undertaking any further search for documents than it has already undertaken or caused to be undertaken) both (a) are or were previously within its control and (b) are adverse.*"[377] A document is 'adverse' if "*it or any information it contains contradicts or materially damages the disclosing party's contention or version of events on an issue in dispute, or supports the contention or version of events of an opposing party on an issue in dispute*".[378] The duty to disclose adverse documents applies throughout the proceedings[379] and irrespective of any order for Extended Disclosure: "*if adverse documents in the control of a party come to its knowledge at a later date they must (unless*

---

374 Paragraph 4.4 of CPR Practice Direction 51AD.

375 See "*CPR Part 7 claims: particulars of claim and Initial Disclosure*", under "Evidence/Pleadings" above.

376 Paragraph 3.1(2) of CPR Practice Direction 51AD.

377 Paragraph 2.8 of CPR Practice Direction 51AD.

378 Paragraph 2.7 of CPR Practice Direction 51AD.

379 Paragraph 3.3 of CPR Practice Direction 51AD.

privileged) be disclosed without delay".[380]

(d) A party wishing to seek disclosure of documents in addition to, or as an alternative to, Initial Disclosure must request 'Extended Disclosure'.[381] This is done by completing a 'Disclosure Review Document' in advance of the first case management conference in accordance with paragraph 7 of CPR Practice Direction 51U (no application notice is required).[382] An order for Extended Disclosure will only be made where the court "*is persuaded that it is appropriate to do so in order fairly to resolve one or more of the Issues for Disclosure*".[383] The order "*must be reasonable and proportionate having regard to the overriding objective*",[384] including the seven factors listed in paragraph 6.4 of CPR Practice Direction 51AD.[385] The 'Issues for Disclosure' are "*those key issues in dispute, which the parties consider will need to be determined by the court with some reference to contemporaneous documents in order for there to be a fair*

---

380 Paragraph 9.3 of CPR Practice Direction 51AD.

381 Paragraph 6.1 of CPR Practice Direction 51AD.

382 *Ibid.*

383 Paragraph 6.3 of CPR Practice Direction 51AD.

384 Paragraph 6.4 of CPR Practice Direction 51AD.

385 These are:

(1) the nature and complexity of the issues in the proceedings;

(2) the importance of the case, including any non-monetary relief sought;

(3) the likelihood of documents existing that will have probative value in supporting or undermining a party's claim or defence;

(4) the number of documents involved;

(5) the ease and expense of searching for and retrieval of any particular document (taking into account any limitations on the information available and on the likely accuracy of any costs estimates);

(6) the financial position of each party; and

(7) the need to ensure the case is dealt with expeditiously, fairly and at a proportionate cost.

resolution of the proceedings";[386] however, this does not extend "*to every issue which is disputed in the statements of case by denial or non-admission.*"[387] The parties are required to identify and to try to agree the List of Issues for Disclosure in section 1A of the Disclosure Review Document.[388] In relation to each Issue for Disclosure, the parties must also consider which of the five 'Disclosure Models' identified in paragraph 8 of CPR Practice Direction 51AD should apply.[389] Although the parties may agree that a particular Model should apply to a particular Issue for Disclosure, no Model will in fact apply without the approval of the court,[390] who will usually consider whether to make an order for Extended Disclosure and, if so, on what terms at the first case management conference.

(e) Appendix 5 to Practice Direction 57AD contains provisions "*for a simplified disclosure regime for Less Complex Claims*".[391] These are defined as claims which by virtue of their "*nature, value, complexity and the likely volume of Extended Disclosure may not benefit from the full procedure set out in the main body of Practice Direction 57AD*".[392] If the value of the claim is less than £1m, the claim should be treated as a Less Complex Claim unless its nature, complexity and/or the likely volume of Extended Disclosure indicate to the contrary.[393] A claim may be treated as a Less Complex Claim either by agreement made between all the parties

386 Paragraph 7.6 of CPR Practice Direction 51AD.

387 *Ibid.*

388 Paragraph 7 of CPR Practice Direction 51AD.

389 See also paragraph 9 of CPR Practice Direction 51AD.

390 Paragraph 8.2 of CPR Practice Direction 51AD.

391 Paragraph 1 of Appendix 5 to CPR Practice Direction 57AD.

392 Paragraph 3 of Appendix 5 to CPR Practice Direction 57AD.

393 Paragraph 4 of Appendix 5 to CPR Practice Direction 57AD.

or by order of the court.[394] An agreement between the parties may be made before or after the claim is issued.[395] If there is no agreement between the parties before the claim is issued, "*the claimant may by letter or in its particulars of claim notify the defendant that it wishes the claim to be treated as a Less Complex Claim. If no such notification is given by the claimant, a defendant may by letter or in its defence notify the claimant that it wishes to threat the claim as a Less Complex Claim*".[396] Such a request must include brief reasons for believing that the claim meets the relevant criteria.[397] If no agreement is reached, the court may make an order of its own volition or on an application made by a party by application notice, which the court will determine in writing without a hearing where possible.[398]

As indicated above, in most rectification claims the key – and possibly the only – documentary evidence is likely to be the will file. In practice, this will usually be disclosed during pre-action correspondence. It also seems likely that in most cases all other relevant documentary evidence will be disclosed either pre-action or during Initial Disclosure. As a result, there may be no need for any Extended Disclosure. However, where some further disclosure is envisaged, the parties may want to consider agreeing that the claim be treated as a Less Complex Claim, as the simplified disclosure regime should be suitable in most rectification claims, and is likely to be more streamlined and thus less costly that the 'full' regime imposed by CPR Practice Direction 57AD.

Depending on the circumstances, it may also be worth considering whether disclosure should be sought from a non-party pursuant to CPR

---

394 Paragraph 5 of Appendix 5 to CPR Practice Direction 57AD.

395 Paragraph 6 of Appendix 5 to CPR Practice Direction 57AD.

396 Paragraph 7 of Appendix 5 to CPR Practice Direction 57AD.

397 Paragraph 8 of Appendix 5 to CPR Practice Direction 57AD.

398 Paragraph 9 of Appendix 5 to CPR Practice Direction 57AD.

rule 31.17.

Witness statements

CPR Part 8 claims

In CPR Part 8 claims, witness statements will have already been filed and served at the early stages of the proceedings (as discussed above).

CPR Part 7 claims

In CPR Part 7 claims, directions for the exchange of witness statements are normally given at the CCMC. Who should be asked to give evidence and what that topics that evidence should cover will depend on the particular circumstances of the case. In general terms, the topics which the evidence is likely to have to cover are the same which the particulars of claim should cover, viz.:

(a) the claimant's role and the capacity in which he brings the claim;

(b) the factual background;

(c) the current drafting of the will and its construction;

(d) what the testator's intentions are alleged to have been;

(e) how the current drafting of the will fails to give effect to the testator's intentions, and whether this is due to a clerical error and/or a failure to understand the testator's instructions;

(f) how the court is being asked to rectify the will;

(g) the position of the other interested parties;

(h) the approximate value of the estate or fund in issue.

In cases involving a professionally prepared will, the key witness evidence is generally likely to be that of the individual or individuals who were involved in taking instructions for will, drafting it and arranging its execution. Indeed, in some cases the draftsman may be the only witness.[399] Depending on how involved they were, the attesting witnesses may also be able to shed light on the testator's intentions and on the will making process.

If the testator discussed his intentions with family and/or friends (who may or may not be beneficiaries or intended beneficiaries of his will), these individuals may also be able to give evidence on the issue.

CPR Practice Direction 57AC, which applies to "*trial witness statements*"[400] in the Business and Property Courts, does not apply to claims for the rectification of wills, unless the court orders otherwise.[401]

Disposal hearing/trial

At the disposal hearing (in CPR Part 8 claims) or trial (in CPR Part 7 claims), the court will hear the argument in favour and against rectification. In CPR Part 8 claims, directions will have previously been given as to whether there should be oral evidence and cross-examination

---

399 See e.g. *Re Bimson* [2010] EWHC 3679 (Ch) at [6].

400 Defined by paragraph 1.2 of CPR Practice Direction 57AC as "*a witness statement that is served pursuant to an order made under rule 32.4(2), or pursuant to rule 8.5 or an order made under rule 8.6(1)(b), or that is prepared for the trial of an unfair prejudice petition or a contributory's just and equitable winding up petition, including supplemental or reply witness statements where allowed by the court*".

401 Paragraph 1.3(6) of CPR Practice Direction 57AC provides that the Practice Direction does not apply to "*proceedings falling within CPR Part 57, which applies to [...] claims for the rectification of wills*", unless the court orders otherwise. Accordingly, it appears that the guidance in paragraph 18.28 of the Chancery Guide (which applies to the preparation of "*trial witness statements in a rectification claim*") does not apply to a claim for the rectification of a will.

of any of the witnesses (e.g. the draftsman).[402]

Disposal hearings/trials in rectification claims are generally listed in public, i.e. in a court which is open to members of the public.[403] Whilst it may be possible in some cases to persuade a court to list the claim in private pursuant to CPR rule 39.2(3),[404] or to impose some other less extensive reporting restriction,[405] a party seeking such an order is likely to have to show compelling reasons why the court should depart from the principle of open justice.[406]

---

402 See paragraph 13.33 of the Chancery Guide.

403 Under the general rule in CPR rule 39.2(1).

404 CPR rule 39.2 requires the court to sit in private if it is satisfied (i) that "*it is necessary to sit in private to secure the proper administration of justice*" and (ii) that one or more of the 7 sub-rules of CPR rule 39.2(3) is engaged. Of those sub-rules, those which may be engaged in a rectification claim are likely to be (c), (d) and (g), viz.:

(c) [the hearing] involves confidential information (including information relating to personal financial matters) and publicity would damage that confidentiality;

(d) a private hearing is necessary to protect the interests of any child or protected party; [...]

(g) the court considers [a hearing in private] to be necessary, in the interests of justice."

On the other hand, sub-rule (f) is unlikely to be engaged in contested rectification cases, as that sub-rule is engaged in relation to hearings involving "*<u>uncontentious</u> matters arising in the administration of trusts or in the administration of a deceased person's estate*" (emphasis added).

405 See e.g. *ABC v JKL* [2019] EWHC 2416 (Ch), which involved the rectification of a deed of appointment.

406 See in this regard the Court of Appeal's guidance in *MN v OP* [2019] EWCA Civ 679 regarding privacy and reporting restrictions in the context of applications pursuant to the Variation of Trusts Act 1958.

Judgment

The Master or judge will decide how, when and where to deliver judgment. Judgment may be delivered orally immediately at the conclusion of the hearing (a so-called '*ex tempore*' judgment),[407] or may be reserved. A reserved judgment may be delivered orally at a later date or, more commonly, may be circulated in written draft to the parties and then formally handed down at a subsequent date. Sometimes – particularly in urgent cases – the court may announce its decision and make any necessary order at the conclusion of the hearing and provide its reasoned judgment at a later date.[408]

Costs

As indicated at 3.2.3 above, if the will was professionally prepared and the circumstances indicate that a professional negligence claim against the draftsman is likely, his insurers may have agreed in advance to fund the costs of the rectification claim. Where the claim is unopposed, the court will often be asked to make no order as to costs, on the basis that the parties will recover their costs from the draftsman's insurer as agreed.[409]

On the other hand, if the rectification claim is contested, the general rule (which applies in all civil litigation) is that the unsuccessful party will be ordered to pay the costs of the successful party.[410] However, costs are ultimately in the discretion of the court,[411] and the court may therefore decide to depart from that starting point and make a different costs order. In general terms, in deciding costs the court will try to ensure that the

407 See e.g. *Slattery v Jagger* [2015] EWHC 3976 (Ch).

408 See e.g. *ABC v JKL* [2019] EWHC 2416 (Ch) at [4].

409 See e.g. *Re Bimson* [2010] EWHC 3679 (Ch) at [23] and *Gerling v Gerling* [2010] EWHC 3661 (Ch) at [50].

410 CPR rule 44.2.(2)(a).

411 Section 51(1) of the Senior Courts Act 1981.

costs are in fact borne by the negligent draftsman and/or (in a contested case) by the party who has lost, and not by the successful party. In deciding precisely how this should be achieved, the court will have to take into account all of the circumstances, including the parties' respective interests under the will and who would in fact bear the costs if the costs are ordered to be paid out of the estate.[412] It may also be possible to seek a non-party costs order against the firm responsible for the negligent drafting.[413]

Order

If the rectification claim succeeds, the order will need to make it clear precisely how the will is being rectified. It will usually be sensible for one of the recitals to record that the court was satisfied that the will is so expressed that it fails to carry out the testator's intentions in consequence of a clerical error or of a failure to understand the testator's instructions (as the case may be).

How the rectification is best recorded in the order will depend on precisely what the rectification consists of. In general terms, it is suggested that:

(a) if the rectification is straightforward and can be clearly described in few words, this can be done in the body of the order (e.g. "pursuant to section 20(1)(b) of the Administration of Justice Act 1982, the Will is rectified by the replacement in clause 3 of the word "patricians" with the word "people");[414]

412 See e.g. and *Marley v Rawlings (costs)* [2014] UKSC 51 and *Slattery v Jagger* [2015] EWHC 3976 (Ch) at [103]-[112].

413 See CPR rule 46.2. Such an order was sought e.g. in *Royal Commonwealth Society for the Blind v Beasant* [2021] EWHC 352 (Ch) at [19]-[48] (the costs order was not considered on appeal: [2022] EWHC 1319 (Ch) at [35]).

414 See Example 6.

(b) however, if the rectification is less straightforward, it is likely to be sensible for the body of the order to refer to a schedule (e.g. by providing: "pursuant to section 20(1)(b) of the Administration of Justice Act 1982, the Will is rectified in the manner set out in the Schedule hereto"), and for the schedule to then set out the rectified version of the relevant provisions of the will.

A copy of every order made for the rectification of a will must be sent to the Principal Registry of the Family Division for filing, and a memorandum of the order must be endorsed on, or permanently annexed to, the grant under which the estate is administered.[415] The order should contain a provision to that effect.

Paragraphs 16.8 to 16.22 of the Chancery Guide contain guidance in relation to the drafting, filing and sealing of orders following a hearing; paragraph 16.23 contains an example form of order.

Appeals

A party who is dissatisfied with the court's decision must obtain the court's permission in order to appeal it.[416] The court will only grant permission to appeal if it considers that the appeal would have a real prospect of success, or that there is some other compelling reason for the appeal to be heard.[417]

Although this is not strictly required, it is generally sensible for a party who wishes to appeal to first seek permission from the lower court.[418] This is usually done when judgment is delivered or handed down and consequential issues, such as the terms of the order giving effect to the

415 Paragraph 11 of CPR Practice Direction 57.

416 CPR rule 52.3(1).

417 CPR rule 52.6(1).

418 Pursuant to CPR rule 52.3(2)(a); see e.g. *In re T (A Child)* [2002] EWCA Civ 1736 at [12]-[13].

judgment and costs, are decided.[419]

If the lower court refuses permission, or if permission was not sought from it, permission must be sought from the appeal court by filing an Appellant's Notice.[420] Unless the court orders otherwise, the time limit for doing so is "*21 days after the date of the decision of the lower court*".[421] That is a relatively short time limit, which cannot be extended by agreement between the parties,[422] and it must be borne in mind that the period starts to run from the date of the decision of the lower court and not, if later, the date on which consequential matters are decided or the date on which the order giving effect to the decision is approved and sealed.[423] If – as is quite common – the lower court's judgment is circulated to the parties in draft and then formally handed down in the absence of the parties, and a hearing to decide consequential matter is arranged at a later date, the lower court should be asked to direct[424] that the 21-day period will only start to run from the date of the later hearing, rather than from the date on which judgment was handed down.[425]

---

419 See paragraph 12.91 of the Chancery Guide.

420 CPR rules 52.3(2)(b) and 52.12(1).

421 CPR rule 52.12(2)(b).

422 CPR rule 52.15(2).

423 See e.g. *Sayers v Clarke Walker (A Firm)* [2002] EWCA Civ 645 at [8]-[9] and *Owusu v Jackson* [2002] EWCA Civ 877 at [24]-[27].

424 Pursuant to CPR 52.12(2)(a).

425 See e.g. *Jackson v Marina Homes Ltd* [2007] EWCA Civ 1404 at [8]. This is envisaged by paragraph 12.91 of the Chancery Guide.

Compromise

In some cases it may be possible to compromise a rectification claim after proceedings have been issued.[426] The mechanism by which the compromise should be implemented will inevitably depend on its terms and on the particular circumstances of the case. In most cases, the following will have to be considered:

(a) Whether the compromise has any tax implications and, if so, whether it is desirable to implement it by way of a deed of variation which can be 'read back' for IHT and/or CGT purposes.[427]

(b) Whether a court order rectifying the will is required, and if so whether the court can be asked to make the order by consent without hearing full argument. In *Burford (Fareham) Ltd v Christian Vision*[428] (which involved the rectification of a deed of assignment of warranties) the court held that there is no "*blanket rule that rectification should not be ordered by consent*"[429] and that the question is one of the court's discretion. However, it should be borne in mind that this jurisdiction is exercised sparingly. In this regard, paragraphs 18.23 and 18.24 of the Chancery Guide provide: "*It is not the practice of the court to make an order for rectification by default or by consent or without a hearing save in exceptional cases. In all cases, even if unopposed, the court will not make an order without being satisfied that it is justified by the evidence. The court will therefore wish to scrutinise carefully the changes that are proposed and the reasons for them*".

426 The circumstances in which it may be possible to resolve a rectification issue without the need for court proceedings are considered at 3.2.2 above.

427 See section 142 of the Inheritance Tax Act 1984 and section 62 of the Taxation of Chargeable Gains Act 1992.

428 [2005] EWHC 2533 (Ch).

429 [2005] EWHC 2533 (Ch) at [7].

(c) Whether the court's approval of the compromise is required, which will be the case where one or more of the parties is a minor,[430] an adult who lacks capacity to conduct litigation[431] and/or a party who has been appointed to represent others pursuant to CPR rule 19.9.[432]

Paragraphs 16.36 to 16.41 of the Chancery Guide contain guidance in relation to consent orders.

430 CPR rule 21.10.

431 *Ibid.*

432 CPR rule 19.9(5).

CHAPTER FOUR

CONSTRUCTION OF OTHER TRUST INSTRUMENTS

4.1 The law

In *Rafferty v Philp*[433] Norris J cited with approval the following passage from *Lewin on Trusts*:[434]

> *Lifetime settlements are no different from other documents in that the subjective intentions of their authors are irrelevant. What counts is the objective meaning that the words of the document convey to the court when considered as a whole in the light of the surrounding circumstances.*

In *Marley v Rawlings*[435] (which concerned a will) the Supreme Court provided the following general guidance in relation to the modern approach to the construction of different types of documents:[436]

> *19. When interpreting a contract, the court is concerned to find the intention of the party or parties, and it does this by identifying the meaning of the relevant words, (a) in the light of (i) the natural and ordinary meaning of those words, (ii) the overall purpose of the*

---

433 [2011] EWHC 709 (Ch).

434 [2011] EWHC 709 (Ch) at [23].

435 [2014] UKSC 2.

436 Other leading authorities on the modern approach to construction generally include *Chartbrook Ltd v Persimmon Homes Ltd* [2009] UKHL 38, *Rainy Sky SA v Kookmin Bank* [2011] UKSC 50, *Arnold v Britton* [2015] UKSC 36 and *Wood v Capita Insurance Services Ltd* [2017] UKSC 24.

document, (iii) any other provisions of the document, (iv) the facts known or assumed by the parties at the time that the document was executed, and (v) common sense, but (b) ignoring subjective evidence of any party's intentions. [...]

20. When it comes to interpreting wills, it seems to me that the approach should be the same. Whether the document in question is a commercial contract or a will, the aim is to identify the intention of the party or parties to the document by interpreting the words used in their documentary, factual and commercial context. As Lord Hoffmann said in Kirin-Amgen Inc v Hoechst Marion Roussel Ltd [2005] 1 All ER 667, para 64, "No one has ever made an acontextual statement. There is always some context to any utterance, however meagre." To the same effect, Sir Thomas Bingham MR said in Arbuthnott v Fagan [1995] CLC 1396, 1400 that "courts will never construe words in a vacuum".

21. Of course, a contract is agreed between a number of parties, whereas a will is made by a single party. However, that distinction is an unconvincing reason for adopting a different approach in principle to interpretation of wills: it is merely one of the contextual circumstances which has to be borne in mind when interpreting the document concerned. Thus, the court takes the same approach to interpretation of unilateral notices as it takes to interpretation of contracts: see Mannai Investment Co Ltd v Eagle Star Life Assurance Co Ltd [1997] AC 749, [...]

22. Another example of a unilateral document which is interpreted in the same way as a contract is a patent—see the approach adopted by Lord Diplock in Catnic Components Ltd v Hill & Smith Ltd [1982] RPC 183, 243, cited with approval, expanded, and applied in Kirin-Amgen at paras 27–32 by Lord Hoffmann. A notice and a patent are both documents intended by its originator to convey information, and so, too, is a will.

> *23. In my view, at least subject to any statutory provision to the contrary, the approach to the interpretation of contracts as set out in the cases discussed in para 19 above is therefore just as appropriate for wills as it is for other unilateral documents.*

Several cases since *Marley v Rawlings* have confirmed that the approach identified by the Supreme Court in that case applies to the construction of unilateral trust instruments such as declarations of trust in a family context,[437] and

Section 21 of the Administration of Justice Act 1982 only applies to wills.[438] As a result, when construing trust instruments other than wills, the distinction between evidence of the settlor's subjective intention (which is not admissible) and other evidence of the so-called 'factual matrix' surrounding the making of the instrument (which is) can be significant. Moreover, it may not always be easy to determine what evidence is in fact relevant to the 'factual matrix'.[439]

---

437 *Millar v Millar* [2018] EWHC 1926 (Ch) at [17]-[23], and in particular at [23]; *Public Trustee v Harrison-Mills* [2018] EWHC 166 (Ch) at [18] (the Court of Appeal overturned the decision on costs, but not on construction: [2019] EWCA Civ 966); *First National Trustco (UK) Ltd v Page* at [68]-[70] (affirmed by the Court of Appeal: [2020] EWCA Civ 107 at [30]-[33]); *Armstrong v Armstrong* [2019] EWHC 2259 (Ch) at [21]-[22]; *Bowack v Saxton* [2020] EWHC 1049 (Ch) at [25]-[26]; *Fafalios v Apodiacos* [2020] EWHC 1189 (Ch) at [30]-[34]; *A-G v Zedra Fiduciary Services (UK) Ltd* [2020] EWHC 2988 (Ch) at [43]-[44]; *PTNZ v AS* [2020] EWHC 3114 (Ch) at [36]-[45]; *Womble Bond Dickinson (Trust Corp) Ltd v Glenn* [2021] EWHC 624 (Ch) at [17]; *Re BetIndex Ltd* [2021] EWHC 1542 (Ch) at [24]-[26]; *Womble Bond Dickinson (Trust Corp) Ltd v No Named Defendant* [2022] EWHC 43 (Ch) at [25]-[28]; *Swissindependent Trustees SA v Sofer* [2023] EWHC 12 (Ch) at [23]-[30].

438 This is discussed at 2.1.

439 See e.g. *Public Trustee v Harrison-Mills* [2018] EWHC 166 (Ch), in which the court concluded that there was no admissible evidence of the 'factual matrix' surrounding the making of the two documents the court

In *Re Hand*[440] the court accepted that human rights considerations can be relevant to the construction of a will. The reference in a 1946 will to "*children*" *prima facie* had to be construed as excluding adopted children as a result of the Adoption of Children Act 1926, which treated adopted children as children of their natural, rather than their adoptive, parents for succession purposes. Although that position had been reversed in 1950, it had been preserved in relation to existing dispositions. However, the court concluded that it was required by the Human Rights Act 1998 to read down the relevant preserving legislation,[441] and to construe "*children*" as including two adopted children so as not to breach their human rights.[442] The full impact of this decision is yet to be explored.[443] The earlier decision in *Re Erskine 1948 Trust*[444] indicates that human rights considerations can be equally relevant to the construction of other trust instruments.

was being asked to construe, and decided that the documents had to be construed by considering their wording only (at [18]-[21]). (The Court of Appeal overturned the decision on costs, but not on construction: [2019] EWCA Civ 966.)

440 [2017] EWHC 533 (Ch).

441 Paragraph 6(1) of Schedule 2 to the Adoption Act 1976.

442 The relevant human rights were the right to respect for private and family life, protected by article 8 of the European Convention on Human Rights, and the right not to be discriminated against on the on the ground of "*birth or other status*", protected by article 14.

443 See e.g. *PQ v RS* [2019] EWHC 1643 (Ch), in which Chief Master Marsh expressed no view as to whether *Re Hand* had been correctly decided (at [24]). See also *Re JC Druce Settlement* [2019] EWHC 3701 (Ch) and *Goodrich v AB* [2022] EWHC 81 (Ch), in which *Re Hand* was followed.

444 [2012] EWHC 732 (Ch).

4.2 Practice and procedure

4.2.1 Who is affected?

The first question trustees should ask themselves when faced with a construction problem is: who is affected by it?

The reason for this is that construction problems have a right answer – and one, or possibly several, wrong ones. Therefore trustees should not try to decide themselves what they think the answer is and then act on that basis. If they do and if they proceed on the basis of an answer which later turns out to be the wrong one, they can be personally liable for breach of trust (i.e. for having administered and/or distributed the trust fund incorrectly).

It follows that the main concern for trustees faced with a construction problem is to ensure that before they take any step based on a particular construction, they protect themselves from potential personal liability for breach of trust. They can do this by obtaining either the binding consent of all affected beneficiaries or authorisation from the court. To get to that position, the trustees will first have to establish who the affected beneficiaries are.

Needless to say, the answer to this will depend on the particular circumstances, and can vary widely. In simple terms, the way to go about ascertaining the affected beneficiaries is to consider the different possible constructions (which may be two or more) and then consider who would benefit under each possible construction, as illustrated by the following examples.

<u>Example 7</u>

In 1968 Dr Bartolo settled a valuable investment portfolio to be held on trust for Marcellina for life, and following her death "*for such child or children of mine as shall then be living, if more than one in equal shares absolutely*", and in default for Count Almaviva absolutely.

Dr Bartolo had only one child, Figaro, who was born out of wedlock.

Following Marcellina's death, there are two possible constructions:

(a) Figaro qualifies as a "*child*" of Dr Bartolo and is therefore entitled to the trust fund; or

(b) Figaro does not qualify as a "*child*" of Dr Bartolo because he is illegitimate, and the trust fund therefore passes to Count Almaviva.

The affected beneficiaries are therefore:

(a) Figaro; and

(b) Count Almaviva.

<u>Example 8</u>[445]

Rigoletto and his late wife owned their home as tenants in common in equal shares. By her will, she left her 50% share in the property to her daughter, Gilda. After receiving tax advice, in 2005 Gilda settled the 50% share in the property she had inherited from her mother on trust for Rigoletto for life, and in remainder for herself, subject to an overriding discretionary power of appointment in favour of a class including herself, her spouse and her children and remoter issue.

Rigoletto and Gilda have recently changed advisors and their new solicitors, Marullo & Co, have discovered that the 2005 trust deed contains a settlor exclusion clause.

There are two possible constructions:

(a) the settlor exclusion clause applies and takes precedence over Gilda's interests; or

445 This example is loosely based on the facts of *Millar v Millar* [2018] EWHC 1926 (Ch).

(b) the settlor exclusion clause does not apply.

The affected beneficiaries are therefore:

(a) Rigoletto;

(b) Gilda; and

(c) the discretionary class of Gilda's spouse and her children and remoter issue.

Example 9

Shortly before his death, Sarastro executed a deed of trust by which he settled a temple he owned on trust for Pamina for life and thereafter to "*those members of the Enlightened Brotherhood to whom I was particularly close*". A few weeks later he died intestate.

The issue is whether the gift in remainder:

(a) is valid and takes effect; or

(b) is void for uncertainty, and thus gives rise to a resulting trust and in turn a partial intestacy.

The affected beneficiaries are therefore:

(a) the members of the intended class; and

(b) Sarastro's intestacy beneficiaries.

If the construction problem affects the amount of tax payable, some thought should be given to whether it is also necessary to involve HMRC.

The corollary to the above is that trustees should bear in mind that they have no personal interest in how the construction problem is resolved between the affected beneficiaries. It is generally not for the trustees to try to second guess what the settlor might have intended, nor to form a view as to which of the affected beneficiaries is more 'worthy' or 'deserving'. The trustees should remain neutral and impartial, and simply do what they are told, either by a unanimous binding agreement reached by all of the affected beneficiaries, or by the court.[446]

4.2.2 Can the problem be resolved by agreement?

In principle, a construction problem can be resolved by the unanimous agreement of all of the beneficiaries affected by it. Therefore, once the trustees have identified all of the affected beneficiaries, the next question they should ask themselves is: can the problem be resolved by agreement?

Suppose that in Example 7 above Figaro and Count Almaviva reach an agreement as to how to divide the trust fund between them. They are the only two parties affected by the uncertainty. If they are able to agree what should happen to the trust fund, then provided they are both capacitous adults, they can resolve the construction problem between themselves without having to go to court. The trustees' only concern will be to ensure that the agreement is properly documented so that they cannot later be criticised by Figaro or Count Almaviva for acting in accordance with it.

Resolving the problem by agreement is usually significantly cheaper and quicker than asking the court to do so. However, as indicated above, if the construction problem affects the amount of tax payable, some thought should be given to whether it is also necessary to obtain the agreement of HMRC.

In practice, construction problems are generally only resolved by

446 See e.g. the will construction cases of *Re Aspinall* [2017] EWHC 454 (Ch), in which the executors as claimants brought the proceedings and then let the rival beneficiaries (who had been joined as defendants) advance the two construction arguments (see [11]); and *Wales v Dixon* [2020] EWHC 1979 (Ch), in which the PRs adopted the same neutral stance and the court dispensed with their attendance at the disposal hearing (see [4]).

agreement in the most straightforward cases. Two reasons can be identified for this. First, beneficiaries often have different views about what the settlor did or did not intend, and are therefore simply unable to reach an agreement. Secondly, to avoid exposing themselves to potential personal liability to disappointed beneficiaries, trustees must obtain the binding consent of all of the beneficiaries who are affected by the construction problem. This will not be possible if the construction problem affects beneficiaries who are minors, unborn, lack capacity and/or cannot be found. As those types of beneficiaries are unable to give the trustees their binding consent, in cases in which they are affected, the court's intervention is likely to be necessary.

A useful way to explore whether the construction problem can be resolved by agreement is for the trustees, who are often the first to spot the problem, to obtain advice from counsel on the construction problem and then share that advice with all affected beneficiaries and canvass their views. If the trust incorporates clause 12.3 of the STEP Standard Provisions (2nd edition), the trustees should consider obtaining the advice of counsel of "*at least five years' standing*" if they want to rely on the protection from liability afforded by that clause.[447]

---

447 Clause 12.3 and the following two clauses provide:

12.3 A Trustee shall not be liable for acting in accordance with the advice of counsel, of at least five years' standing, with respect to the Trust. The Trustees may in particular conduct legal proceedings in accordance with such advice without obtaining a court order. A Trustee may recover from the Trust Fund any expenses where he has acted in accordance with such advice.

12.4 Clause 12.3 does not apply:

12.4.1 in relation to a Trustee who knows or has reasonable cause to suspect that the advice was given in ignorance of material facts;

12.4.2 if proceedings are pending to obtain the decision of the court on the matter;

12.4.3 in relation to a Trustee who has a personal interest in the subject matter of the advice; or

This process should help both the trustees and all the affected beneficiaries to understand their respective positions, which in turn should inform all involved whether there is any hope of the construction problem being resolved by agreement and, if so, how this might be achieved. Depending on the circumstances, the affected beneficiaries may wish to try to reach an agreement by, for example, negotiating in correspondence, at a round-table meeting or at a mediation.

As indicated above, trustees should bear in mind that they have no personal interest in how the construction problem is resolved between the affected beneficiaries. Their focus should be to ensure:

(a) that they obtain the binding consent of all affected beneficiaries so they are protected from potential personal liability for breach of trust (i.e. for having distributed to the wrong person); and

(b) that the agreement is one which the trustees can in fact implement. For example, the trustees should consider whether the agreement has tax consequences and, if so, how these should be addressed.

However, if all affected beneficiaries manage to reach a binding agreement which the trustees can implement, it is not for the trustees to 'approve' or 'disapprove' of it in any moral or ethical sense, e.g. on the basis that they think the settlor would or would not have liked it. It also follows from this that trustees are generally not required to actively participate in any negotiations between the affected beneficiaries; indeed, trustees should ensure they do not incur unnecessary costs by doing so.

In cases in which professional negligence proceedings against the draftsman have also been threatened or are on foot, it may be sensible to

---

12.4.4 in relation to a Trustee who has committed a breach of trust relating to the subject matter of the advice.

12.5 Clause 12.3 does not prejudice any right of any Person to follow property or income into the hands of any Person, other than a purchaser, who may have received it.

try to compromise those proceedings at the same time.

There are two further tools which can help achieve a pragmatic solution without the court's intervention in a suitable case. The first is the possibility of the trustees agreeing to distribute on a particular basis provided the recipient beneficiaries in return provide the trustees with suitable indemnities, possibly backed by security. Such indemnities would be designed to protect the trustees against the risk that they may be personally liable to disappointed beneficiaries if the basis on which they have distributed subsequently turns out to be wrong. The second is the possibility of obtaining insurance to provide the trustees with that same protection.

Whether either of these tools is a useful one will depend on all of the particular surrounding circumstances. As a rather crude rule of thumb, it is suggested that the greater the financial value of the construction problem, the less likely these tools are to provide a practical solution. This is because the greater the amount of money that turns on the construction problem, the greater the potential liability of the trustees, and thus the more nervous both the beneficiaries and any insurance company will be in providing trustees with adequate protection. Further, in high value cases there is less of a risk of the trust fund being significantly depleted by the costs involved in making a court application, which might also point towards such ab application being the better option.

4.2.3 Professional negligence

If the trust instrument was professionally prepared, it may be possible to argue that the construction problem amounts to professional negligence by the draftsman. If so, a professional negligence claim against the draftsman is usually threatened, and sometimes issued, before a construction claim is brought.

Depending on the circumstances, if both the professional negligence claim and the construction claim have merit, the draftsman's insurers might agree to fund the construction claim, particularly if the costs involved in doing so are likely to be lower than their potential exposure in the event the professional negligence claim is successful.[448]

4.2.4 Court intervention: section 48 of the Administration of Justice Act 1985

A construction problem will usually be incapable of resolution by agreement without the court's intervention for one of two reasons (and sometimes both):

(a) all affected beneficiaries cannot reach an agreement; or

(b) all adult capacitous affected beneficiaries have reached an agreement, but the problem also affects beneficiaries who are minors, unborn, lack capacity and/or cannot be found.

Section 48 of the Administration of Justice Act 1985 ("AJA") contains a mechanism which can be useful in the latter situation (but not the former). The section provides:

> ***48.— Power of High Court to authorise action to be taken in reliance on counsel's opinion.***
>
> *(1) Where—*
>
> *(a) any question of construction has arisen out of the terms of a will or a trust; and*
>
> *(b) an opinion in writing given by a person who has a 10 year High Court qualification, within the meaning of section 71 of the Courts and Legal Services Act 1990, has been obtained on that question by the personal representatives or trustees under the will or trust,*

448 See e.g. the will rectification case of *Re Bimson* [2010] EWHC 3679 (Ch) at [23].

> *the High Court may, on the application of the personal representatives or trustees and without hearing argument, make an order authorising those persons to take such steps in reliance on the said opinion as are specified in the order.*
>
> *(2) The High Court shall not make an order under subsection (1) if it appears to the court that a dispute exists which would make it inappropriate for the court to make the order without hearing argument.*

There are two important points to note in relation to this mechanism. First, the procedure cannot be used where "*a dispute exists which would make it inappropriate for the court to make the order without hearing argument*" (section 48(2) AJA). That will generally be the case where two or more affected beneficiaries are actively advancing two or more competing constructions, both of which are "*reasonably tenable*"[449]. However, it may also be the case where two conflicting opinions have been obtained from two different counsel as to the correct construction and the court feels it cannot resolve the conflict without hearing argument, as in *Greenwold v Pike*.[450]

Secondly, it is important to understand the nature of an order made under section 48 AJA and distinguish it from an order made at the conclusion of a contested construction claim (which is considered in the next section). An order made under section 48 AJA permits the trustees to proceed in accordance with counsel's opinion, and protects them from personal liability for breach of trust if counsel's opinion later turns out to be wrong. However, it does not require the court to determine the construction problem itself, nor therefore to decide whether counsel's opinion is correct. It is therefore an order which is akin to a *Re*

449 Paragraph 25.58 of the Chancery Guide. The paragraph, which is set out in full below, provides that the court may order a party who disagreed with the opinion when having "*no reasonably tenable argument [to the] contrary*" to pay "*all or part of any costs thrown away*".

450 [2007] EWHC 2202 (Ch).

Benjamin[451] order (which authorises PRs to proceed on the footing that certain facts which cannot be established with certainty are correct).[452]

The significance of this is that an order made under section 48 AJA therefore leaves open the possibility that an affected beneficiary may subsequently[453] bring a contested construction claim and the court may at that stage determine that the opinion from counsel (in accordance with which the trustees have proceeded) is wrong. If this were to happen, the trustees will be protected from personal liability for breach of trust because they have acted as authorised by the court's order (viz. in accordance with counsel's opinion). However, it would be open to the disappointed beneficiary to try to recover from the recipient beneficiaries any property which was distributed to them in accordance with the construction which the court has subsequently determined is wrong (subject to any applicable defences, such as laches and limitation).[454]

The question whether the mechanism provided by section 48 AJA should be used despite the fact that it carries this risk is generally answered by weighing up that risk against the costs saving in not having a fully contested construction claim. The mechanism provided by section 48 AJA is likely to be attractive if the trust fund is small and the capacitous adult beneficiaries are therefore keen to ensure that it is not depleted by a fully contested construction claim and/or the circumstances suggest that the risk of any beneficiary subsequently bringing a challenge is small or negligible. On the other hand, if the trust fund is large and/or it is thought that there is a serious risk that a beneficiary may subsequently

---

451 [1902] 1 Ch 723.

452 The classic example is an order authorising PRs to distribute the estate on the footing that a beneficiary who cannot be found predeceased the testator (which were the circumstances in *Re Benjamin* itself).

453 E.g. after he has attained majority.

454 The leading authority on this difficult topic remains the House of Lords decision in *Ministry of Health v Simpson* [1951] AC 251. In relation to the limitation period applicable to this sort of claim, see *Davies v Sharples* [2006] EWHC 362 (Ch).

bring a challenge, it may be worth incurring the extra cost of having a fully contested construction claim so as to have the construction problem resolved once and for all. For relatively rare examples of reported decisions in which the High Court made an order under section 48 AJA, see *Re Duffy*[455] and *Clarke-Sullivan v Clarke-Sullivan*.[456]

The CPR contain some procedural rules which apply to a claim for an order under section 48 AJA. Such a claim must be made in the High Court[457] and must be brought in the Chancery Division,[458] i.e. what has now become the Property, Trusts and Probate List (ChD) of the Business and Property Courts. It must be brought by the trustees[459] and can be brought either in the Rolls Building in London or in one of the District Registries (Birmingham, Bristol, Cardiff, Leeds, Liverpool, Manchester and Newcastle-upon-Tyne).[460]

Rule 64.3 CPR requires such a claim to be made by way of a CPR Part 8 claim form.[461] Paragraph 5 of CPR Practice Direction 64A provides:

> *A Part 8 claim form for an application by trustees under section 48 of the Administration of Justice Act 1985 (power of High Court to authorise action to be taken in reliance on legal opinion) may be issued*

---

455 [2013] EWHC 2395 (Ch).

456 [2021] EWHC 4 (Ch).

457 This is required by section 48(1) AJA itself, which confers jurisdiction to make the relevant order on the High Court.

458 CPR rule 64.1(3).

459 This is required by section 48(1) AJA itself, which refers to "*the application of the personal representatives or trustees*".

460 Paragraph 1.3 of the Chancery Guide. Appendix C to the Chancery Guide ('Chancery Business outside the Rolls Building') contains helpful information regarding Chancery business outside London, including contact details of the various District Registries.

461 CPR rule 64.3 applies to claims under section 48 AJA as a result of CPR rule 64.2(a).

without naming a defendant, under rule 8.2A. No separate application for permission under rule 8.2A need be made.[462]

Chapter 25 of the Chancery Guide provides the following detailed procedural guidance, which helpfully lists the topics which need to be addressed in the witness statement filed in support of the claim:[463]

Applications under section 48 of the Administration of Justice Act 1985

25.49 The jurisdiction conferred on the High Court by section 48 of the Administration of Justice Act 1985 to authorise action based on a written legal opinion about an issue of construction of a trust document may be invoked by trustees where such a question has arisen out of the terms of a trust.

25.50 Whilst the jurisdiction is particularly well suited to construction issues arising in relation to a trust of modest value where a conventional inter partes application would be prohibitively expensive, it may be (and has been) successfully invoked in other cases. It is intended to be used in clear cases only.

25.51 Applications under section 48 of the Administration of Justice Act 1985 should be made by Part 8 claim form (PD 64A 5).

25.52 The claim should be supported by a witness statement to which are exhibited: (a) copies of all relevant documents; (b) instructions to a person with a 10-year High Court qualification within the meaning

462 This is confirmed by paragraph 13.37(e) of the Chancery Guide. Consistently with this, CPR rule 64.4 expressly states that its provisions (which govern who should be a party to a claim to which Section I of CPR Part 64 applies) do not apply to a claim under section 48 AJA.

463 This derives (with necessary modifications) from *Practice Direction (Chancery: Construction Summons)* [1987] 1 WLR 251.

of the Courts and Legal Services Act 1990 (the 'qualified person'); (c) the qualified person's opinion; and (d) draft terms of the desired order.

25.53 The application is for an order to authorise the trustees to act on the basis of a legal opinion, which may deal with construction issues; it should not seek a decision of the court itself on the construction of any instrument.

25.54 The court may consider that, as a matter of discretion, it would be preferable to have the issue finally and bindingly resolved at a substantive hearing, as opposed to its merely being made the subject of directions to the trustees. This is more likely where conflicting opinions have been expressed by different counsel advising the trustees: see Greenwold v Pike [2007] EWHC 2202 (Ch).

25.55 The witness statement (or exhibits thereto) should state: (a) the reason for the application; (b) the names of all persons who are, or may be, affected by the order sought; (c) all surrounding circumstances admissible and relevant in construing the document; (d) the date of qualification of the qualified person and his or her experience in the construction of trust documents; (e) the approximate value of the fund or property in question; (f) whether it is known to the applicant that a dispute exists and, if so, details of such dispute; and (g) what steps are proposed to be taken in reliance on the opinion.

25.56 The Master will consider the claim, and, if necessary, direct service of notices under CPR 19.8A[464] *or request further information. It is important that the evidence explains how those potentially affected have been identified, and what steps have been taken to consult them on the order sought. If the court is satisfied that the order sought is*

464 With effect from 6th April 2023, what used to be CPR rule 19.8A became rule 19.13: see rules 1(1) and 12(14) of the Civil Procedure (Amendment) Rules 2023 (SI 2023/105).

> *appropriate, it will be made without a hearing and sent to the claimant.*
>
> *25.57 If following service of notices under rule 19.8A*[465] *any acknowledgment of service is received, the claimant must apply to the Master (on notice to the parties who have so acknowledged service) for directions. The Master will ordinarily direct that the case proceeds as a Part 8 claim.*
>
> *25.58 If on the hearing of the claim the court is of the opinion that any party who entered an acknowledgment of service has no reasonably tenable argument contrary to the qualified person's opinion, in the exercise of the court's discretion it may order such party to pay all or part of any costs thrown away.*

Because applications pursuant to section 48 AJA are only suitable in non-contentious cases (as explained above), the incidence of the costs of the proceedings is also likely to be agreed in advance between the trustees and the adult capacitous affected beneficiaries. The usual agreement is likely to be that the costs of the proceedings will be borne by the trust as an administration expense. As the only active parties will be the trustees and the application must be uncontested (because the procedure is otherwise unsuitable), the costs should be relatively modest.

4.2.5 Court intervention: construction claim in the Chancery Division

If the affected beneficiaries cannot reach an agreement and the mechanism provided by section 48 AJA cannot be used or is considered undesirable,[466] the solution will be to ask the court to resolve the construction problem by way of a contested construction claim.

---

465 Ibid.

466 E.g. because it is desirable to resolve the construction problem once and for all.

Starting the claim

A claim asking the court to resolve a construction problem is a claim "*for the court to determine [a] question arising in [...] (ii) the execution of a trust*" within CPR rule 64.2(a). Indeed, it is highly likely to be one of the types of claims which are listed in paragraph 1(1) of CPR Practice Direction 64A as examples of claims which may be made under CPR rule 64.2(a), viz.:

> *(1) a claim for the determination of any of the following questions –*
>
> *(a) any question as to who is included in any class of persons having –*
>
> *[...]*
>
> *(iii) a beneficial interest in any property subject to a trust;*
>
> *(b) any question as to the rights or interests of any person claiming –*
>
> *[...]*
>
> *(iii) to be beneficially entitled under a trust;*

As a result, Section I of CPR Part 64 applies to such a claim, which in turn means the claim must be made by issuing a CPR Part 8 claim form.[467]

The claim is started by filing a CPR Part 8 claim form and accompanying evidence (considered below). Particulars of claim are not required.[468] Claims brought by CPR Part 8 are automatically allocated to the multi-track.[469]

---

467 CPR rule 64.3. See also paragraph 13.2(a) of the Chancery Guide.

468 CPR rule 8.9(a), which disapplies CPR Part 16; see also paragraph 13.14 of the Chancery Guide.

469 CPR rule 8.9(c); see also paragraph 13.14 of the Chancery Guide.

Claim form N208 must be used.[470] CPR rule 8.2 provides that the claim form must state:

(a) that CPR Part 8 applies;

(b) the question which the claimant wants the court to decide, or the remedy which the claimant is seeking and the legal basis for the claim to that remedy;

(c) if the claim is being made under an enactment, what that enactment is;

(d) if the claimant is claiming in a representative capacity, what that capacity is; and

(e) if the defendant is sued in a representative capacity, what that capacity is.

Although in some cases rectification will not be relevant, claims for construction and rectification are often brought in the alternative.[471] A construction problem may also arise in the context of another dispute, such as a professional negligence claim. In these sorts of circumstances, the procedural rules governing any other claim must also be borne in mind. Where the construction problem is one of several aspects in dispute, it may be worth considering whether the court should be asked to deal with any aspect as a preliminary issue.[472]

470 Paragraph 13.6 of the Chancery Guide.

471 See e.g. *Millar v Millar* [2018] EWHC 1926 (Ch) and *Armstrong v Armstrong* [2019] EWHC 2259 (Ch).

472 As was done in the context of wills in *Burnard v Burnard* [2014] EWHC 340 (Ch) (see [7]) and *Tish v Olley* [2018] EWHC 1069 (Ch) (see [1]).

Parties

Determining who should be made a party to a construction claim often requires some careful thought. In general, it is useful to bear in mind that:

(a) the court will expect someone to argue in favour of each of the various possible constructions (which may be two or more);

(b) it is generally desirable to take steps to ensure that everyone affected by the construction problem will be bound by the court's order;[473]

(c) the trustees should generally remain neutral in their capacity as trustees and not argue in favour of one of the possible constructions;

(d) however, where the claim is unopposed and/or no beneficiary with a contrary interest wishes to take an active role, it may be incumbent on the trustees as "*watchdog*"[474] for unrepresented or unborn beneficiaries to assist the court by "*bringing to the court's attention any relevant legal propositions or argument affecting the position of unrepresented beneficiaries or parties*"[475] to ensure the court is able to reach the right result; and

(e) if the construction problem affects the amount of tax payable, it may be necessary to notify, and perhaps even join, HMRC.

As a starting point, CPR rule 64.4(1) provides the following rules in

473 See e.g. *Millar v Millar* [2018] EWHC 1926 (Ch), in which the court noted that the claimants had not joined or sought a representation order in respect of a class of spouses who had a contingent interest, who would therefore not be bound by the court's order (at [9]).

474 *Re Druce's Settlement Trusts* [1962] 1 WLR 363 at 370.

475 *State Street Bank & Trust Co v Sompo Japan Insurance Inc* [2010] EWHC 1461 (Ch) at [30]. See also e.g. *Re Hemming* [2008] EWHC 8565 (Ch) at [40].

relation to who the parties should be:

> *(1) In a claim to which this Section applies, other than an application under section 48 of the Administration of Justice Act 1985 –*
>
> *(a) all the trustees must be parties;*
>
> *(b) if the claim is made by trustees, any of them who does not consent to being a claimant must be made a defendant; and*
>
> *(c) the claimant may make parties to the claim any persons with an interest in or claim against the estate, or an interest under the trust, who it is appropriate to make parties having regard to the nature of the order sought.*

The claim can generally be brought either by the trustees, or by one or more of the beneficiaries.

All trustees must be parties (CPR rule 64.4(1)(a) and (b) above), which is unsurprising given that they need to be bound by the order. What may be less clear is how to ensure that all affected beneficiaries are joined or are otherwise bound by the court's order.

In cases involving a limited number of affected beneficiaries, the answer may be fairly straightforward. The simplest example is where there are two possible constructions and the only affected beneficiaries are capacitous adults, as in Example 7 above (assuming Figaro and Count Almaviva are capacitous adults). In such cases, either the trustees bring the claim and join the affected beneficiaries as defendants,[476] or one of the affected beneficiaries can bring the claim and join the trustees and the other affected beneficiaries as defendants. In either case, the trustees should generally adopt a neutral stance and let the affected beneficiaries advance the two alternative construction arguments. Exceptionally, the particular circumstances may mean that it is convenient for the trustees

476 See e.g. *Re Erskine 1948 Trust* [2012] EWHC 732 (Ch) at [5].

to advance one of the construction arguments; if so, they should ensure that they do so without jeopardising their neutrality.[477]

Where one or more of the affected beneficiaries is a minor or lacks capacity and is to be a party to the claim, that beneficiary will need a litigation friend (unless, in the case of a minor, the court makes an order permitting the child to conduct proceedings without a litigation friend).[478] CPR Part 21 contains detailed guidance on the procedure for the appointment of a litigation friend.

On the other hand, the position may be more complicated where the construction problem affects a large number of beneficiaries (e.g. large classes) and/or where some of the affected beneficiaries are minors, unborn, lack capacity and/or cannot be found. In Example 9 above, the class of intestacy beneficiaries may be large and/or its members difficult to trace, and it may be difficult to ascertain all members of the other class. In these sorts of cases, there is likely to be a tension between on the one hand ensuring that everyone who has an interest is properly represented and has an opportunity to be heard, and on the other trying to avoid depleting the estate or trust by incurring significant costs tracing and communicating with large classes of beneficiaries.

How the balance should be struck will inevitably depend on the circumstances of the particular case. In complicated cases, the provisionsof CPR rule 19.9[479] and/or 19.13[480] can be of considerable

477 See e.g. the wills cases of *Re Wippell* [2018] EWHC 730 (Ch) at [8] and *Jeffreys v Scruton* [2020] EWHC 536 (Ch) at [4]; and *PTNZ v AS* [2020] EWHC 3114 (Ch) at [8] and [86].

478 CPR rule 21.2(1).

479 With effect from 6th April 2023, what used to be CPR rule 19.7 became rule 19.9: see rules 1(1) and 12(10) of the Civil Procedure (Amendment) Rules 2023 (SI 2023/105).

480 With effect from 6th April 2023, what used to be CPR rule 19.8A became rule 19.13: see rules 1(1) and 12(14) of the Civil Procedure (Amendment) Rules 2023 (SI 2023/105).

assistance.[481] These govern respectively the appointment of a party to represent the interests of others, and the service of proceedings and/or orders on non-parties so as to bind them. (The ability to issue a CPR Part 8 claim form without naming a defendant pursuant to CPR rule 8.2A can be useful where a claim is brought pursuant to section 48 AJA.[482] However, it is difficult to envisage a situation in which a construction claim will be issued without naming at least one defendant.)[483]

CPR rule 19.9(2) provides:

> *The court may make an order appointing a person to represent any other person or persons in the claim where the person or persons to be represented –*
>
> *(a) are unborn;*
>
> *(b) cannot be found;*
>
> *(c) cannot easily be ascertained; or*

---

481 The relevance of these rules to claims concerning trusts is highlighted by paragraphs 25.10 to 25.14 of the Chancery Guide, considered below. Note that CPR rule 19.8, which is entitled "*Representative parties with same interest*", does not apply to claims "*about [...] (b) property subject to a trust, or (c) the meaning of a document, including a statute*": see CPR rules 19.8(5) and 19.9(1). (CPR rule 19.8 used to be CPR rule 19.6 until it was renumbered with effect from 6th April 2023: see rules 1(1) and 12(9) of the Civil Procedure (Amendment) Rules 2023 (SI 2023/105)).

482 See 2.2.4 above.

483 Permission to issue the claim without naming a defendant was given in the will construction case of *Re Harte* [2015] EWHC 2351 (Ch). However, the claimant executors were then directed to take reasonable steps to trace the testatrix's statutory next of kin and to serve notices pursuant to CPR rule 19.8A (now CPR rule 19.13) on various people and charities (see [2]-[4]).

(d) are a class of persons who have the same interest in a claim and –

(i) one or more members of that class are within sub-paragraphs (a), (b) or (c); or

(ii) to appoint a representative would further the overriding objective.

This caters for several different scenarios:

(a) is self-explanatory;

(b) covers situations in which it is clear who the affected beneficiary is, but (reasonable) attempts to find him have proved unsuccessful;

(c) covers situations in which it is not clear who the affected beneficiary is, nor can this be easily clarified;

(d) covers two alternative situations where a class of persons has the same interest in the claim:

   (i) is self-explanatory;

   (ii) is potentially wide and flexible. It can be used, for example, where there is a large class of affected beneficiaries scattered around the world, all of whom have the same interest, and it would further the overriding objective to appoint one of them to represent the whole class (e.g. by reducing procedural delay and costs) – ideally one who can be served within the jurisdiction.[484]

CPR rule 19.9(3) provides that an application for a representation order under CPR rule 19.9(2) may be made "*by any person who seeks to be appointed under the order or any party to the claim*", and may be made "*at*

484 For an example, see *Public Trustee v Harrison* [2018] EWHC 166 (Ch) at [8].

any time before or after the claim has started". CPR rule 19.9(4) provides that the application notice for such an order must be served on:

> *(a) all parties to the claim, if the claim has started;*
>
> *(b) the person sought to be appointed, if that person is not the applicant or a party to the claim; and*
>
> *(c) any other person as directed by the court.*

It is important to note that where the court has made a representation order under CPR rule 19.9, the court's approval is required to settle the claim.[485] This is to safeguard the position of the represented parties and to ensure their representative does not enter into a compromise which is disadvantageous to them: CPR rule 19.9(6) gives the court jurisdiction to approve a settlement "*where it is satisfied that the settlement is for the benefit of all represented persons*".

In relation to CPR rule 19.9, the Chancery Guide explains: "*Where the claim relates to the internal affairs of the trust or estate it may be appropriate for a representation order to be made so that the interests of all classes of beneficiaries are represented and protected but they are also all bound by the decision.*"[486]

CPR rule 19.13 provides:

> *Power to make judgements binding on non-parties*
>
> *(1) This rule applies to any claim relating to –*

---

485 CPR rule 19.9(5).

486 Paragraph 25.11 of the Chancery Guide. (The paragraph refers to "*CPR 19.7*", which was the old numbering of the rule before it was renumbered rule 19.9 with effect from 6th April 2023: see rules 1(1) and 12(10) of the Civil Procedure (Amendment) Rules 2023 (SI 2023/105))).

[…]

(b) property subject to a trust; or

(c) the sale of any property.

(2) The court may at any time direct that notice of–

(a) the claim; or

(b) any judgment or order given in the claim,

be served on any person who is not a party but who is or may be affected by it.

(3) An application under this rule –

(a) may be made without notice; and

(b) must be supported by written evidence which includes the reasons why the person to be served should be bound by the judgment in the claim.

(4) Unless the court orders otherwise –

(a) a notice of a claim or of a judgment or order under this rule must be –

> *(i) in the form required by the practice direction;*
>
> *(ii) issued by the court; and*
>
> *(iii) accompanied by a form of acknowledgment of service with any necessary modifications;*

(b) a notice of a claim must also be accompanied by –

> *(i) a copy of the claim form; and*

(ii) such other statements of case, witness statements or affidavits as the court may direct; and

(c) a notice of a judgment or order must also be accompanied by a copy of the judgment or order.

(5) If a person served with notice of a claim files an acknowledgment of service of the notice within 14 days they will become a party to the claim.

(6) If a person served with notice of a claim does not acknowledge service of the notice they will be bound by any judgment given in the claim as if they were a party.

(7) If, after service of a notice of a claim on a person, the claim form is amended so as substantially to alter the relief claimed, the court may direct that a judgment shall not bind that person unless a further notice, together with a copy of the amended claim form, is served on them.

(8) Any person served with a notice of a judgment or order under this rule –

(a) shall be bound by the judgment or order as if they had been a party to the claim; but

(b) may, provided they acknowledge service –

(i) within 28 days after the notice is served on them, apply to the court to set aside or vary the judgment or order; and

(ii) take part in any proceedings relating to the judgment or order.

(9) The following rules of Part 10 (acknowledgment of service) apply –

(a) rule 10.4; and

(b) rule 10.5, subject to the modification that references to the defendant are to be read as references to the person served with the notice.

(10) A notice under this rule is issued on the date entered on the notice by the court.

The procedure in CPR rule 19.13 can be useful to bind interested beneficiaries who do not want to take an active role in the proceedings, such as the adult children of an 'active' interested beneficiary who are content to simply support their parent's position. However, it suggests that it is unlikely to be a good idea to press on with the proceedings and to then try to rely on CPR rule 19.13 to serve a judgment or order on an interested beneficiary who it is thought will want to actively have a say. In such cases there is a risk that such a beneficiary will then apply to set aside the judgment or order (pursuant to CPR rule 19.13(8)(b)) to, in effect, re-open the case to advance his argument, and this could significantly increase the overall costs. In this sort of situation it is likely to be preferable to ensure that such a beneficiary is able to actively participate from the outset.

It should be borne in mind that the issue of representation is likely to be considered by the court at the first directions hearing, at which creative and pragmatic solutions can be considered with the Master, particularly in complex cases.[487]

---

487 See e.g. the will case of *Re Harte* [2015] EWHC 2351 (Ch), in which the PRs were initially given permission to issue the construction and rectification claims without naming a defendant (pursuant to CPR rule 8.2A), and were then given directions as to the steps they should take to ascertain the intestacy beneficiaries (including by advertisement) and as to the parties to whom they should give notice of the proceedings pursuant to CPR rule 19.8A (see [3]-[4]); and *Womble Bond Dickinson (Trust Corp) Ltd v No Named Defendant* [2022] EWHC 43 (Ch), in which the trustees of an employee benefit trust were given permission to issue the construction claim without naming a defendant, and the court directed their solicitors to instruct a separate counsel to advance the

Limitation

No limitation period applies to construction claims. However, a time limit or limitation period may be relevant if the dispute involves one or more other claims to which a time limit or limitation period does apply, such as a professional negligence claim.

Which court

The County Court appears to have jurisdiction to determine a construction problem if the value of the trust fund does not exceed £350,000.[488] However, in practice most construction claims are issued in the High Court, where they must be brought in the Chancery Division,[489] i.e. what has now become the Property, Trusts and Probate List (ChD) of the Business and Property Courts. If it is to be issued in the High Court, a construction claim can be issued either in the Rolls Building in London or in one of the District Registries (Birmingham, Bristol, Cardiff, Leeds, Liverpool, Manchester and Newcastle-upon-Tyne).[490]

---

opposing arguments effectively as Advocate to the Court, given that there was no individual who could obviously be appointed to represent all of the beneficiaries: see [6].

488 Section 23 of the County Courts Act 1984 and article 3 of the County Court Jurisdiction Order 2014 (SI 2014/503). This assumes that the relevant construction claim is a type of "*proceedings for the execution of any trust*" within section 23(b).

489 CPR rule 64.1(3). See also section 61 and paragraphs 1(c) and 1(d) of Schedule 1 to the Senior Courts Act 1981.

490 Paragraph 1.3 of the Chancery Guide. Appendix C to the Chancery Guide ('Chancery Business outside the Rolls Building') contains helpful information regarding Chancery business outside London, including contact details of the various District Registries.

Evidence

The claimant must file the evidence on which he intends to rely when his claim form is issued[491] (unless the claimant only intends to rely on the evidence contained in the claim form itself, which it is suggested is unlikely to be the case in construction claims). This will generally be in the form of one or more witness statements. CPR Practice Direction 57AC, which applies to "*trial witness statements*"[492] in the Business and Property Courts, does not apply to proceedings under CPR Part 64, unless the court orders otherwise.[493] The claimant's evidence must be served on the defendant with the claim form.[494]

The contents of the witness statement(s) will of course depend on the circumstances of the particular case, and on whether the claimant is a neutral trustee who is simply explaining the construction problem to the court, or an interested beneficiary who is advancing a particular construction. In general terms, the topics which one should consider covering in the evidence filed in support of the claim are likely to be:

(a) the claimant's role and the capacity in which he brings the claim;

(b) the factual background (or 'factual matrix');

(c) the construction problem;

(d) how the trust document was prepared;

---

491 CPR rule 8.5(1); see also paragraph 13.10 of the Chancery Guide.

492 Defined by paragraph 1.2 of CPR Practice Direction 57AC as "*a witness statement that is served pursuant to an order made under rule 32.4(2), or pursuant to rule 8.5 or an order made under rule 8.6(1)(b), or that is prepared for the trial of an unfair prejudice petition or a contributory's just and equitable winding up petition, including supplemental or reply witness statements where allowed by the court*".

493 Paragraph 1.3(8) of CPR Practice Direction 57AC.

494 CPR rule 8.5(2).

(e) the position of the other interested parties;

(f) the approximate value of the fund in issue.[495]

If the trust document was professionally prepared, some thought should be given as to whether evidence should be obtained from the draftsman responsible for preparing it (if available) and, if so, as to who should call the draftsman as a witness.[496] As indicated above, it must be borne in mind that evidence of the settlor's subjective intention is not admissible to help resolve construction problems.

It should also be borne in mind that the CPR requires witness statements to be in the witness's own words[497] and that construction problems are usually issues of law rather than fact. The temptation to include in a witness statement extensive legal submissions and references to case law should generally be resisted, particularly in witness statements of lay witnesses; these are properly a matter for skeleton arguments and submissions.

Prospective (or pre-emptive) costs orders

In some construction cases it may be appropriate to consider at an early stage of the proceedings whether a mechanism should be put in place for the costs of one or more of the parties to be paid out of the estate or trust fund in any event irrespective of the outcome.[498] This can be either by way of a contractual agreement by the trustees or by a so-called prospective (or pre-emptive) costs order by the court. This issue tends to arise primarily in pension cases, where an individual pension scheme

495 Paragraph 25.4 of the Chancery Guide.

496 See e.g. the will construction case of *Re McKay* [2023] EWHC 642 (Ch) at [39]-[40].

497 Paragraph 18.1 of CPR Practice Direction 32; see also paragraph 8.1 of the Chancery Guide.

498 The costs orders which are likely to be made at the conclusion of the proceedings are considered at "Costs" below.

member may be made a party to complex litigation as representative of other scheme members, and it may be unfair for him to have to bear his costs personally at least until the conclusion of the litigation, which can create a cash flow problem.[499] However, the issue is unlikely to arise in claims concerning the correct construction of a family trust.

Where the issue does arise, the eight sub-paragraphs of paragraph 6 of CPR Practice Direction 64A contain some detailed guidance about prospective costs orders, as do paragraphs 25.30 to 25.32 of the Chancery Guide. A model form of prospective costs order is appended to CPR Practice Direction 64A.

Costs management

CPR rule 3.12 makes it clear that costs management does not apply to CPR Part 8 claims unless the court orders that it should pursuant to CPR rule 3.12(1A).[500] Paragraph 5(e) of CPR Practice Direction 3D provides that an order for costs management may be "*particularly appropriate*" in "*any Part 8 or other claims or applications involving a substantial dispute of fact and/or likely to require oral evidence and/or extensive disclosure*". The Chancery Guide also provides that: "*It is the court's experience that it is often helpful for costs budgets to be exchanged in cases in the ChD B&PCs London even if costs budgeting would not otherwise apply. Parties should consider exchanging costs budgets and/or opting into costs management even in cases which are outside the costs management regime. If the parties agree that a costs management order should be made, a consent order should be lodged in advance of the CMC including proposed directions for costs*

499 The principles governing the making of a prospective costs order have been considered in a line of pensions cases which includes *McDonald v Horn* [1995] 1 All ER 961 and *IBM United Kingdom Pensions Trust Ltd v Metcalfe* [2012] EWHC 125 (Ch). In the context of pensions, see also paragraph 26.30 of the Chancery Guide.

500 In relation to which see also and paragraph 2 of CPR Practice Direction 3D. This is reiterated by paragraph 13.30 of the Chancery Guide.

management".[501]

A party seeking an order that costs management should apply to the proceedings should "*give notice to the other parties and the court well in advance of the directions hearing and explain, preferably in a witness statement, why such an order is sought*".[502]

In trust construction claims an obligation to file and serve a costs budget may be imposed by paragraph 5 of CPR Practice Direction 3E.[503] Significantly, the obligation applies early on in the proceedings when the party files his evidence (as explained below).

Section II of Practice Direction 3E is entitled '*Costs Capping in Relation to Trust Funds*'; paragraph 5 is the Section's only paragraph. It supplements CPR rules 3.19 to 3.21 and paragraphs 1 to 4 of Practice Direction 3E,[504] which govern costs capping orders generally. The provisions of the paragraph are designed to "*enable the parties to consider whether to apply for, and the court to consider whether to make of its own initiative, a costs capping order in relation to proceedings relating to trust funds*".[505]

The obligation to file and serve a costs budget is imposed by paragraphs 5.4 and 5.5, which provide:

> *5.4 Any party to such proceedings who intends to apply for an order for the payment of costs out of the trust fund must file and serve on all other parties written notice of that intention together with a budget of the costs likely to be incurred by that party.*

501 Paragraph 6.31 of the Chancery Guide.

502 Paragraph 13.31 of the Chancery Guide.

503 Paragraph 25.15 of the Chancery Guide draws attention to this.

504 Paragraph 5.3 of CPR Practice Direction 3E.

505 Paragraph 5.2 of CPR Practice Direction 3E.

> *5.5 The documents mentioned in paragraph 5.4 must be filed and served –*
>
> *[…]*
>
> *(b) in a Part 8 claim, with the evidence (or, if a defendant does not intend to serve and file evidence, with the acknowledgement of service).*

Finally, paragraph 5.6 provides that when the proceedings first come before the court for directions, the court may make a costs capping order of its own initiative, whether or not any party has applied for such an order.

In most construction claims, all parties will seek an order that their costs of the proceedings be paid out of the trust fund[506] – or at least will "*intend*" to apply for such an order when the proceedings are started and/or when the relevant party files his evidence. This appears to trigger the obligation (imposed by paragraph 5.4) to file and serve on all other parties both "*written notice of that intention*" and a budget "*of the costs likely to be incurred by that party*".

On the other hand, costs capping orders are rare in construction claims (other than in pension cases), and anecdotal evidence suggests that this provision is rarely (if ever) complied with or enforced in practice in such claims. It is also unclear what the sanction for non-compliance is (if any). However, the provision is there, and practitioners ought to be aware of it, at least unless and until it is amended by the Civil Procedure Rule Committee.

Service

The usual rules for service contained in the CPR – mostly in CPR Part 6 – apply to claims for the construction of a trust instrument. If it is necessary to seek the court's permission to serve the claim form out of the

506 See further under "Costs" below.

jurisdiction pursuant to CPR rule 6.36, the grounds listed in paragraph 3.1 of CPR Practice Direction 6B which are likely to be relevant are grounds (11) to (12D):

> *Claims about property within the jurisdiction*
>
> *(11) The subject matter of the claim relates wholly or principally to property within the jurisdiction, provided that nothing under this paragraph shall render justiciable the title to or the right to possession of immovable property outside England and Wales.*
>
> *Claims about trusts etc.*
>
> *(12) A claim is made in respect of a trust which is created [...] by a written instrument, or created orally and evidenced in writing, and which is governed by the law of England and Wales.*
>
> *(12A) A claim is made in respect of a trust which is created [...] by a written instrument, or created orally and evidenced in writing, and which provides that jurisdiction in respect of such a claim shall be conferred upon the courts of England and Wales.*
>
> *(12B) A claim is made in respect of a trust which is created [...] by a written instrument [...] and which expressly or impliedly designates England and Wales as the principal place of administration.*
>
> *(12C) A claim is made in respect of a trust created in the jurisdiction.*
>
> *(12D) A claim is made for a declaration that no trust has arisen where, if the trust was found to have arisen, it would comply with one of the conditions set out in paragraph (12), (12A), (12B) or (12C).*

Responding to the claim

A defendant who wishes to respond to the claim must file an acknowledgment of service in the relevant practice form (viz. form N210) not more than 14 days after service of the claim form on him.[507] At the same time he must also serve his acknowledgment of service on the claimant and on any other party.[508] If he fails to do so, the defendant may attend the hearing of the claim but may not take part in the hearing unless the court gives permission.[509] As the Chancery Guide makes clear, these are "*serious consequences*".[510]

Defendants who acknowledge service but do not intend to file any evidence should notify the court in writing when they file their acknowledgment of service that they do not intend to file evidence. This "*enables the court to know what each defendant's intention is when it considers the file and avoids delay*".[511]

CPR rule 8.8(1) provides that where a defendant "*contends that the CPR Part 8 procedure should not be used because there is (a) a substantial dispute of fact and (b) the use of the Part 8 procedure is not required or permitted by a rule or practice direction, he must state his reasons when he files his acknowledgment of service*". This is unlikely to apply in construction claims, as such claims tend not to involve substantial disputes of fact, and in any event must be started by issuing a Part 8 claim form as a result of CPR rule 64.3. However, in cases in which the dispute does involve a dispute of fact, it may be appropriate for directions to be given for the

---

507 CPR rule 8.3(1); see also paragraph 13.8 of the Chancery Guide. Note that different (longer) periods apply if the proceedings have been served on the defendant out of the jurisdiction: see CPR rules 8.3(3) and 10.3(2).

508 CPR rule 8.3(1).

509 CPR rule 8.4(2).

510 Paragraph 13.8 of the Chancery Guide.

511 Paragraph 13.15 of the Chancery Guide.

claim to proceed as, in effect, a hybrid claim, as explained below.[512]

A defendant who wishes to rely on written evidence must file it when he files his acknowledgment of service,[513] and must at the same time serve a copy of his evidence on the other parties.[514] The defendant may not rely on any written evidence which has not been served in accordance with these rules at the hearing of the claim unless the court gives permission.[515]

As the time limit for the defendant to file and serve his evidence is quite short (viz. 14 days from service of the claim on him), CPR rule 8.5(9) allows the parties to "*agree in writing on an extension of time of not more than 14 days for serving and filing evidence from the defendant*". Such an agreement must be filed at court by the defendant at the same time as he files his acknowledgment of service.[516] The Chancery Guide recognises that it is "*not unusual for an extension of time to be agreed between the parties for the service of evidence*".[517]

If a defendant requires more time to file his evidence, he should apply to the court for an extension of time by way of an application pursuant to CPR Part 23.[518] If the parties are in agreement that such an extension should be granted, the application should be made by filing a consent order.[519] If there is no agreement, an application "*should be made to a Master using the urgent applications procedure set out in paragraphs 15.11 to 15.14 [of the Chancery Guide] but does not need to be certified as urgent business. When issuing the application the applicant should add 'Urgent*

512 See "Directions hearing" below.

513 CPR rule 8.5(3); see also paragraph 13.10 of the Chancery Guide.

514 CPR rule 8.5(4).

515 CPR rule 8.6(1).

516 CPR rule 8.5(10).

517 Paragraph 13.11 of the Chancery Guide.

518 CPR rule 8.5(8).

519 As to which, see paragraphs 16.36 to 16.41 of the Chancery Guide.

Application EOT' to the comment box on CE-File to assist the court staff to process the application promptly".[520] The Chancery Guide indicates that "*[i]n substantial matters the court will normally be willing to grant a reasonable extension*".[521]

As for the claimant's evidence, the contents of any witness statement(s) adduced by a defendant will of course depend on the circumstances of the particular case. In general terms, the topics one should consider covering are likely to be the same as those to be covered by the claimant in his evidence (discussed above).

Default and summary judgment

It is not possible to obtain judgment in default in a claim commenced by pursuant to CPR Part 8[522] or a claim which seeks declaratory relief.[523] Construction claims are usually both.

If the claim is unopposed and is brought by way of CPR Part 8 proceedings, it will generally be unnecessary to apply for summary judgment, and the claimant can instead ask the court to list the claim for a disposal hearing, as Chief Master Marsh explained in *Sovereign Trustees Ltd v Lewis*:[524]

> "*Part 8 claims are markedly different to Part 7 claims. Although there is no bar to issuing a Part 24 application [i.e. an application for*

520 Paragraph 15.28 of the Chancery Guide.

521 Paragraph 13.11 of the Chancery Guide.

522 CPR rules 8.1(5) and 12.2(b); see also paragraph 5.9 and 13.4 of the Chancery Guide.

523 Paragraph 5.7 of the Chancery Guide provides: "*Declaratory relief and relief by way of rectification will not be granted without evidence and will not ordinarily be appropriate for resolution by way of default judgment.*".

524 [2016] EWHC 2593 (Ch) at [3]. However, see also *Guthrie v Morel* [2015] EWHC 3172 (Ch), where summary judgment was granted in a contested will construction claim.

> *summary judgment] in a Part 8 claim, it will rarely be necessary for the claimant to do so where it is seeking judgment on the whole of the claim. In part this is because the second limb of CPR 24.2 will normally have no application because there will be no 'trial' as such. Part 8 claims are normally resolved at a 'disposal hearing'. This is made clear by paragraph 8.1 of Practice Direction 8A which states:*
>
> *'8.1 The court may on the hearing date –*
>
> *(i) proceed to hear the case and dispose of the claim;*
>
> *(ii) give case management directions.'*
>
> *It follows that in most Part 8 claims, where the relief sought is unopposed, or cannot realistically be opposed, it will suffice for the claimant to ask the court to fix a disposal hearing at which the court may determine whether or not the relief sought by the claimant should be granted.*"[525]

Claimant's evidence in reply

If the claimant wishes to rely on further written evidence in reply to the defendant's evidence, he must file it within 14 days of service of the defendant's evidence on him,[526] and he must also serve a copy of it on the other parties "*within the same time limit*".[527] In the same way as a defendant, a claimant may not rely on any written evidence which has not been served in accordance with these rules at the hearing of the claim unless the court gives permission.[528]

As that time limit is also quite short, CPR rule 8.5(9) allows the parties

525 Although paragraph 8.1 of CPR Practice Direction 8A has since been repealed, it is suggested that the reasoning remains valid.

526 CPR rule 8.5(5).

527 CPR rule 8.5(6).

528 CPR rule 8.6(1).

to "*agree in writing on an extension of time [...] of not more than 28 days for filing and serving evidence in reply*". Such an agreement must be filed at court "*within 48 hours of the agreement*".[529] As indicated above, the Chancery Guide recognises that it is "*not unusual for an extension of time to be agreed between the parties for the service of evidence*".[530]

If a claimant requires more time to file his evidence in reply to the defendant's, he too should apply to the court for an extension of time by way of an application pursuant to CPR Part 23.[531] The guidance considered above in the context of the defendant's evidence applies equally to applications for extensions of time by claimants in relation to their evidence in reply. In particular, it should be noted that the Chancery Guide indicates that "*[i]n substantial matters the court will normally be willing to grant a reasonable extension*".[532]

Directions hearing

Claims issued under the Part 8 procedure are treated as having been allocated to the multi-track and CPR Part 26 ('*Case Management – Preliminary Stage*') does not apply.[533] No directions questionnaires are required.[534]

The court file will generally be considered by the assigned Master[535] after the time for acknowledgment of service has expired, or, if the time for serving the defendant's evidence has been extended, after the expiry of that period. If a defendant has not acknowledged service, the assigned

529 CPR rule 8.5(10).

530 Paragraph 13.11 of the Chancery Guide.

531 CPR rule 8.5(8).

532 Paragraph 13.11 of the Chancery Guide.

533 CPR rule 8.9(c); see also paragraph 13.14 of the Chancery Guide.

534 Paragraph 13.14 of the Chancery Guide.

535 Or District Judge of the High Court if the claim is in one of the District Registries.

Master will typically make an order in the form of CH44.[536] This is an order which directs a defendant who intends to contest the claim to file and serve an acknowledgment of service and evidence by a specified date, failing which he shall not be entitled to rely on any evidence at the disposal hearing unless the court gives permission.[537]

If 21 days after the expiry of any extended period for service of evidence no notice of a directions hearing has been received, the claimant should contact the court by letter filed on CE-File together, if appropriate, with a draft order substantially in form CH44, requesting either a directions or disposal hearing. The letter should provide dates to avoid, and a realistic time estimate for both the hearing and any pre-reading.[538]

At that stage the Master will consider whether the claim and decide:

(a) Whether the claim may be capable of being dealt with 'on paper', i.e. on the papers without a hearing.[539] The Chancery Guide makes it clear that "*[d]isposal without a hearing is exceptional*"[540] and indicates that if the claimant considers that a hearing is not required, and the defendant has filed an acknowledgment of service saying the claim will not be defended, the claimant may ask the court to consider whether the claim may be dealt with on paper.[541] Examples provided by the Chancery Guide are: "*some Norwich Pharmacal applications, some claims for relief where the court has directed that the claim need not name a defendant, and some unopposed applications for relief such as applications for a vesting*

536 Paragraph 13.15 of the Chancery Guide.

537 A specimen CH44 order is available on the Government website: https://www.gov.uk/government/publications/form-ch44-order-for-disposal-hearing (accessed 31st May 2023).

538 Paragraph 13.16 of the Chancery Guide.

539 Paragraph 13.18(a) of the Chancery Guide.

540 Paragraph 13.18(a)(i) of the Chancery Guide.

541 Ibid.

order";[542] and in the trusts context, a claim "*for approval of a sale, purchase, compromise or other transaction by a trustee, provided the claim is able to satisfy the court that there is no conflict of interest or prejudice to beneficiaries*".[543] It is suggested that a construction claim is unlikely to be dealt with in this way.

(b) If not, whether directions may be given without a hearing. The Chancery Guide explains: "*In most Part 8 claims, the Master will either make an order for directions at the point of initial review or direct that a hearing is fixed. If directions are given at that stage they will usually give notice of a disposal hearing and give directions concerning further evidence to be filed. The court will give notice of the hearing to all the parties, and the notice or order will specify to whom the notice has been sent*".[544]

(c) Whether the claim is likely to be referred to a different level of judge for disposal.[545]

A directions hearing with a time estimate of half a day or less (and no more than 90 minutes pre-reading) will take place remotely unless the court orders otherwise.[546] It is suggested that this is likely to be the case in most construction claims. If a party considers that the directions hearing should take place using a format other than the default format, they should CE-File and serve on the other parties a letter setting out their alternative proposal, together with brief reasons, within 7 days of receipt of the Notice of Hearing.[547] Appendix Z to the Chancery Guide contains helpful guidance on the preparation and conduct of remote or

542 Paragraph 13.18(a)(ii) of the Chancery Guide.

543 Paragraph 25.9 of the Chancery Guide.

544 Paragraph 13.18(b) of the Chancery Guide.

545 Paragraph 13.18(c) of the Chancery Guide.

546 Paragraph 13.19 of the Chancery Guide.

547 Ibid.

hybrid hearings.

The Chancery Guide explains that at a directions hearing, "*the court will generally wish to establish whether:*

> *(a) the court has all the evidence it will need (including expert evidence)*
>
> *(b) the claim is ready for a disposal hearing;*
>
> *(c) any witnesses will need to attend the final hearing for cross-examination, in which case the court will give directions with a view to fixing the period during which the case will be heard;*
>
> *the disposal hearing should be dealt with by a Master or by a [High Court Judge], Section 9 Judge or Deputy [High Court Judge].*"[548]

It is suggested that in a construction claim, the court is likely to consider the following at a directions hearing:

(a) Evidence, including whether directions should be given for the filing of any further evidence (in addition to the evidence which will already have been filed by that point) and whether any witnesses should be required to attend to give oral evidence and be cross-examined at the disposal hearing.[549] In general, the CPR Part 8 procedure is designed for claims which do not involve substantial disputes of fact, and the starting point in CPR Part 8 claims seems to be that there should be no oral evidence at the disposal hearing unless the court orders otherwise.[550] Furthermore, claims

548 paragraph 13.20 of the Chancery Guide.

549 CPR rule 8.6(2) provides "*The court may require or permit a party to give oral evidence at the hearing*" and CPR rule 8.6(3) provides "*The court may give directions requiring the attendance for cross-examination of a witness who has given written evidence*".

550 See paragraph 13.13 of the Chancery Guide: "*Part 8 claims will generally be disposed of on written evidence without cross-examination. The witness*

concerning the construction of a trust instrument rarely turn on conflicting factual evidence, particularly given that extrinsic evidence of the settlor's subjective intention is inadmissible.[551] It is therefore rare for directions to be given for oral evidence and cross-examination in claims concerning the construction of trust instruments.

(b) Representation of the parties, such as whether any litigation friend needs to be appointed and/or whether any representation order should be made and/or notice given pursuant to CPR rule 19.13 (as to which, see <u>Parties</u> above).

(c) Directions in relation to the disposal hearing, such as directions about when and how the disposal hearing should be listed, its time estimate, and the level of judge required.

   (i) As regards listing, if there is to be no oral evidence at the disposal hearing, then "*a trial will be listed before the relevant level of judge as directed by a Master*".[552] However, if oral evidence is required at the disposal hearing, then the listing of the trial will involve a two-stage

---

statements together with the claim form should be sufficient in most cases to define the issues".

551 This can be contrasted with claims for the construction of wills, where such evidence may be admissible if section 21 of the Administration of Justice Act 1982 is engaged. See e.g. *Hives v Machin* [2017] EWHC 1414 (Ch), in which the judge heard and considered conflicting oral evidence as to the testatrix's intentions, but ultimately concluded that section 21 AJA was not engaged and that such evidence was therefore inadmissible (see in particular [39] to [59]); and *Re Nodes* [2021] EWHC 1057 (Ch), where the court rejected the evidence as to the testator's intentions given by the draftsman, and preferred that given by the testator's widow.

552 Paragraph 12.24 of the Chancery Guide.

procedure.[553] First, a trial window, usually of 3 months, will be specified during which the trial is to take place. Then the parties should provide the court with an agreed list of dates to avoid, and the court will then proceed to fix a date for the start of the trial.[554]

(ii) As regards time estimate, this is likely to depend in particular on the number and complexity of the construction arguments which are being advanced, and on whether extrinsic evidence is admissible pursuant to section 21 AJA and, if so, whether that evidence consists of live oral evidence from witnesses who will be cross-examined.

(iii) As regards level of judge, CPR rule 2.4 provides that in proceedings in the High Court, any act which may be performed by the court may be performed "*by any judge, Master, Registrar in Bankruptcy or District Judge*".[555] Section II of CPR Practice Direction 2B does not impose any restriction on the jurisdiction of Masters or District Judges in relation to construction claims. On the contrary, the Chancery Guide provides: "*Most claims relating to trusts, estates and charities will be disposed of by a Master. The master will only release a claim to be heard by a High Court Judge if, exceptionally, the claim is of particularly high value, complexity, or legal novelty*".[556]

(d) 'Housekeeping' directions to prepare the case for the disposal

553 See paragraphs 12.16 to 12.23 of the Chancery Guide.

554 Paragraph 12.17 of the Chancery Guide.

555 Note the reference to 'District Judge' here is to a District Judge of the High Court (who is broadly the equivalent in the District Registries of a Master in London), not to a District Judge of the County Court.

556 Paragraph 25.2 of the Chancery Guide.

hearing, such as directions relating to the hearing bundle,[557] skeleton arguments,[558] and other documents such as dramatis personae, chronologies, lists of issues,[559] reading lists[560] and bundles of authorities.[561] As regards the latter, it is important to bear in mind that the court is being asked to construe the particular trust instrument in question (or one of its provisions) in the circumstances in which it was made, and is therefore unlikely to be assisted by the citation of numerous authorities which have construed similar provisions in different wills made in different circumstances. The Privy Council made this clear in the will case of *Sammut v Manzi*:[562]

> *There were placed before their Lordships no less than 17 decided cases, some of which involved decisions on wording that bore some similarity with that used in the present case. Little assistance in construing a will is likely to be gained by consideration of how other judges have interpreted similar wording in other cases. Counsel rightly recognised that the starting point must be to look at the natural meaning of the wording of the will to be construed without reference to other decisions or to prima facie principles of construction.*

---

557 Detailed rules in relation to hearing bundles are contained in paragraph 27 of CPR Practice Direction 32 and are supplemented by the guidance contained in Chapter 12 of, and Appendix X to, the Chancery Guide.

558 In relation to which see paragraphs 12.49 to 12.51 of, and Appendix Y to, the Chancery Guide.

559 In relation to which see paragraphs 12.52 to 12.55 of the Chancery Guide.

560 In relation to which see paragraph 12.56 to 12.58 of the Chancery Guide.

561 In relation to which see paragraph 12.59 to 12.61 of the Chancery Guide.

562 [2009] 1 WLR 1834 at [3]-[4].

(e) Whether the court should make a costs capping order of its own initiative pursuant to CPR rules 3.19 to 3.21. These are rare in practice in construction claims.

Disclosure

The disclosure process in the Business and Property Courts was substantially overhauled with the coming into effect of CPR Practice Direction 57AD on 1st October 2022.[563] However, the Practice Direction does not apply to claims proceeding under CPR Part 8 "*unless the court orders otherwise*".[564]

Given the disclosure obligations already imposed by CPR Part 8, it is suggested that orders for extended disclosure pursuant to CPR Practice Direction 57AD are likely to be rare in construction claims. Some support for this can be found in paragraph 13.25 of the Chancery Guide: "*PD 57AD does not apply to Part 8 claims when issued, and it is rare for an order for disclosure to be made in a Part 8 claim. However, if any form of disclosure is ordered the court will adopt such parts of PD 57AD as are appropriate (and CPR 31 does not apply)*".

Disposal hearing

At the disposal hearing, the court will hear the competing construction arguments, which may be two or, sometimes, more.

Disposal hearings in construction claims are generally listed in public, i.e. in a court which is open to members of the public.[565] Whilst it may be possible in some cases to persuade a court to list the claim in private pursuant to CPR rule 39.2(3),[566] or to impose some other less extensive

563 This followed a pilot introduced with effect from 1st January 2019 by what was CPR Practice Direction 51U.

564 Paragraph 1.4(7) of CPR Practice Direction 57AD.

565 Under the general rule in CPR rule 39.2(1).

566 CPR rule 39.2 requires the court to sit in private if it is satisfied (i) that

reporting restriction, a party seeking such an order is likely to have to show compelling reasons why the court should depart from the principle of open justice.[567]

Judgment

The Master or judge will decide how, when and where to deliver judgment. Judgment may be delivered orally immediately at the conclusion of the hearing (a so-called '*ex tempore*' judgment), or may be reserved. A reserved judgment may be delivered orally at a later date or, more commonly, may be circulated in written draft to the parties and then formally handed down at a subsequent date.

"*it is necessary to sit in private to secure the proper administration of justice*" and (ii) that one or more of the 7 sub-rules of CPR rule 39.2(3) is engaged. Of those sub-rules, those which may be engaged in a construction claim are likely to be (c), (d) and (g), viz.:

(c) [the hearing] involves confidential information (including information relating to personal financial matters) and publicity would damage that confidentiality;

(d) a private hearing is necessary to protect the interests of any child or protected party; [...]

(g) the court considers [a hearing in private] to be necessary, in the interests of justice."

On the other hand, sub-rule (f) is unlikely to be engaged where the correct construction is in dispute, as that sub-rule is engaged in relation to hearings involving "*uncontentious matters arising in the administration of trusts or in the administration of a deceased person's estate*" (emphasis added).

567 See in this regard the Court of Appeal's guidance in *MN v OP* [2019] EWCA Civ 679 regarding privacy and reporting restrictions in the context of applications pursuant to the Variation of Trusts Act 1958, which was subsequently applied by Chief Master Marsh in *MN v OP* [2019] EWHC 1643 (Ch) (although the same letters were used to anonymise the parties in both cases, the two cases were unrelated).

Costs

In *Re Buckton*,[568] Kekewich J identified the following two classes of cases in which he considered it appropriate to order that all parties' costs be paid out of the estate or trust (instead of following the general rule, now contained in CPR rule 44.2(2)(a), that the unsuccessful party will be ordered to pay the costs of the successful party):

> *In a large proportion of the summonses adjourned into Court for argument the applicants are trustees of a will or settlement who ask the Court to construe the instrument of trust for their guidance, and in order to ascertain the interests of the beneficiaries, or else ask to have some question determined which has arisen in the administration of the trusts. In cases of this character I regard the costs of all parties as necessarily incurred for the benefit of the estate, and direct them to be taxed as between solicitor and client and paid out of the estate. It is, of course, possible that trustees may come to the Court without due cause. A question of construction or of administration may be too clear for argument, or it may be the duty of trustees to inform a claimant that they must administer their trust on the footing that his claim is unfounded, and leave him to take whatever course he thinks fit. But, although I have thought it necessary sometimes to caution timid trustees against making applications which might with propriety be avoided, I act on the principle that trustees are entitled to the fullest possible protection which the Court can give them, and that I must give them credit for not applying to the Court except under advice which, though it may appear to me unsound, must not be readily treated as unwise. I cannot remember any case in which I have refused to deal with the costs of an application by trustees in the manner above mentioned.*
>
> *There is a second class of cases differing in form, but not in substance, from the first. In these cases it is admitted on all hands, or it is apparent from the proceedings, that although the application is made, not by trustees (who are respondents), but by some of the beneficiaries, yet it is*

568 [1907] 2 Ch 406.

> *made by reason of some difficulty of construction, or administration, which would have justified an application by the trustees, and it is not made by them only because, for some reason or other, a different course has been deemed more convenient. To cases of this class I extend the operation of the same rule as is observed in cases of the first class. The application is necessary for the administration of the trust, and the costs of all parties are necessarily incurred for the benefit of the estate regarded as a whole.*

Construction claims generally fall in either the first or the second class of cases identified in *Re Buckton* (depending on whether the claim is brought by the trustees or a beneficiary). As a result, the general starting point is that the costs of all of the parties will be payable out of the trust.[569]

Costs are however ultimately in the discretion of the court,[570] and the court may therefore decide to depart from that starting point and make a different costs order. It may decide to do so, for example, if it considers that the unreasonable conduct of one of the parties has materially increased costs unnecessarily,[571] or that the construction problem was not in fact a problem at all because one of the possible constructions was unarguable.[572]

---

569 In the will case of *Wales v Dixon* [2020] EWHC 1979 (Ch) the court encouraged the parties to agree such an order, indicating that it would be prepared to carry out a summary assessment if the costs could not be agreed: see [35].

570 Section 51(1) of the Senior Courts Act 1981.

571 See *Harrison-Mills v Public Trustee* [2019] EWCA Civ 966 at [66].

572 In *Re Buckton* [1907] 2 Ch 406 Kekewich J acknowledged the possibility that trustees "*may come to the Court without due cause*". However, his subsequent comments suggest that cases in which PRs or trustees will be deprived of their costs as a result will be rare: "*although I have thought it necessary sometimes to caution timid trustees against making applications which might with propriety be avoided, I act on the principle that trustees are entitled to the fullest possible protection which the Court can give them,*

In general terms, in deciding costs the court will try to ensure that the costs are in fact borne by the negligent draftsman and/or (in a contested case) by the party who has lost, and not by the successful party. In deciding precisely how this should be achieved, the court will have to take into account all of the circumstances, including the parties' respective interests under the will and who would in fact bear the costs if the costs are ordered to be paid out of the trust.[573] As indicated at 4.2.3 above, in cases involving professional negligence, the draftsman's insurers may have agreed in advance to pay the costs of the construction claim.[574] Alternatively, it may be possible to seek a non-party costs order against the firm responsible for the negligent drafting.[575]

Order

In construction claims the order which gives effect to the judgment will generally consist of two parts:

(a) a declaration by which the court formally declares the correct meaning of the trust instrument, or of one or more of its provisions; and

(b) an order directing the trustees to administer the trust in question

---

and that I must give them credit for not applying to the Court except under advice which, though it may appear to me unsound, must not be readily treated as unwise." See also *Harrison-Mills v Public Trustee* [2019] EWCA Civ 966 at [59].

573 See e.g. the wills cases of *Marley v Rawlings (costs)* [2014] UKSC 51 and *Slattery v Jagger* [2015] EWHC 3976 (Ch) at [103]-[112].

574 See e.g. the will case of *Slattery v Jagger* [2015] EWHC 3976 (Ch) at [103]-[112] (which involved both a construction and a rectification claim).

575 See CPR rule 46.2. Such an order was sought e.g. in *Royal Commonwealth Society for the Blind v Beasant* [2021] EWHC 352 (Ch) at [19]-[48] (the costs order was not considered on appeal: [2022] EWHC 1319 (Ch) at [35]).

in accordance with the declaration.

CPR Practice Direction 40E contains guidance in relation to reserved judgments. Paragraphs 16.8 to 16.22 of the Chancery Guide contain guidance in relation to the drafting, filing and sealing of orders following a hearing; paragraph 16.23 contains an example form of order.

Appeals

A party who is dissatisfied with the court's decision must obtain the court's permission in order to appeal it.[576] The court will only grant permission to appeal if it considers that the appeal would have a real prospect of success, or that there is some other compelling reason for the appeal to be heard.[577]

Although this is not strictly required, it is generally sensible for a party who wishes to appeal to first seek permission from the lower court.[578] This is usually done when judgment is delivered or handed down and consequential issues, such as the terms of the order giving effect to the judgment and costs, are decided.[579]

If the lower court refuses permission, or if permission was not sought from it, permission must be sought from the appeal court by filing an Appellant's Notice.[580] Unless the court orders otherwise, the time limit for doing so is "*21 days after the date of the decision of the lower court*".[581] That is a relatively short time limit, which cannot be extended by

576 CPR rule 52.3(1).

577 CPR rule 52.6(1).

578 Pursuant to CPR rule 52.3(2)(a); see e.g. *In re T (A Child)* [2002] EWCA Civ 1736 at [12]-[13].

579 See paragraph 12.91 of the Chancery Guide.

580 CPR rules 52.3(2)(b) and 52.12(1).

581 CPR rule 52.12(2)(b).

agreement between the parties,[582] and it must be borne in mind that the period starts to run from the date of the decision of the lower court and not, if later, the date on which consequential matters are decided or the date on which the order giving effect to the decision is approved and sealed.[583] If – as is quite common – the lower court's judgment is circulated to the parties in draft and then formally handed down in the absence of the parties, and a hearing to decide consequential matter is arranged at a later date, the lower court should be asked to direct[584] that the 21-day period will only start to run from the date of the later hearing, rather than from the date on which judgment was handed down.[585]

Compromise

In some cases it may be possible to compromise a construction claim after proceedings have been issued.[586] The mechanism by which the compromise should be implemented will inevitably depend on its terms and on the particular circumstances of the case. In most cases, the following will have to be considered:

(a) Whether the compromise has any tax implications and, if so, how these should be addressed.

(b) Whether a declaration by the court as to the correct construction of the trust instrument, or of one or more of its provisions, is required or desirable, and if so whether the court can be asked to make it by consent without hearing full argument in accordance

582 CPR rule 52.15(2).

583 See e.g. *Sayers v Clarke Walker (A Firm)* [2002] EWCA Civ 645 at [8]-[9] and *Owusu v Jackson* [2002] EWCA Civ 877 at [24]-[27].

584 Pursuant to CPR 52.12(2)(a).

585 See e.g. *Jackson v Marina Homes Ltd* [2007] EWCA Civ 1404 at [8]. This is envisaged by paragraph 12.91 of the Chancery Guide.

586 The circumstances in which it may be possible to resolve a construction issue without the need for court proceedings are considered at 4.2.2 above.

with the principles in *Hayim v Couch*,[587] *Pavilion Property Trustees Ltd v Permira Advisers LLP*[588] and *Singh v Singh*.[589] It should be borne in mind that this jurisdiction tends to be exercised sparingly.

(c) Whether the court's approval of the compromise is required, which will be the case where one or more of the parties is a minor,[590] an adult who lacks capacity to conduct litigation[591] and/or a party who has been appointed to represent others pursuant to CPR rule 19.9.[592]

Paragraphs 16.36 to 16.41 of the Chancery Guide contain guidance in relation to consent orders.

---

587 [2009] EWHC 1040 (Ch) at [12]-[18].

588 [2014] EWHC 145 (Ch) at [9]-[10].

589 [2014] EWHC 2762 (Ch) at [5]-[9].

590 CPR rule 21.10.

591 *Ibid.*

592 CPR rule 19.9(5).

CHAPTER FIVE

RECTIFICATION OF OTHER TRUST INSTRUMENTS

5.1 The law

The equitable jurisdiction to rectify other unilateral[593] trust instruments, such as trust deeds,[594] is well established.[595] In *Allnutt v Wilding*[596] the Court of Appeal explained the nature of the jurisdiction as follows: "*rectification is about putting the record straight. In the case of a voluntary settlement, rectification involves bringing the trust document into line with the true intentions of the settlor as held by him at the date when he executed the document. This can be done by the court when, owing to a mistake in the*

---

593 The rectification of bilateral documents, such as contracts, is a large topic in itself which is outside the scope of this book.

594 Other documents which can be rectified pursuant to this jurisdiction include: deeds of appointment: see e.g. *A v D* [2017] EWHC 2222 (Ch), *Ware v Ware* [2021] EWHC 694 (Ch) and *Hopes v Burton* [2022] EWHC 2770 (Ch); deeds of revocation and appointment: see e.g. *RBS Trustees (CI) Ltd v Stubbs* [2017] EWHC 180 (Ch); deeds of variation: see e.g. *Giles v Royal National Institute for the Blind* [2014] EWHC 1373 (Ch) and *Morrell v Morrell* [2021] EWHC 117 (Ch). The court has no jurisdiction to rectify an incorrect tax return: *Webster v Webster* [2020] EWHC 2275 (Ch).

595 An early example of the jurisdiction being referred to is *Walker v Armstrong* (1856) 8 DeGM&G 531. In *Re Butlin's Settlement* [1976] Ch 251 Brightman J (as he then was) held there was "*no doubt*" that the court has power to rectify a settlement "*notwithstanding that it is a voluntary settlement and not the result of a bargain, such as an ante-nuptial marriage settlement*" (at 260F).

596 [2007] EWCA Civ 412.

drafting of the document, it fails to record the settlor's true intentions. The mistake may, for example, consist of leaving out words that were intended to be put into the document, or putting in words that were not intended to be in the document; or through a misunderstanding by those involved about the meanings of the words or expressions that were used in the document. Mistakes of this kind have the effect that the document, as executed, is not a true record of the settlor's intentions."[597]

In *Giles v Royal National Institute for the Blind*,[598] Barling J summarised four criteria which the court must apply when deciding whether to rectify a unilateral document (derived primarily from the Court of Appeal's decision in *Racal Group Services Ltd v Ashmore*):[599]

> *(1) While equity has power to rectify a written instrument so that it accords with the true intention of its maker, as a discretionary remedy rectification is to be treated with caution. One aspect of that caution is that the claimant's case should be established by clear evidence of the true intention to which effect has not been given in the instrument. Such proof is on the civil standard of balance of probability. But as the alleged true intention of necessity contradicts the written instrument, there must be convincing proof to counteract the evidence of a different intention represented by the document itself;*
>
> *(2) There must be a flaw in the written document such that it does not give effect to the parties'/donor's agreement/intention, as opposed to the parties/donor merely being mistaken as to the consequences of what they*

---

597 [2007] EWCA Civ 412 at [11]. This echoes the Court of Appeal's earlier decision in *Racal Group Services Ltd v Ashmore* [1995] STC 1151, where the following passage from *Snell's Principles of Equity* (29th ed., 1990) was cited with approval (at 1154h): "*What is rectified is not a mistake in the transaction itself, but a mistake in the way in which that transaction has been expressed in writing*".

598 [2014] EWHC 1373 (Ch). The case involved the rectification of a deed of variation of a will.

599 [1995] STC 1151.

have agreed/intended; for example it is not sufficient merely that the document fails to achieve the desired fiscal objective;

(3) The specific intention of the parties/donor must be shown; it is not sufficient to show that the parties did *<u>not</u>* *intend what was recorded; they also have to show what they did intend, with some degree of precision;*

(4) There must be an issue capable of being contested between the parties notwithstanding that all relevant parties consent. This criterion has been much criticised: the purpose of it, and its actual content and scope, are by no means clear. In Racal Peter Gibson LJ expressly approved the following summary of the principle by Vinelott J in the same case. Vinelott J stated that the court must be satisfied:

"that there is an issue capable of being contested, between the parties or between a covenantor or a grantor and the person he intended to benefit, it being irrelevant first that rectification of the document is sought or consented to by them all, and second that rectification is desired because it has beneficial fiscal consequences. On the other hand, the court will not order rectification of a document as between the parties or as between a grantor or covenantor and an intended beneficiary, if their rights will be unaffected and if the only effect of the order will be to secure a fiscal benefit."

Whilst all four points are important, it is worth commenting further on (3) in particular. In order to succeed, the party seeking rectification has to establish with sufficient cogency and precision not just that something has gone wrong, but also what the document maker's[600] actual intention in fact was. This is because the court will only rectify the document in a particular way if it is satisfied that, once it has done so, the rectified document will accurately reflect the maker's actual intention. Whilst establishing that something has gone wrong can be fairly straightforward,

600 This will often be the settlor in the case of a trust deed, or the trustee(s) in relation to other documents such as a deed of appointment.

establishing the maker's actual intention can prove a stumbling block. This is particularly the case where the maker has a particular fiscal objective in mind, but may have delegated the precise mechanics of how to achieve that objective to his advisers. In those cases, it may be straightforward to establish that something has gone wrong where the fiscal objective has not been achieved, but it may be difficult (or even impossible) to establish with sufficient cogency and precision what the maker actually intended the document to say. This is because the maker may never in fact have given the precise mechanics particular thought and/or may have been content to follow the advice as to the precise mechanics given by his advisers. This sort of problem is illustrated by, for example, both *Racal Group Services Ltd v Ashmore*[601] and *Allnutt v Wilding*,[602]. In both cases the rectification claim failed because, although the court was satisfied that something had gone wrong, the party seeking rectification was unable to establish with sufficient cogency and precision what the maker's actual intention had in fact been.[603]

The Court of Appeal in *Day v Day*[604] made it clear that in cases involving voluntary instruments, what is relevant is "*the subjective intention of the settlor*"[605] and it is "*not a legal requirement for rectification of a voluntary settlement that there is any outward expression or objective communication of the settlor's intention equivalent to the need to show an outward expression of accord for rectification of a contract for mutual mistake*".[606] In order to ascertain the maker's intention at the time the instrument was made, it is

601 [1995] STC 1151.

602 [2007] EWCA Civ 412.

603 See *Racal Group Services Ltd v Ashmore* [1995] STC 1151 at 1160b-e; *Allnutt v Wilding* [2007] EWCA Civ 412 at [20]-[21] and [26]. A claim to rectify a deed of appointment failed for similar reasons in *Laird v Simcock* [2022] EWHC 1865 (Ch): see [54] and [56].

604 [2013] EWCA Civ 280.

605 [2013] EWCA Civ 280 at [22].

606 *Ibid.*

legitimate to have regard to conduct which post-dates the instrument.[607]

No limitation period applies to a claim for the rectification of a trust instrument other than a will.[608] However, as the remedy is equitable, it seems likely that the court could refuse to grant relief on the grounds of acquiescence and/or laches.[609] The interests of third parties will also be relevant.[610] In cases involving professionally prepared instruments in which professional negligence proceedings are likely to be relevant, regard must be had to the limitation period which applies to those proceedings.

5.2 Practice and procedure

5.2.1 Who is affected?

The first question trustees should ask themselves when faced with a rectification problem is: who is affected by it?

The main concern for trustees faced with a possible rectification problem

607 See e.g. *Gallaher v Gallaher Pensions Ltd* [2005] EWHC 42 (Ch) at [141], *Merchant Navy Officers Pension Fund Trustees v Watkins* [2013] EWHC 4741 (Ch) at [20], *Saga Group Ltd v Paul* [2016] EWHC 2344 (Ch) at [43], *Sovereign Trustees Ltd v Lewis* [2016] EWHC 2593 (Ch) at [15(iii)] and *A v D* [2017] EWHC 2222 (Ch) at [50].

608 See e.g. *Oatley v Oately* [2014] EWHC 1956 (Ch) where a trust deed was rectified 19 years after it was made notwithstanding that the problem had first been spotted, and rectification considered, over 4 years before the rectification claim was issued, and *Unipart Group Ltd v UGC Pension Trustees Ltd* [2018] EWHC 2124 (Ch) where a deed governing a pension scheme was rectified 16 years after it was made notwithstanding that the problem had arguably first been spotted over 10 years before the rectification claim was issued.

609 See e.g. *Snell's Equity*, 34th ed., at 16-025. See also *Oatley v Oately* [2014] EWHC 1956 (Ch), where the court indicated that "*in the light of the fact that rectification is a discretionary equitable remedy, it is relevant to take into account when determining whether to exercise the discretion, any delay and the effect of that delay before the remedy has been sought*" (at [86]).

610 *Ibid.*

is to ensure that before they take any step based on a particular provision of the trust instrument, they protect themselves from potential personal liability for breach of trust, which they can do by obtaining either the binding consent of all affected beneficiaries or authorisation from the court. To get to that position, the trustees will first have to establish who the affected beneficiaries are.

Needless to say, the answer to this will depend on the particular circumstances, and can vary widely. In simple terms, the way to go about ascertaining the affected beneficiaries is to consider the different possible outcomes depending on whether the trust instrument is or is not rectified (which may be two or more) and then consider who would benefit in each situation, as illustrated by the following examples.

Example 10

Wotan decides to make provision for his ten daughters by settling the benefit of a life insurance policy on trust for them. At the meeting with his solicitor, Mr Mime of Fasolt & Fafner Solicitors, Wotan gives Mr Mime a piece of paper on which he has written the names of his ten daughters; nine names appear on the front, and the final name on the back.

After the meeting, Mr Mime drafts a trust deed using a precedent from his firm's database and posts it to Wotan with instructions on how to execute it, which Wotan does.

Following Wotan's death it transpires that clause 5 of the trust deed identifies the beneficiaries as "*my daughters Gerhilde, Ortlinde, Waltraute, Schwertleite, Helmwige, Siegrune, Grimgerde and Roßweiße*". However, Wotan's tenth daughter, Brünnhilde – whose name appeared on the back of the piece of paper – has been omitted.

The issue is whether clause 5 should be rectified by adding Brünnhilde.

The affected beneficiaries are therefore Wotan's ten daughters.

Example 11

Just over 10 years ago, Mimì unexpectedly inherited from a distant cousin two semi-detached houses on the same street: numbers 21 and 27 Cold Hand Lane. For the past 10 years, Mimì and her partner Rodolfo have been living at 21 Cold Hand Lane, which is the larger of the two properties (having been extended into the loft by Mimì late cousin). The other property has been let out to tenants, Marcello and Musetta, with whom Mimì and Rodolfo have become close friends.

Musetta has recently lost her job and she and Marcello, who is a stay at home dad, are struggling financially. To help them, Mimì instructs her solicitor, Mr Murger of Illica & Giacosa Solicitors, to settle 27 Cold Hand Lane on trust for Marcello and Musetta during their joint lives; thereafter the property is to pass to such of Mimì's children and remoter issue as are then living, if more than one in equal shares.

Some years after executing the deed, Mimì decides to make a will. As part of this process, it transpires that the trust deed identifies the trust property as 21 (rather than 27) Cold Hand Lane. The title number in the deed is also the title number of number 21 rather than that of number 27.

The issue is whether the trust deed should be rectified to correct the house number and title number.

The affected beneficiaries are Mimì, Rodolfo, their children and remoter issue, and Marcello and Musetta.

Example 12

Don Giovanni instructs his solicitor, Lorenzo Da Ponte, to create a discretionary trust for the benefit of all of his former girlfriends, explaining that his trusted servant, Leporello, has their details. Mr Da Ponte liaises with Leporello and prepares a trust deed, which lists the names of 2,065 beneficiaries in a 52-page schedule. A few days after executing the trust deed, Don Giovanni dies of food poisoning.

It subsequently transpires that the trust instrument does not contain any discretionary power, and instead requires the trustees to hold the trust fund on trust for 125 years, and only then to distribute it to such of the beneficiaries who are alive, if more than one in equal shares, or in default to the Red Cross.

The issue is whether the trust instrument should be rectified by the insertion of discretionary powers which the trustees can exercise in favour of the beneficiaries during the trust period. The affected beneficiaries are therefore the 2,065 listed beneficiaries and the Red Cross.

If the rectification problem affects the amount of tax payable, some thought should be given to whether it is also necessary to involve HMRC.[611]

The corollary to the above is that trustees should bear in mind that they have no personal interest in how the rectification problem is resolved between the affected beneficiaries. It is not for the trustees to try to second guess what the settlor might have intended, nor to form a view as to which of the affected beneficiaries is more 'worthy' or 'deserving'. The trustees should remain neutral and impartial, and simply do what they are told, either by a unanimous binding agreement reached by all of the affected beneficiaries, or by the court.

5.2.2 Can the problem be resolved by agreement?

Some rectification problems can be resolved by the unanimous agreement of all of the beneficiaries affected by it. Therefore, once the trustees have identified all of the affected beneficiaries, the next question they should

---

611 Paragraph 18.26 of the Chancery Guide provides: "*If there are fiscal consequences which will arise from the changes to the document, HMRC (or any appropriate foreign tax body or bodies) should be notified, preferably before the claim is issued, and invited to confirm whether they wish to be joined as a party to the claim in order to make representations. The evidence in support of the claim should include such notification, and the position of HMRC (or any appropriate foreign tax body or bodies)*".

ask themselves is: can the problem be resolved by agreement?

Suppose that in Example 10 above, Wotan's ten daughters agree to split the trust fund between all of them equally (including Brünnhilde). They are the only individuals affected by the uncertainty. If they are all capacitous adults and agree what should happen, they can resolve the construction problem between themselves without having to go to court. The trustees' only concern will be to ensure that the agreement is properly documented so that they cannot later be criticised by any of the ten daughters for acting in accordance with it.

Resolving the problem by agreement is usually significantly cheaper and quicker than asking the court to do so. However, as indicated above, if the rectification problem affects the amount of tax payable, some thought should be given to whether it is also necessary to obtain the agreement of HMRC.

In practice, rectification problems are generally only resolved by agreement in the most straightforward cases. Two reasons can be identified for this. First, beneficiaries often have different views about what the settlor did or did not intend, and are therefore simply unable to reach an agreement. Secondly, to avoid exposing themselves to potential personal liability to disappointed beneficiaries, trustees must obtain the binding consent of all of the beneficiaries who are affected by the problem. This will not be possible if the problem affects beneficiaries who are minors, unborn, lack capacity and/or cannot be found. As those types of beneficiaries are unable to give the trustees their binding consent, in cases in which they are affected, the court's intervention will be necessary.

A useful way to explore whether the rectification problem can be resolved by agreement is for the trustees, who are often the first to spot the problem, to obtain advice from counsel on the rectification problem and then share that advice with all affected beneficiaries and canvass their views. If the trust document incorporates clause 12.3 of the STEP Standard Provisions (2nd edition), the trustees should consider obtaining the advice of counsel of "*at least five years' standing*" if they want to rely on the protection from liability afforded by that clause.[612]

This process should help both the trustees and all affected beneficiaries understand their respective positions, which in turn should inform all involved whether there is any hope of the rectification problem being resolved by agreement and, if so, how this might be achieved. Depending on the circumstances, the affected beneficiaries may wish to try to reach an agreement by, for example, negotiating in correspondence, at a round-table meeting or at a mediation.

As indicated above, trustees should bear in mind that they have no personal interest in how the rectification problem is resolved between the affected beneficiaries. The focus of the trustees should be to ensure:

(a) that they obtain the binding consent of all affected beneficiaries so they are protected from potential personal liability for breach of trust (i.e. for having distributed to the wrong person); and

---

612 Clause 12.3 and the following two clauses provide:

12.3 A Trustee shall not be liable for acting in accordance with the advice of counsel, of at least five years' standing, with respect to the Trust. The Trustees may in particular conduct legal proceedings in accordance with such advice without obtaining a court order. A Trustee may recover from the Trust Fund any expenses where he has acted in accordance with such advice.

12.4 Clause 12.3 does not apply:

12.4.1 in relation to a Trustee who knows or has reasonable cause to suspect that the advice was given in ignorance of material facts;

12.4.2 if proceedings are pending to obtain the decision of the court on the matter;

12.4.3 in relation to a Trustee who has a personal interest in the subject matter of the advice; or

12.4.4 in relation to a Trustee who has committed a breach of trust relating to the subject matter of the advice.

12.5 Clause 12.3 does not prejudice any right of any Person to follow property or income into the hands of any Person, other than a purchaser, who may have received it.

(b) that the agreement is one which the trustees can in fact implement. For example, the trustees should consider whether the agreement has tax consequences and, if so, how these should be addressed.

However, if all affected beneficiaries manage to reach a binding agreement which the trustees can implement, it is not for the trustees to 'approve' or 'disapprove' of it in any moral or ethical sense, e.g. on the basis that they think the settlor would or would not have liked it. It also follows from this that trustees are generally not required to actively participate in any negotiations between the affected beneficiaries; indeed, trustees should ensure they do not incur unnecessary costs by doing so.

In cases in which professional negligence proceedings against the draftsman have also been threatened or are on foot, it may be sensible to try to compromise the professional negligence at the same time.

There are two further tools which can help achieve a pragmatic solution without the court's intervention in a suitable case. The first is the possibility of the trustees agreeing to distribute on a particular basis provided the recipient beneficiaries in return provide the trustees with suitable indemnities, possibly backed by security. Such indemnities would be designed to protect the trustees against the risk that they may be personally liable to disappointed beneficiaries if the basis on which they have distributed subsequently turns out to be wrong. The second is the possibility of obtaining insurance to provide the trustees with that same protection.

Whether either of these tools is a useful one will depend on all of the particular surrounding circumstances. As a rather crude rule of thumb, it is suggested that the greater the financial value of the rectification problem, the less likely these tools are to provide a practical solution. This is because the greater the amount of money that turns on the rectification problem, the greater the potential liability of the trustees, and thus the more nervous both the beneficiaries and any insurance company will be in providing trustees with adequate protection. Further, in high value cases there is less of a risk of the trust fund being significantly depleted by the costs involved in making a court application, which might also point towards such an application being the better option.

5.2.3 Professional negligence

If the trust instrument was professionally prepared, it may be possible for a disappointed beneficiary to argue that the rectification problem amounts to professional negligence by the draftsman and seek damages on the basis of *White v Jones*.[613] In these sorts of circumstances, the disappointed beneficiary is usually under a duty to mitigate his loss by seeking to rectify the will before pursuing professional negligence proceedings against the draftsman[614] (although if limitation is a concern, a limitation standstill may have to be agreed, or the professional negligence claim issued protectively and stayed,).

Depending on the circumstances, if both the professional negligence claim and the rectification claim have merit, the draftsman's insurers might agree to fund the rectification claim, particularly if the costs involved in doing so are likely to be lower than their potential exposure in the event the professional negligence claim is successful.[615]

---

613 [1995] 2 AC 207.

614 See e.g. *Walker v Geo H Medlicott & Son* [1999] 1 WLR 727 and *Horsfall v Haywards* [1999] 1 FLR 1182. See also *Grattan v McNaughton* [2001] WTLR 1305 in which the claimant was criticised for pursuing the professional negligence claim first up to and including trial, and only once that claim had been dismissed, pursuing a rectification claim based on the same evidence which she had issued only 14 days before the trial of the professional negligence claim. Although no application to strike out the rectification claim on the grounds that it was an abuse of process was pursued, the judge indicated that he would have been "*provisionally very attracted to it*" as it could not be "*in the public interest to permit virtually the same issues in relation to the drafting of the will to be litigated twice*".

615 See e.g. *Re Bimson* [2010] EWHC 3679 (Ch) at [23].

5.2.4 Court intervention: rectification claims in the Chancery Division[616]

Notifying HMRC

The Chancery Guide provides: "*If there are fiscal consequences which will arise from the changes to the document, HMRC (or any appropriate foreign tax body or bodies) should be notified, preferably before the claim is issued, and invited to confirm whether they wish to be joined as a party to the claim in order to make representations. The evidence in support of the claim should include such notification, and the position of HMRC (or any appropriate foreign tax body or bodies)*".[617]

Starting the claim

In many cases rectification claims are brought by way of CPR Part 8 proceedings. This may be because the claim is not opposed by the beneficiaries who are capacitous adults, but it also affects beneficiaries who are minors, unborn, lack capacity and/or cannot be found, and/or it is necessary to obtain a court order granting rectification because the drafting problem has tax consequences.[618] This may also be done because the rectification claim is being brought together with one or more other claims – typically a construction claim[619] – which must be brought by way of a CPR Part 8 claim (see 4.2.4.). In this sort of situation, the procedural rules governing the other claim(s) must also be borne in mind.

---

616 Rectification cannot be obtained by way of an application pursuant to section 48 AJA (discussed in section 4.2.4), no matter how strong the claim and/or clear the evidence: see *Greenwold v Pike* [2007] EWHC 2002 (Ch) at [5] and *Clarke-Sullivan v Clarke-Sullivan* [2021] EWHC at [25] and [62(3)].

617 Paragraph 18.26 of the Chancery Guide.

618 See e.g. *Racal Group Services Ltd v Ashmore* [1995] STC 1151 and *Allnutt v Wilding* [2007] EWCA Civ 412.

619 See e.g. *Millar v Millar* [2018] EWHC 1926 (Ch) and *Armstrong v Armstrong* [2019] EWHC 2259 (Ch).

The Chancery Guide exhorts parties to a rectification claim to "*give careful consideration to whether the claim should be brought under the Part 7 or Part 8 procedure*".[620] It also indicates that where a rectification claim is brought by CPR Part 8 proceedings and there are therefore no particulars of claim, "*the claimant should [...] consider whether to prepare a document which summarises the claim to be provided to the court and the parties with the claim form*".[621]

Some thought should also be given as to whether the court should be asked to deal with any aspects in dispute as a preliminary issue.[622]

On the other hand, if the rectification claim is brought on its own and is opposed, it is likely to involve a substantial dispute of fact, and it is therefore likely to be more appropriate for the claim to be brought as a CPR Part 7 claim rather than a CPR Part 8 claim.[623]

<u>Parties</u>

Determining who should be made a party to a rectification claim often requires some careful thought. In general, it is useful to bear in mind that:

(a) if the rectification problem is being resolved by way of a contested rectification claim, it should be clear that there are at least two opposing parties, and who they are; they will need to be joined;

(b) the court will want to ensure that everyone affected by the

---

620 Paragraph 18.21 of the Chancery Guide.

621 Paragraph 18.22 of the Chancery Guide.

622 As in *Burnard v Burnard* [2014] EWHC 340 (Ch) (see [7]).

623 CPR rule 8.1(2). In *Kelly v Brennan* [2020] EWHC 245 (Ch) the claim was brought by CPR Part 8 (see [3]) despite the fact that rectification was the only relief sought and that the claim was opposed. However, the defendants' position appears to have evolved over time (see [5]-[7]) and there was perhaps no substantial dispute of fact.

rectification problem has an opportunity to be heard;

(c) in a contentious situation, the trustees should generally remain neutral in their capacity as trustees and not advocate in favour or against rectification, and should instead let the opposing beneficiaries fight it out;

(d) however, where the claim is unopposed and/or no beneficiary with a contrary interest wishes to take an active role, it may be incumbent on the trustees as "*watchdog*"[624] for unrepresented or unborn beneficiaries to assist the court by "*bringing to the court's attention any relevant legal propositions or argument affecting the position of unrepresented beneficiaries or parties*"[625] to ensure the court is able to reach the right result; and

(e) as indicated above, if the rectification problem affects the amount of tax payable, it may be necessary to notify, and perhaps even join, HMRC.[626]

(f) All of the current trustees should be joined as a party to a rectification claim to ensure they are bound by the order. What may be less clear is how to ensure that all affected beneficiaries are joined and are able to have their say.

In cases involving a limited number of affected beneficiaries, the answer may be fairly straightforward. The simplest example is where there are two possible outcomes and the only affected beneficiaries are capacitous adults, as in Example 10 above (assuming the ten daughters are all capacitous adults). In such cases, it may be sensible for the trustees to leave it to the beneficiary who would benefit from the rectification to

---

624 *Re Druce's Settlement Trusts* [1962] 1 WLR 363 at 370.

625 *State Street Bank & Trust Co v Sompo Japan Insurance Inc* [2010] EWHC 1461 (Ch) at [30]. See also e.g. *Re Hemming* [2008] EWHC 8565 (Ch) at [40].

626 See "Notifying HMRC" above.

bring the claim, and to join both the trustees and the other affected beneficiaries as defendants. As the contest is in substance between the affected beneficiaries, the trustees should adopt a neutral stance and let the affected beneficiaries advance the two alternative arguments.

Where one or more of the affected beneficiaries is a minor or lacks capacity and is to be a party to the claim, that beneficiary will need a litigation friend (unless, in the case of a minor, the court makes an order permitting the child to conduct proceedings without a litigation friend).[627] CPR Part 21 contains detailed guidance on the procedure for the appointment of a litigation friend.

On the other hand, the position may be more complicated where the rectification problem affects a large number of beneficiaries (e.g. large classes) – as in Example 12 above – and/or where some of the affected beneficiaries are minors, unborn, lack capacity and/or cannot be found (which could also be a problem in Example 12). In these sorts of cases, there is likely to be a tension between on the one hand ensuring that everyone who has an interest is properly represented and has an opportunity to be heard, and on the other trying to avoid depleting the estate or trust by incurring significant costs tracing and communicating with large classes of beneficiaries.

How the balance should be struck will inevitably depend on the circumstances of the particular case. In complicated cases, the provisions of CPR rule 19.9[628] and/or 19.13[629] can be of considerable assistance.[630]

---

627 CPR rule 21.2(1).

628 With effect from 6th April 2023, what used to be CPR rule 19.7 became rule 19.9: see rules 1(1) and 12(10) of the Civil Procedure (Amendment) Rules 2023 (SI 2023/105).

629 With effect from 6th April 2023, what used to be CPR rule 19.8A became rule 19.13: see rules 1(1) and 12(14) of the Civil Procedure (Amendment) Rules 2023 (SI 2023/105).

630 The relevance of these rules to claims concerning estates and trusts is highlighted by paragraphs 25.10 to 25.14 of the Chancery Guide,

These govern respectively the appointment of a party to represent the interests of others and the service of proceedings and/or orders on non-parties so as to bind them. In a suitable case, the ability to issue a CPR Part 8 claim form without naming a defendant pursuant to CPR rule 8.2A may also be useful.[631]

CPR rule 19.9(2) provides:

> *The court may make an order appointing a person to represent any other person or persons in the claim where the person or persons to be represented –*
>
> *(a) are unborn;*
>
> *(b) cannot be found;*
>
> *(c) cannot easily be ascertained; or*
>
> *(d) are a class of persons who have the same interest in a claim and –*
>
> > *(i) one or more members of that class are within sub-paragraphs (a), (b) or (c); or*

---

considered below. Note that CPR rule 19.8, which is entitled "*Representative parties with same interest*", does not apply to claims "*about (a) the estate of a deceased person, (b) property subject to a trust, or (c) the meaning of a document, including a statute*": see CPR rules 19.8(5) and 19.9(1). (CPR rule 19.8 used to be CPR rule 19.6 until it was renumbered with effect from 6th April 2023: see rules 1(1) and 12(9) of the Civil Procedure (Amendment) Rules 2023 (SI 2023/105)).

631 Permission to issue the claim without naming a defendant was given in the will construction case of *Re Harte* [2015] EWHC 2351 (Ch). However, the claimant executors were then directed to take reasonable steps to trace the testatrix's statutory next of kin and to serve notices pursuant to CPR rule 19.8A (now CPR rule 19.13) on various people and charities (see [2]-[4]).

(ii) to appoint a representative would further the overriding objective.

This caters for several different scenarios:

(a) is self-explanatory;

(b) covers situations in which it is clear who the affected beneficiary is, but (reasonable) attempts to find him have proved unsuccessful;

(c) covers situations in which it is not clear who the affected beneficiary is, nor can this be easily clarified;

(d) covers two alternative situations where a class of persons has the same interest in the claim:

 (i) is self-explanatory;

 (ii) is potentially wide and flexible. It can be used, for example, where there is a large class of affected beneficiaries scattered around the world, all of whom have the same interest, and it would further the overriding objective to appoint one of them to represent the whole class (e.g. by reducing procedural delay and costs) – ideally one who can be served within the jurisdiction.[632]

CPR rule 19.9(3) provides that an application for a representation order under CPR rule 19.9(2) may be made "*by any person who seeks to be appointed under the order or any party to the claim*", and may be made "*at any time before or after the claim has started*". CPR rule 19.9(4) provides that the application notice for such an order must be served on:

632 For an example, see *Public Trustee v Harrison* [2018] EWHC 166 (Ch) at [8].

(a) all parties to the claim, if the claim has started;

(b) the person sought to be appointed, if that person is not the applicant or a party to the claim; and

(c) any other person as directed by the court.

It is important to note that where the court has made a representation order under CPR rule 19.9, the court's approval is required to settle the claim.[633] This is to safeguard the position of the represented parties and to ensure their representative does not enter into a compromise which is disadvantageous to them: CPR rule 19.9(6) gives the court jurisdiction to approve a settlement "*where it is satisfied that the settlement is for the benefit of all represented persons*".

In relation to CPR rule 19.9, the Chancery Guide explains: "*Where the claim relates to the internal affairs of the trust or estate it may be appropriate for a representation order to be made so that the interests of all classes of beneficiaries are represented and protected but they are also all bound by the decision.*"[634]

Finally, CPR rule 19.13 provides:

Power to make judgements binding on non-parties

(1) This rule applies to any claim relating to –

[…];

633 CPR rule 19.9(5).

634 Paragraph 25.11 of the Chancery Guide. (The paragraph refers to "*CPR 19.7*", which was the old numbering of the rule before it was renumbered rule 19.9 with effect from 6th April 2023: see rules 1(1) and 12(10) of the Civil Procedure (Amendment) Rules 2023 (SI 2023/105))).

(b) property subject to a trust; or

(c) the sale of any property.

(2) The court may at any time direct that notice of –

(a) the claim; or

(b) any judgment or order given in the claim,

be served on any person who is not a party but who is or may be affected by it.

(3) An application under this rule –

(a) may be made without notice; and

(b) must be supported by written evidence which includes the reasons why the person to be served should be bound by the judgment in the claim.

(4) Unless the court orders otherwise –

(a) a notice of a claim or of a judgment or order under this rule must be –

(i) in the form required by the practice direction;

(ii) issued by the court; and

(iii) accompanied by a form of acknowledgment of service with any necessary modifications;

(b) a notice of a claim must also be accompanied by –

(i) a copy of the claim form; and

(ii) such other statements of case, witness statements or affidavits as the court may direct; and

(c) a notice of a judgment or order must also be accompanied by a copy of the judgment or order.

(5) If a person served with notice of a claim files an acknowledgment of service of the notice within 14 days they will become a party to the claim.

(6) If a person served with notice of a claim does not acknowledge service of the notice they will be bound by any judgment given in the claim as if they were a party.

(7) If, after service of a notice of a claim on a person, the claim form is amended so as substantially to alter the relief claimed, the court may direct that a judgment shall not bind that person unless a further notice, together with a copy of the amended claim form, is served on them.

(8) Any person served with a notice of a judgment or order under this rule –

(a) shall be bound by the judgment or order as if he had been a party to the claim; but

(b) may, provided they acknowledges service –

> *(i) within 28 days after the notice is served on them, apply to the court to set aside or vary the judgment or order; and*
>
> *(ii) take part in any proceedings relating to the judgment or order.*

(9) The following rules of Part 10 (acknowledgment of service) apply –

(a) rule 10.4; and

(b) rule 10.5, subject to the modification that references to the defendant are to be read as references to the person served with the notice.

(10) A notice under this rule is issued on the date entered on the notice by the court.

The procedure in CPR rule 19.13 can be useful to bind interested beneficiaries who do not want to take an active role in the proceedings, such as the adult children of an 'active' interested beneficiary who are content to simply support their parent's position. However, it suggests that it is unlikely to be a good idea to press on with the proceedings and to then try to rely on CPR rule 19.13 to serve a judgment or order on an interested beneficiary who it is thought will want to actively have a say. In such cases there is a risk that such a beneficiary will then apply to set aside the judgment or order (pursuant to CPR rule 19.13(8)(b)) to, in effect, re-open the case to advance his argument, and this could significantly increase the overall costs. In this sort of situation it is likely to be preferable to ensure that such a beneficiary is able to actively participate from the outset.

It should be borne in mind that the issue of representation is likely to be considered by the court at the first directions hearing, at which creative and pragmatic solutions can be considered with the Master, particularly in complex cases.[635]

---

635 See e.g. the will case of *Re Harte* [2015] EWHC 2351 (Ch), in which the PRs were initially given permission to issue the construction and rectification claims without naming a defendant (pursuant to CPR rule 8.2A), and were then given directions as to the steps they should take to ascertain the intestacy beneficiaries (including by advertisement) and as to the parties to whom they should give notice of the proceedings pursuant to CPR rule 19.8A (see [3]-[4]) and *Womble Bond Dickinson (Trust Corp) Ltd v No Named Defendant* [2022] EWHC 43 (Ch), in which the trustees of an employee benefit trust were given permission to issue the construction claim without naming a defendant, and the court directed their solicitors to instruct a separate counsel to advance the opposing arguments effectively as Advocate to the Court, given that there was no individual who could obviously be appointed to represent all of the beneficiaries: see [6].

Limitation

As indicated above, it seems no limitation period applies to a claim for the rectification of a trust instrument. However, as the remedy is equitable, it seems likely that the court could refuse to grant relief on the grounds of acquiescence and/or laches.[636] The interests of third parties will also be relevant.[637]

Which court

The County Court appears to have jurisdiction to determine a claim for the rectification of a trust instrument if the value of the trust fund does not exceed £350,000.[638] However, in practice rectification claims are invariably issued in the Chancery Division of the High Court,[639] i.e. what has now become the Property, Trusts and Probate List (ChD) of the Business and Property Courts. A rectification claim can be issued either in the Rolls Building in London or in one of the District Registries (Birmingham, Bristol, Cardiff, Leeds, Liverpool, Manchester and Newcastle-upon-Tyne).[640]

636 See e.g. *Snell's Equity*, 34th ed., at 16-025.

637 *Ibid.*

638 Section 23 of the County Courts Act 1984 and article 3 of the County Court Jurisdiction Order 2014 (SI 2014/503). This assumes that the rectification claim in question is a type of "*proceedings for relief against [...] mistake*" within section 23(g).

639 Section 61 and paragraph 1(g) of Schedule 1 to the Senior Courts Act 1981; see also paragraph 18.16 of the Chancery Guide.

640 Paragraph 1.3 of the Chancery Guide. Appendix C to the Chancery Guide ('Chancery Business outside the Rolls Building') contains helpful information regarding Chancery business outside London, including contact details of the various District Registries.

Evidence/Pleadings

A distinction needs to be drawn between rectification claims brought by way of a CPR Part 8 claim and those brought by way of a CPR Part 7 claim.[641]

CPR Part 8 claims: evidence

If the rectification claim is brought by way of a CPR Part 8 claim, the claimant must file the evidence on which he intends to rely when his claim form is issued[642] (unless the claimant only intends to rely on the evidence contained in the claim form itself, which it is suggested is unlikely to be the case in rectification claims). This will generally be in the form of one or more witness statements. The claimant's evidence must be served on the defendant with the claim form.[643]

CPR Practice Direction 57AC applies to "*trial witness statements*"[644] in the Business and Property Courts. This appears to include claims for rectification of unilateral trust documents (other than wills).[645] Paragraph 18.28 of the Chancery Guide provides: "*When preparing trial witness statements in a rectification claim, careful thought needs to be given to compliance with (or dispensation from) the requirements of PD 57AC. This*

---

641 See "Starting the claim" above.

642 CPR rule 8.5(1); see also paragraph 13.10 of the Chancery Guide.

643 CPR rule 8.5(2).

644 Defined by paragraph 1.2 of CPR Practice Direction 57AC as "*a witness statement that is served pursuant to an order made under rule 32.4(2), or pursuant to rule 8.5 or an order made under rule 8.6(1)(b), or that is prepared for the trial of an unfair prejudice petition or a contributory's just and equitable winding up petition, including supplemental or reply witness statements where allowed by the court*".

645 Paragraph 1.3(6) of CPR Practice Direction 57AC provides that the Practice Direction does not apply to "*proceedings falling within CPR Part 57, which applies to [...] claims for the rectification of wills*", unless the court orders otherwise.

is a particularly important consideration in rectification claims where the passage of time or the nature of the rectification sought may mean that there is no witness able to give evidence as to the relevant events and/or where it is necessary for a witness to express a belief as to whether there has been a mistake and/or to explain what happened". In an appropriate case, it may be possible to ask the court to dispense with the requirements of CPR Practice Direction 57AC by making an application without notice and asking that it be determined without a hearing.[646]

The contents of the witness statement(s) will of course depend on the circumstances of the particular case. In general terms, the topics which one should consider covering in the evidence filed in support of the claim are likely to be:

(a) the claimant's role and the capacity in which he brings the claim;

(b) the factual background;

(c) the current drafting of the trust instrument and its construction;

(d) what the maker's intentions are alleged to have been;

(e) how the current drafting of the trust instrument fails to correctly record the maker's intentions;

(f) how the court is being asked to rectify the trust instrument;[647]

(g) the position of the other interested parties;

---

646 See paragraphs 4.2 and 4.4 of CPR Practice Direction 57AC.

647 Paragraph 18.27 of the Chancery Guide encourages "*[c]laimants (and any parties agreeing or consenting to the claim) [...] to consider carefully the form of order sought in advance of issuing the claim*" and "*how the document in respect of which rectification is sought is intended to be treated (i.e. whether the order will be indorsed on the document to be rectified, and, if so, how)*". It also points out that the court "*is likely to wish to make the minimum possible changes in order to rectify the document in question*".

(h) the approximate value of the estate or fund in issue.[648]

If the trust instrument was professionally prepared, some thought should be given as to whether evidence should be obtained from the draftsman responsible for preparing it (if available) and, if so, as to who should call the draftsman as a witness.[649]

It should be borne in mind that the CPR requires witness statements to be in the witness's own words.[650] Furthermore, the temptation to include in a witness statement extensive legal submissions and references to case law should generally be resisted, particularly in witness statements of lay witnesses; these are properly a matter for skeleton arguments and submissions.

CPR Part 7 claims: particulars of claim and Initial Disclosure

If the rectification claim is brought by way of a CPR Part 7 claim,[651] the particulars of claim must either be contained in or served with the claim form, or be served on the defendant within 14 days after service of the claim form, subject to them being served no later than the latest time for serving the claim form.[652] The contents of the particulars of claim will of course depend on the circumstances of the particular case. In general terms, the topics which the party seeking rectification should consider covering in the particulars of claim are likely to be the same as those the claimant's evidence should over in CPR Part 8 claims, viz.:

648 Paragraph 25.4 of the Chancery Guide.

649 See e.g. the will rectification case of *Re McKay* [2023] EWHC 642 (Ch) at [39]-[40].

650 Paragraph 18.1 of CPR Practice Direction 32; see also paragraph 3.3 of CPR Practice Direction 57AC and paragraph 8.1 of the Chancery Guide and paragraph .

651 See "Starting the claim" above.

652 CPR rule 7.4.

(a) the claimant's role and the capacity in which he brings the claim;

(b) the factual background;

(c) the current drafting of the trust instrument and its construction;

(d) what the maker's intentions are alleged to have been;

(e) how the current drafting of the trust instrument fails to correctly record the maker's intentions;

(f) how the court is being asked to rectify the trust instrument;[653]

(g) the position of the other interested parties;

(h) the approximate value of the estate or fund in issue.

As well as the rules in CPR rule 16.4 and CPR Practice Direction 16, the drafting guidelines contained in paragraphs 4.2 to 4.9 of the Chancery Guide apply to particulars of claim.

In claims proceeding under CPR Part 7,[654] paragraph 5.1 of CPR Practice Direction 57AD requires the claimant to provide at the same time as his statement of case "*an Initial Disclosure List of Documents that lists and is accompanied by copies of:*

(1) the key documents on which it has relied (expressly or otherwise) in support of the claims or defences advanced in its statement of case (and

---

653 Paragraph 18.27 of the Chancery Guide encourages "*[c]laimants (and any parties agreeing or consenting to the claim) [...] to consider carefully the form of order sought in advance of issuing the claim*" and "*how the document in respect of which rectification is sought is intended to be treated (i.e. whether the order will be indorsed on the document to be rectified, and, if so, how)*". It also points out that the court "*is likely to wish to make the minimum possible changes in order to rectify the document in question*".

654 CPR Practice Direction 57AD does not apply to claims proceeding under CPR Part 8, unless otherwise ordered: see paragraph 1.4(7).

including the documents referred to in that statement of case); and

(2) the key documents that are necessary to enable the other parties to understand the claim or defence they have to meet.

Initial Disclosure is not required where a party concludes and states in writing, approaching the matter in good faith, that giving Initial Disclosure would involve it or any other party providing more than the larger of about 1,000 pages or 200 documents.[655]

The parties can also agree in writing prior to the commencement of proceedings that Initial Disclosure should not apply; however, they should only do so with good reason, as the court may review the parties' reasons for disapplying Initial Disclosure at the first case management conference and may set aside such an agreement aside if it considers that Initial Disclosure "*is likely to provide significant benefits and the costs of providing Initial Disclosure are unlikely to be disproportionate to such benefits*".[656]

A party may also apply to the court for directions limiting or abrogating the obligation to provide Initial Disclosure, for example where complying with the obligation "*will incur disproportionate cost or be unduly complex*".[657]

Prospective (or pre-emptive) costs orders

In some rectification cases it may be appropriate to consider at an early stage of the proceedings whether a mechanism should be put in place for the costs of one or more of the parties to be paid out of the estate or trust fund in any event irrespective of the outcome.[658] This can be either by

655 Paragraph 5.3(3) of CPR Practice Direction 57AD.

656 Paragraph 5.8 of CPR Practice Direction 51AD.

657 Paragraph 5.10 of CPR Practice Direction 57AD.

658 The costs orders which are likely to be made at the conclusion of the proceedings are considered at "Costs" below.

way of a contractual agreement by the PRs or by a so-called prospective (or pre-emptive) costs order by the court. This issue tends to arise primarily in pension cases, where an individual pension scheme member may be made a party to complex litigation as representative of other scheme members, and it may be unfair for him to have to bear his costs personally at least until the conclusion of the litigation, which can create a cash flow problem.[659]

Where the issue arises, the eight sub-paragraphs of paragraph 6 of CPR Practice Direction 64A contain some detailed guidance about prospective costs orders, as do paragraphs 25.30 to 25.32 of the Chancery Guide. A model form of prospective costs order is appended to CPR Practice Direction 64A.

Costs management

CPR Part 8 claims

CPR rule 3.12 makes it clear that costs management does not apply to CPR Part 8 claims unless the court orders that it should pursuant to CPR rule 3.12(1A).[660] Paragraph 5(e) of CPR Practice Direction 3D provides that an order for costs management may be "*particularly appropriate*" in "*any Part 8 or other claims or applications involving a substantial dispute of fact and/or likely to require oral evidence and/or extensive disclosure*". The Chancery Guide also provides that: "*It is the court's experience that it is often helpful for costs budgets to be exchanged in cases in the ChD B&PCs London even if costs budgeting would not otherwise apply. Parties should consider exchanging costs budgets and/or opting into costs management even in cases which are outside the costs management regime. If the parties agree*

659 The principles governing the making of a prospective costs order have been considered in a line of pensions cases which includes *McDonald v Horn* [1995] 1 All ER 961 and *IBM United Kingdom Pensions Trust Ltd v Metcalfe* [2012] EWHC 125 (Ch).

660 In relation to which see also and paragraph 2 of CPR Practice Direction 3D. This is reiterated by paragraph 13.30 of the Chancery Guide.

that a costs management order should be made, a consent order should be lodged in advance of the CMC including proposed directions for costs management".[661]

A party seeking an order that costs management should apply to the proceedings should "*give notice to the other parties and the court well in advance of the directions hearing and explain, preferably in a witness statement, why such an order is sought*".[662]

CPR Part 7 claims

If a rectification claim is brought by way of CPR Part 7 proceedings, it is likely to be a multi-track claim and costs management is likely to apply to it, unless the court dispenses with costs management pursuant to CPR rule 3.12(e). It seems likely that the court will only do so if it is satisfied that the litigation can be conducted justly and at proportionate cost in accordance with the overriding objective without costs management.[663] Costs budgets and budget discussion reports will have to be filed and exchanged in accordance with the procedure contained in Section II of CPR Part 3.

Service

The usual rules for service contained in the CPR – mostly in CPR Part 6 – apply to claims for the rectification of a trust instrument. If it is necessary to seek the court's permission to serve the claim form out of the jurisdiction pursuant to CPR rule 6.36, the grounds listed in paragraph 3.1 of CPR Practice Direction 6B which are likely to be relevant are grounds (11) to (12A):

---

661 Paragraph 6.31 of the Chancery Guide.

662 Paragraph 13.31 of the Chancery Guide.

663 This is the basis on which the court can decide (pursuant to CPR rule 3.15(2)) not to make a costs management order even where costs budgets have been filed.

> *Claims about property within the jurisdiction*
>
> *(11) The subject matter of the claim relates wholly or principally to property within the jurisdiction, provided that nothing under this paragraph shall render justiciable the title to or the right to possession of immovable property outside England and Wales.*
>
> *Claims about trusts etc.*
>
> *(12) A claim is made in respect of a trust which is created [...] by a written instrument, or created orally and evidenced in writing, and which is governed by the law of England and Wales.*
>
> *(12A) A claim is made in respect of a trust which is created [...] by a written instrument, or created orally and evidenced in writing, and which provides that jurisdiction in respect of such a claim shall be conferred upon the courts of England and Wales.*

Responding to the claim

CPR Part 8 claims: defendant's acknowledgment of service and evidence

A defendant who wishes to respond to the claim must file an acknowledgment of service in the relevant practice form (viz. form N210) not more than 14 days after service of the claim form on him.[664] At the same time he must also serve his acknowledgment of service on the claimant and on any other party.[665] If he fails to do so, the defendant may attend the hearing of the claim but may not take part in the hearing unless the court gives permission.[666] As the Chancery Guide makes clear,

664 CPR rule 8.3(1); see also paragraph 13.8 of the Chancery Guide. Note that different (longer) periods apply if the proceedings have been served on the defendant out of the jurisdiction: see CPR rules 8.3(3) and 10.3(2).

665 CPR rule 8.3(1).

666 CPR rule 8.4(2).

these are "*serious consequences*".[667]

The defendant must indicate in his acknowledgment of service whether he contests the claim, and if he seeks a different remedy from that set out in the claim form, what that remedy is.[668] There is no need to file a defence, as CPR Part 15 does not apply to claims brought pursuant to CPR Part 8.[669]

Defendants who acknowledge service but do not intend to file any evidence should notify the court in writing when they file their acknowledgment of service that they do not intend to file evidence. This "*enables the court to know what each defendant's intention is when it considers the file and avoids delay*".[670]

CPR rule 8.8(1) provides that where a defendant "*contends that the CPR Part 8 procedure should not be used because there is (a) a substantial dispute of fact and (b) the use of the Part 8 procedure is not required or permitted by a rule or practice direction, he must state his reasons when he files his acknowledgment of service*". In such cases, it may be appropriate for directions to be given for the claim to proceed as, in effect, a hybrid claim, as explained below.[671]

A defendant who wishes to rely on written evidence must file it when he files his acknowledgment of service,[672] and must at the same time serve a copy of his evidence on the other parties.[673] The defendant may not rely on any written evidence which has not been served in accordance with

---

667 Paragraph 13.8 of the Chancery Guide.

668 CPR rule 8.3(2).

669 CPR rule 8.9(a); see also paragraph 13.9 of the Chancery Guide.

670 Paragraph 13.15 of the Chancery Guide.

671 See "Directions hearing" below.

672 CPR rule 8.5(3); see also paragraph 13.10 of the Chancery Guide.

673 CPR rule 8.5(4).

these rules at the hearing of the claim unless the court gives permission.[674]

As the time limit for the defendant to file and serve his evidence is quite short (viz. 14 days from service of the claim on him), CPR rule 8.5(9) allows the parties to "*agree in writing on an extension of time of not more than 14 days for serving and filing evidence from the defendant*". Such an agreement must be filed at court with the acknowledgment of service.[675] The Chancery Guide recognises that it is "*not unusual for an extension of time to be agreed between the parties for the service of evidence*".[676]

If a defendant requires more time to file his evidence, he should apply to the court for an extension of time by way of an application pursuant to CPR Part 23.[677] If the parties are in agreement that such an extension should be granted, the application should be made by filing a consent order.[678] If there is no agreement, an application "*should be made to a Master using the urgent applications procedure set out in paragraphs 15.11 to 15.14 [of the Chancery Guide] but does not need to be certified as urgent business. When issuing the application the applicant should add 'Urgent Application EOT' to the comment box on CE-File to assist the court staff to process the application promptly*".[679] The Chancery Guide indicates that "*[i]n substantial matters the court will normally be willing to grant a reasonable extension*".[680]

As for the claimant's evidence, the contents of any witness statement(s) adduced by a defendant will of course depend on the circumstances of the particular case. In general terms, the topics one should consider

674 CPR rule 8.6(1).

675 CPR rule 8.5(10).

676 Paragraph 13.11 of the Chancery Guide.

677 CPR rule 8.5(8).

678 As to which, see paragraphs 16.36 to 16.41 of the Chancery Guide.

679 Paragraph 15.28 of the Chancery Guide.

680 Paragraph 13.11 of the Chancery Guide.

covering are likely to be the same as those to be covered by the claimant in his evidence (discussed above). An aspect which can give rise to conflicting factual evidence is the extrinsic evidence of the maker's intention. This might be the case, for example, where that evidence consists of conversations the maker had with different people at different times about his intentions, which are inconsistent with one another;[681] or where the draftsman gives evidence as to the maker's intentions which conflicts with that given by the maker's family members, friends and/or business associates.[682]

CPR Part 7 claims: defendant's acknowledgement of service and defence

In most cases,[683] a defendant who wishes to defend a CPR Part 7 claim must either file a defence within 14 days of service of the particulars of claim on him,[684] or file an acknowledgment of service within in the same period[685] and then file a defence within 28 days of service of the particulars of claim.[686] A copy of the defence must also be served on the other parties.[687] The parties can agree to extend these time limits by up

681 See e.g. the will rectification case of *Hives v Machin* [2017] EWHC 1414 (Ch), in which the judge heard and analysed conflicting oral evidence as to the testatrix's intentions, but ultimately concluded that section 21 AJA was not engaged and such evidence was therefore inadmissible (see in particular [39] to [59]).

682 See e.g. the will rectification case of *Re Nodes* [2021] EWHC 1057 (Ch), where the evidence as to the testator's intentions given by the draftsman conflicted with that given by the testator's widow and his long-term business associate.

683 Special time limits apply, for example, where the proceedings are served on the defendant out of the jurisdiction: see e.g. CPR rules 10.3(2) and 15.4(2).

684 CPR rule 15.4(1)(a).

685 CPR rule 10.3(1).

686 CPR rule 15.4(1)(b).

687 CPR rule 15.6.

to 28 days;[688] if they do, the defendant must notify the court of the agreement in writing.[689]

At the same time as filing a defence, the defendant should consider whether he wishes or needs to bring a counterclaim. This is because the defendant can bring a counterclaim against the claimant by filing particulars of the counterclaim[690] without the court's permission if the counterclaim is filed at the same time as the defence;[691] however, the defendant will need the court's permission if the counterclaim is filed at any other time.[692] Whether it is necessary to bring a counterclaim will depend on the particular circumstances of the litigation and on the relief the defendant is seeking from the court. For example, if a defendant who is resisting a rectification claim is a beneficiary of a trust created by a deed which does not cause any construction problems, it may be sufficient for him to simply file a defence denying that the claimant is entitled to the rectification he seeks (and thus impliedly asking the court to dismiss the claimant's rectification claim). On the other hand, if for example the defendant wishes to ask the court to rectify the trust instrument in a different way from that which the claimant is arguing for, and/or wishes to ask the court to determine the meaning of a particular provision of the trust instrument, then it may be necessary for him to both defend the claimant's rectification claim and bring a counterclaim.

As well as the rules in CPR rule 16.5 and CPR Practice Direction 16, the drafting guidelines contained in paragraphs 4.2 to 4.12 of the Chancery Guide apply to defences.

In claims proceeding under CPR Part 7,[693] paragraph 5.1 of CPR

---

688 CPR rule 15.5(1).

689 CPR rule 15.5(2).

690 CPR rule 20.4(1).

691 CPR rule 20.4(2)(a).

692 CPR rule 20.4(2)(b).

693 CPR Practice Direction 57AD does not apply to claims proceeding

Practice Direction 57AD requires the defendant to provide at the same time as his statement of case 'Initial Disclosure'. This is considered in more detail above.[694]

Default and summary judgment

It is generally not possible to obtain judgment in default in a rectification claim. The Chancery Guide explains that: "*It is not the practice of the court to make an order for rectification by default or by consent or without a hearing save in exceptional cases. In all cases, even if unopposed, the court will not make an order without being satisfied that it is justified by the evidence. The court will therefore wish to scrutinise carefully the changes that are proposed and the reasons for them.*"[695]

On the other hand, it is generally possible to obtain summary judgment in a rectification claim in an appropriate case. This will usually be where the claim is opposed and is brought by CPR Part 7 proceedings, and the applicant is able to demonstrate that the claim or defence (as the case may be) has no real prospect of success and that there is no other compelling reason why the claim should be disposed of at a trial. However, if the claim is unopposed and is brought by way of CPR Part 8 proceedings, it will generally be unnecessary to apply for summary judgment, and the claimant can instead ask the court to list the claim for a disposal hearing, as Chief Master Marsh explained in *Sovereign Trustees Ltd v Lewis*:[696]

---

under CPR Part 8, unless otherwise ordered: see paragraph 1.4(7).

694 See "*CPR Part 7 claims: particulars of claim and Initial Disclosure*", under "Evidence/Pleadings" above.

695 Paragraphs 18.23 and 18.24 of the Chancery Guide; see also paragraph 5.7: "*Declaratory relief and relief by way of rectification will not be granted without evidence and will not ordinarily be appropriate for resolution by way of default judgment*".

696 [2016] EWHC 2593 (Ch) at [3]. See also paragraph 26.17 of the Chancery Guide in relation to uncontentious claims for the rectification of pension schemes. However, it should be noted that in *The Girls' Day School Trust v GDST Pension Trustees Ltd* [2016] EWHC 1254 (Ch)

> "*Part 8 claims are markedly different to Part 7 claims. Although there is no bar to issuing a Part 24 application [i.e. an application for summary judgment] in a Part 8 claim, it will rarely be necessary for the claimant to do so where it is seeking judgment on the whole of the claim. In part this is because the second limb of CPR 24.2 will normally have no application because there will be no 'trial' as such. Part 8 claims are normally resolved at a 'disposal hearing'. This is made clear by paragraph 8.1 of Practice Direction 8A which states:*
>
> *'8.1 The court may on the hearing date –*
>
> *(i) proceed to hear the case and dispose of the claim;*
>
> *(ii) give case management directions.'*
>
> *It follows that in most Part 8 claims, where the relief sought is unopposed, or cannot realistically be opposed, it will suffice for the claimant to ask the court to fix a disposal hearing at which the court may determine whether or not the relief sought by the claimant should be granted.*"

Claimant's reply

CPR Part 8 claims: claimant's evidence in reply

If the claimant wishes to rely on further written evidence in reply to the defendant's evidence, he must file it within 14 days of service of the defendant's evidence on him,[697] and he must also serve a copy of it on the other parties "*within the same time limit*".[698] In the same way as a defendant, a claimant may not rely on any written evidence which has not been served in accordance with these rules at the hearing of the claim

---

summary judgment was granted without a hearing in an unopposed claim for the rectification of a pension scheme.

697 CPR rule 8.5(5).

698 CPR rule 8.5(6).

unless the court gives permission.[699]

As that time limit is also quite short, CPR rule 8.5(9) allows the parties to "*agree in writing on an extension of time [...] of not more than 28 days for serving and filing evidence in reply*". Such an agreement must be filed at court "*with 48 hours of the agreement*".[700] As indicated above, the Chancery Guide recognises that it is "*not unusual for an extension of time to be agreed between the parties for the service of evidence*".[701]

If a claimant requires more time to file his evidence in reply to the defendant's, he too should apply to the court for an extension of time by way of an application pursuant to CPR Part 23.[702] The guidance considered above in the context of the defendant's evidence applies equally to applications for extensions of time by claimants in relation to their evidence in reply. In particular, it should be noted that the Chancery Guide indicates that "*[i]n substantial matters the court will normally be willing to grant a reasonable extension*".[703]

CPR Part 7 claims: claimant's reply

If the claimant wishes to file a reply, he must file it with his directions questionnaire.[704] The CPR requires the claimant to serve a reply on the other parties "*at the same time it is filed*".[705] However, the Chancery Guide encourages claimants to serve replies before filing directions questionnaires if possible to give the other parties an opportunity to

699 CPR rule 8.6(1).

700 CPR rule 8.5(10).

701 Paragraph 13.11 of the Chancery Guide.

702 CPR rule 8.5(8).

703 Paragraph 13.11 of the Chancery Guide.

704 CPR rule 15.8(a)(i).

705 CPR rule 15.8(a)(ii).

consider the reply before they file their own directions questionnaires.[706]

As well as the rules in CPR rule 16.7 and CPR Practice Direction 16, the drafting guidelines contained in paragraphs 4.2 to 4.12 of the Chancery Guide apply to replies.

Directions and case management

The Chancery Guide encourages parties in all rectification claims – whether proceeding under CPR Part 7 or Part 8 – to "*consider whether it may be of assistance to the court (and the parties) in addition to any witness evidence to seek a direction for a narrative chronology with key documents*".[707] It continues:

> "*If such an order is made the parties should seek to identify and agree the key documents and a narrative chronology with reference where appropriate to those key documents. Where there is disagreement, the narrative chronology should set out each of the parties' positions making clear where there is a divergence between them on a particular issue. A bundle containing that narrative chronology and the key documents should be made available to the judge by any PTR and/or provided with skeleton arguments for trial or final hearing.*"[708]

CPR Part 8 claims

Claims issued under the Part 8 procedure are treated as having been allocated to the multi-track and CPR Part 26 ('*Case Management – Preliminary Stage*') does not apply.[709] No directions questionnaires are required.[710]

---

706 Paragraph 4.12 of the Chancery Guide.

707 Paragraph 18.29 of the Chancery Guide.

708 Ibid.

709 CPR rule 8.9(c); see also paragraph 13.14 of the Chancery Guide.

710 Paragraph 13.14 of the Chancery Guide.

The court file will generally be considered by the assigned Master[711] after the time for acknowledgment of service has expired, or, if the time for serving the defendant's evidence has been extended, after the expiry of that period. If a defendant has not acknowledged service, the assigned Master will typically make an order in the form of CH44.[712] This is an order which directs a defendant who intends to contest the claim to file and serve an acknowledgment of service and evidence by a specified date, failing which he shall not be entitled to rely on any evidence at the disposal hearing unless the court gives permission.[713]

If 21 days after the expiry of any extended period for service of evidence no notice of a directions hearing has been received, the claimant should contact the court by letter filed on CE-File together, if appropriate, with a draft order substantially in form CH44, requesting either a directions or disposal hearing. The letter should provide dates to avoid, and a realistic time estimate for both the hearing and any pre-reading.[714]

At that stage the Master will consider whether the claim and decide:

(a) Whether the claim may be capable of being dealt with 'on paper', i.e. on the papers without a hearing.[715] The Chancery Guide makes it clear that "*[i]t is not the practice of the court to make an order for rectification by default or by consent or without a hearing save in exceptional cases. In all cases, even if unopposed, the court will not make an order without being satisfied that it is justified by the evidence. The court will therefore wish to scrutinise carefully the*

711 Or District Judge of the High Court if the claim is in one of the District Registries.

712 Paragraph 13.15 of the Chancery Guide.

713 A specimen CH44 order is available on the Government website: https://www.gov.uk/government/publications/form-ch44-order-for-disposal-hearing (accessed 31st May 2023).

714 Paragraph 13.16 of the Chancery Guide.

715 Paragraph 13.18(a) of the Chancery Guide.

changes that are proposed and the reasons for them."[716] It is suggested that in most (if not all) will rectification claims, a hearing will be required.

(b) If not, whether directions may be given without a hearing. The Chancery Guide explains: "*In most Part 8 claims, the Master will either make an order for directions at the point of initial review or direct that a hearing is fixed. If directions are given at that stage they will usually give notice of a disposal hearing and give directions concerning further evidence to be filed. The court will give notice of the hearing to all the parties, and the notice or order will specify to whom the notice has been sent*".[717]

(c) Whether the claim is likely to be referred to a different level of judge for disposal.[718] In this regard, the Chancery Guide makes it clear that "*[r]ectification claims will be case managed and determined by a Master save in exceptional cases. In particular, the Master will only refer to a HCJ a claim which is consented to or not opposed if it raises issues of particular complexity or difficulty.*"[719]

A directions hearing with a time estimate of half a day or less (and no more than 90 minutes pre-reading) will take place remotely unless the court orders otherwise.[720] It is suggested that this is likely to be the case in most rectification claims. If a party considers that the directions hearing should take place using a format other than the default format, they should CE-File and serve on the other parties a letter setting out

---

716 Paragraphs 18.23 and 18.24 of the Chancery Guide; see also paragraph 5.7: "*Declaratory relief and relief by way of rectification will not be granted without evidence and will not ordinarily be appropriate for resolution by way of default judgment*".

717 Paragraph 13.18(b) of the Chancery Guide.

718 Paragraph 13.18(c) of the Chancery Guide.

719 Paragraph 18.20 of the Chancery Guide.

720 Paragraph 13.19 of the Chancery Guide.

their alternative proposal, together with brief reasons, within 7 days of receipt of the Notice of Hearing.[721] Appendix Z to the Chancery Guide contains helpful guidance on the preparation and conduct of remote or hybrid hearings.

The Chancery Guide explains that at a directions hearing, "*the court will generally wish to establish whether:*

> *(a) the court has all the evidence it will need (including expert evidence)*
>
> *(b) the claim is ready for a disposal hearing;*
>
> *(c) any witnesses will need to attend the final hearing for cross-examination, in which case the court will give directions with a view to fixing the period during which the case will be heard;*
>
> *(d) the disposal hearing should be dealt with by a Master or by a [High Court Judge], Section 9 Judge or Deputy [High Court Judge].*"[722]

It is suggested that in a rectification claim, the court is likely to consider the following at a directions hearing:

(a) Evidence, including whether directions should be given for the filing of any further evidence (in addition to the evidence which will already have been filed by that point) and whether any witnesses should be required to attend to give oral evidence and be cross-examined at the disposal hearing.[723] If a rectification claim is proceeding pursuant to CPR Part 8 because it is unopposed (at

721 Ibid.

722 paragraph 13.20 of the Chancery Guide.

723 CPR rule 8.6(2) provides "*The court may require or permit a party to give oral evidence at the hearing*" and CPR rule 8.6(3) provides "*The court may give directions requiring the attendance for cross-examination of a witness who has given written evidence*".

least by the affected beneficiaries who are capacitous adults), it is likely to be decided on written evidence only.[724] However, if it is opposed but is proceeding pursuant to CPR Part 8 because it has been brought as an alternative to a construction claim, thought should be given as to whether to seek directions for witnesses (such as the draftsman, if the will was professionally prepared) to be required to attend to give oral evidence and be cross-examined at the disposal hearing.[725] The Chancery Guide provides: "*The evidence in support must establish the common or unilateral mistake on which the claim in rectification is based even where the parties consent to, or do not oppose, the claim. The court may direct that oral evidence be given even where all relevant parties consent (or do not oppose), with or without cross-examination. The court may also wish to hear argument on all relevant matters and may direct that arguments against the remedy are put, including if appropriate by directing that a party take such a role.*"[726] The Chancery Guide also points out that: "*Part 8 is flexible and the court can adopt a hybrid procedure under which limited factual disputes requiring oral evidence or disclosure can be accommodated within Part 8 proceedings – see Vitpol Building Service v Samen [2008] EWHC 2283 (TCC) (paragraph 18)*".[727]

(b) Representation of the parties, such as whether any litigation friend needs to be appointed and/or whether any representation order should be made and/or notice given pursuant to CPR rule 19.13 (as to which, see Parties above).

724 See paragraph 13.3 of the Chancery Guide: "*Part 8 claims will generally be disposed of on written evidence without cross-examination. The witness statements with the claim form should be sufficient in most cases to define the issues*".

725 See e.g. *Re McKay* [2023] EWHC 642 (Ch) at [39]-[40].

726 Paragraph 18.25 of the Chancery Guide.

727 Paragraph 13.28 of the Chancery Guide.

(c) Directions in relation to the disposal hearing, such as directions about when and how the disposal hearing should be listed, its time estimate, and the level of judge required.

(i) As regards listing, if there is to be no oral evidence at the disposal hearing, then "*a trial will be listed before the relevant level of judge as directed by a Master*".[728] However, if oral evidence is required at the disposal hearing, then the listing of the trial will involve a two-stage procedure.[729] First, a trial window, usually of 3 months, will be specified during which the trial is to take place. Then the parties should provide the court with an agreed list of dates to avoid, and the court will then proceed to fix a date for the start of the trial.[730]

(ii) As regards time estimate, this is likely to depend in particular on the number and complexity of the rectification arguments which are being advanced, and on whether there is going to be live oral evidence from witnesses who will be cross-examined.

(iii) As regards level of judge, as indicated above, paragraph 18.20 of the Chancery Guide provides: "*[r]ectification claims will be case managed and determined by a Master save in exceptional cases. In particular, the Master will only refer to a HCJ a claim which is consented to or not opposed if it raises issues of particular complexity or difficulty*". However, for claims proceeding in a District Registry, it should be noted that paragraph 7B.2(e) of CPR Practice Direction 2B provides that a District Judge in a District Registry may not make an order for rectification without

728 Paragraph 12.24 of the Chancery Guide.

729 See paragraphs 12.16 to 12.23 of the Chancery Guide.

730 Paragraph 12.17 of the Chancery Guide.

the consent of the Supervising Judge for the region in which the District Judge is sitting, or their nominee.

(d) 'Housekeeping' directions to prepare the case for the disposal hearing, such as directions relating to the hearing bundle,[731] skeleton arguments,[732] and other documents such as dramatis personae, chronologies, lists of issues,[733] reading lists[734] and bundles of authorities.[735]

CPR Part 7 claims: costs and case management conference

The Chancery Guide provides that all cases "*appropriately issued in the ChD B&PCs London will be automatically allocated to the multi-track*".[736] Once defences have been filed, the court will send the parties a Notice of Proposed Allocation (form N149C) confirming the allocation to multi-track and providing a date for the filing of Directions Questionnaires ("DQs") (form N181).[737] If any defendant fails to file a defence, this may not happen automatically. Therefore if a Notice of Proposed Allocation has not been received within 21 days of the last deadline for filing a defence, the claimant should contact the court by letter filed on CE-file

731 Detailed rules in relation to hearing bundles are contained in paragraph 27 of CPR Practice Direction 32 and are supplemented by the guidance contained in Chapter 12 of, and Appendix X to, the Chancery Guide.

732 In relation to which see paragraphs 12.49 to 12.51 of, and Appendix Y to, the Chancery Guide.

733 In relation to which see paragraphs 12.52 to 12.55 of the Chancery Guide.

734 In relation to which see paragraph 12.56 to 12.58 of the Chancery Guide.

735 In relation to which see paragraph 12.59 to 12.61 of the Chancery Guide.

736 Paragraph 6.4 of the Chancery Guide.

737 *Ibid.*

to request such a Notice.[738]

The parties will then have to file and serve DQs and attempt to agree directions by the date specified in the Notice of Proposed Allocation. Parties can extend the deadline for one or more periods of up to 28 days. To do so, they must file a consent order, which must be approved by the court.[739]

On receipt of the DQs, the court will list a case management conference ("CMC") or a costs and case management conference ("CCMC") with a time estimate of 1½ hours plus 1 hour pre-reading, unless the parties provide a different agreed time estimate.[740]

After the DQs are filed and before the first CMC/CCMC, if any of the following issues are raised in the DQs or in any letter accompanying them, the Master will review the DQs and draft directions and may make and order in respect of such issues in advance of the CMC/CCMC:[741]

(a) Whether the claim should remain in the ChD B&PCs London.

(b) Whether a listing of more than 1½ hours is required for a CCMC or CMC.

(c) The appropriate hearing format for the CMC / CCMC.

(d) Whether cost management applies (if the parties disagree about that: see paragraphs 6.28 and 6.29 of the Chancery Guide) and whether or not a costs management order is required.

(e) (If requested) whether there should be a stay of proceedings, or a

738 Paragraph 6.5 of the Chancery Guide.

739 Paragraph 6.6 of the Chancery Guide.

740 Paragraphs 6.8 and 6.44 of the Chancery Guide.

741 Paragraphs 6.41 and 6.42 of the Chancery Guide.

continuation of an existing stay.

(f) (If requested) whether the claim should be docketed (see Chapter 3 and paragraph 6.25 of the Chancery Guide for further guidance).

A CMC/CCMC with a time estimate of half a day or less (and no more than 90 minutes pre-reading) will take place remotely unless the court orders otherwise.[742] It is suggested that this is likely to be the case in most rectification claims. Appendix Z to the Chancery Guide contains helpful guidance on the preparation and conduct of remote or hybrid hearings.

At the CMC/CCMC, the issues which the court is likely to consider are the same as those which would be considered at a directions hearing if the claim were proceeding as a CPR Part 8 claim (discussed above). However, the sequence of events is likely to be different: in CPR Part 8 claims, by the time the case reaches a directions hearing, witness statements will have already been filed and exchanged, and the relevant documents which the parties wish to rely on will usually have already been disclosed (generally as exhibits to the witness statements). On the other hand, in CPR Part 7 claims, directions for disclosure and witness statements are generally given at the CCMC.

Disclosure

In general terms, in contested rectification claims which involve a professionally prepared trust instrument, the key documentary evidence – and often the only documentary evidence – is usually the file relating to the instrument. Such files are rarely particularly extensive, usually running into the dozens of pages (sometimes into the hundreds, but very rarely into the thousands). As a result, there is normally little difficulty or cost in the file being disclosed in its entirety, usually when the rectification problem is being investigated (and thus before any proceedings are issued).

742 Paragraph 6.44 of the Chancery Guide.

Where a file relates to more than one client – which is not uncommon for example where both members of a couple have undertaken a tax planning exercise at the same time using the same solicitor – it may be necessary to redact privileged information relating to the other client (unless that client waives privilege).

In addition to the file, it may be useful to consider whether there could be any other documentary evidence of the settlor's intentions, for example in any diary or other notes he may have kept (including electronic notes such as draft emails or notes made on a computer or a mobile phone or a tablet). Often settlors do not discuss what they might consider to be their private personal affairs with friends or even family, but another source of documentary evidence of the settlor's intentions could be any correspondence in which these were discussed, including both formal correspondence, such as letters and emails, and more informal communications, such as text messages, WhatsApp messages or other forms of electronic communication.

CPR Part 8 claims

The disclosure process in the Business and Property Courts was substantially overhauled with the coming into effect of CPR Practice Direction 57AD on 1st October 2022.[743] However, the Practice Direction does not apply to claims proceeding under CPR Part 8 "*unless the court orders otherwise*".[744]

Given the disclosure obligations already imposed by CPR Part 8, it is suggested that orders for extended disclosure pursuant to CPR Practice Direction 57AD are likely to be rare in rectification claims proceeding under CPR Part 8. Some support for this can be found in paragraph 13.25 of the Chancery Guide: "*PD 57AD does not apply to Part 8 claims when issued, and it is rare for an order for disclosure to be made in a Part 8*

743 This followed a pilot introduced with effect from 1st January 2019 by what was CPR Practice Direction 51U.

744 Paragraph 1.4(7) of CPR Practice Direction 57AD.

claim. However, if any form of disclosure is ordered the court will adopt such parts of PD 57AD as are appropriate (and CPR 31 does not apply)".

CPR Part 7 claims

As indicated above, the disclosure process in the Business and Property Courts was substantially overhauled with the coming into effect of CPR Practice Direction 57AD on 1st October 2022.[745]

The provisions of Practice Direction 57AD are detailed. In summary, it is suggested that the following points are likely to be particularly relevant in rectification claims.

(a) The Practice Direction imposes a duty to "*to take reasonable steps to preserve documents […] that may be relevant to any issue in the proceedings*".[746] This duty applies to:

  (i) "*[a] person who knows that it is or may become a party to proceedings that have been commenced or who knows that it may become a party to proceedings that may be commenced*";[747] and

  (ii) "*[l]egal representatives who have the conduct of litigation on behalf of a party to proceedings that have been commenced, or who are instructed with a view to the conduct of litigation where their client knows it may become a party to proceedings that have been or may be commenced*".[748]

The duty to preserve documents applies to "*documents which might otherwise be deleted or destroyed in accordance with a document*

745 This followed a pilot introduced with effect from 1st January 2019 by what was CPR Practice Direction 51U.

746 Paragraph 3.1(1) and 3.2(1) of CPR Practice Direction 51AD.

747 Paragraph 3.1 of CPR Practice Direction 51AD.

748 Paragraph 3.2 of CPR Practice Direction 51AD.

retention policy or in the ordinary course of business"[749] and "*[p]reservation includes, in suitable cases, making copies of sources and documents and storing them.*"[750] Legal representatives are also under a duty to notify their client of the duty to preserve documents "*within a reasonable period of being instructed*"[751] and to obtain written confirmation from the client that any document deletion or destruction processes have been suspended for the duration of the proceedings in accordance with paragraphs 4.2 and 4.3 of CPR Practice Direction 51AD.

(b) The Practice Direction creates a new concept of 'Initial Disclosure', which imposes disclosure obligations at the time a party files his statement of case – and thus before any directions for disclosure are given by the court. This is discussed above.[752]

(c) Once proceedings have commenced, the parties are under a duty "*to disclose, regardless of any order for disclosure made, known adverse documents, unless they are privileged*"[753] in accordance with the provisions of the pilot. 'Known adverse documents' are "*documents (other than privileged documents) that a party is actually aware (without undertaking any further search for documents than it has already undertaken or caused to be undertaken) both (a) are or were previously within its control and (b) are adverse.*"[754] A document is 'adverse' if "*it or any information it contains contradicts or materially damages the disclosing party's contention or version of events on an issue in dispute, or supports the contention or version of events of an*

---

749 Paragraph 4.1 of CPR Practice Direction 51AD; see also paragraph 4.2 and 4.3.

750 Paragraph 4.1 of CPR Practice Direction 51AD.

751 Paragraph 4.4 of CPR Practice Direction 51AD.

752 See "*CPR Part 7 claims: particulars of claim and Initial Disclosure*", under "Evidence/Pleadings" above.

753 Paragraph 3.1(2) of CPR Practice Direction 51AD.

754 Paragraph 2.8 of CPR Practice Direction 51AD.

opposing party on an issue in dispute".[755] The duty to disclose adverse documents applies throughout the proceedings[756] and irrespective of any order for Extended Disclosure: "*if adverse documents in the control of a party come to its knowledge at a later date they must (unless privileged) be disclosed without delay*".[757]

(d) A party wishing to seek disclosure of documents in addition to, or as an alternative to, Initial Disclosure must request 'Extended Disclosure'.[758] This is done by completing a 'Disclosure Review Document' in advance of the first case management conference in accordance with paragraph 7 of CPR Practice Direction 51U (no application notice is required).[759] An order for Extended Disclosure will only be made where the court "*is persuaded that it is appropriate to do so in order fairly to resolve one or more of the Issues for Disclosure*".[760] The order "*must be reasonable and proportionate having regard to the overriding objective*",[761] including the seven factors listed in paragraph 6.4 of CPR Practice Direction 51AD.[762]

---

755 Paragraph 2.7 of CPR Practice Direction 51AD.

756 Paragraph 3.3 of CPR Practice Direction 51AD.

757 Paragraph 9.3 of CPR Practice Direction 51AD.

758 Paragraph 6.1 of CPR Practice Direction 51AD.

759 *Ibid.*

760 Paragraph 6.3 of CPR Practice Direction 51AD.

761 Paragraph 6.4 of CPR Practice Direction 51AD.

762 These are:

(1) the nature and complexity of the issues in the proceedings;

(2) the importance of the case, including any non-monetary relief sought;

(3) the likelihood of documents existing that will have probative value in supporting or undermining a party's claim or defence;

(4) the number of documents involved;

The 'Issues for Disclosure' are "*those key issues in dispute, which the parties consider will need to be determined by the court with some reference to contemporaneous documents in order for there to be a fair resolution of the proceedings*";[763] however, this does not extend "*to every issue which is disputed in the statements of case by denial or non-admission.*"[764] The parties are required to identify and to try to agree the List of Issues for Disclosure in section 1A of the Disclosure Review Document.[765] In relation to each Issue for Disclosure, the parties must also consider which of the five 'Disclosure Models' identified in paragraph 8 of CPR Practice Direction 51AD should apply.[766] Although the parties may agree that a particular Model should apply to a particular Issue for Disclosure, no Model will in fact apply without the approval of the court,[767] who will usually consider whether to make an order for Extended Disclosure and, if so, on what terms at the first case management conference.

(e) Appendix 5 to Practice Direction 57AD contains provisions "*for a simplified disclosure regime for Less Complex Claims*".[768] These are defined as claims which by virtue of their "*nature, value, complexity and the likely volume of Extended Disclosure may not benefit from the*

---

(5) the ease and expense of searching for and retrieval of any particular document (taking into account any limitations on the information available and on the likely accuracy of any costs estimates);

(6) the financial position of each party; and

(7) the need to ensure the case is dealt with expeditiously, fairly and at a proportionate cost.

763 Paragraph 7.6 of CPR Practice Direction 51AD.

764 *Ibid.*

765 Paragraph 7 of CPR Practice Direction 51AD.

766 See also paragraph 9 of CPR Practice Direction 51AD.

767 Paragraph 8.2 of CPR Practice Direction 51AD.

768 Paragraph 1 of Appendix 5 to CPR Practice Direction 57AD.

> *full procedure set out in the main body of Practice Direction 57AD*".[769] If the value of the claim is less than £1m, the claim should be treated as a Less Complex Claim unless its nature, complexity and/or the likely volume of Extended Disclosure indicate to the contrary.[770] A claim may be treated as a Less Complex Claim either by agreement made between all the parties or by order of the court.[771] An agreement between the parties may be made before or after the claim is issued.[772] If there is no agreement between the parties before the claim is issued, "*the claimant may by letter or in its particulars of claim notify the defendant that it wishes the claim to be treated as a Less Complex Claim. If no such notification is given by the claimant, a defendant may by letter or in its defence notify the claimant that it wishes to threat the claim as a Less Complex Claim*".[773] Such a request must include brief reasons for believing that the claim meets the relevant criteria.[774] If no agreement is reached, the court may make an order of its own volition or on an application made by a party by application notice, which the court will determine in writing without a hearing where possible.[775]

As indicated above, in most rectification claims the key – and possibly the only – documentary evidence is likely to be the will file. In practice, this will usually be disclosed during pre-action correspondence. It also seems likely that in most cases all other relevant documentary evidence will be disclosed either pre-action or during Initial Disclosure. As a result, there may be no need for any Extended Disclosure. However, where some

769 Paragraph 3 of Appendix 5 to CPR Practice Direction 57AD.

770 Paragraph 4 of Appendix 5 to CPR Practice Direction 57AD.

771 Paragraph 5 of Appendix 5 to CPR Practice Direction 57AD.

772 Paragraph 6 of Appendix 5 to CPR Practice Direction 57AD.

773 Paragraph 7 of Appendix 5 to CPR Practice Direction 57AD.

774 Paragraph 8 of Appendix 5 to CPR Practice Direction 57AD.

775 Paragraph 9 of Appendix 5 to CPR Practice Direction 57AD.

further disclosure is envisaged, the parties may want to consider agreeing that the claim be treated as a Less Complex Claim, as the simplified disclosure regime should be suitable in most rectification claims, and is likely to be more streamlined and thus less costly that the 'full' regime imposed by CPR Practice Direction 57AD.

Depending on the circumstances, it may also be worth considering whether disclosure should be sought from a non-party pursuant to CPR rule 31.17.

Witness statements

CPR Part 8 claims

In CPR Part 8 claims, witness statements will have already been filed and served at the early stages of the proceedings (as discussed above).

CPR Part 7 claims

In CPR Part 7 claims, directions for the exchange of witness statements are normally given at the CCMC. Who should be asked to give evidence and what that topics that evidence should cover will depend on the particular circumstances of the case. In general terms, the topics which the evidence is likely to have to cover are the same which the particulars of claim should cover, viz.:

(a) the claimant's role and the capacity in which he brings the claim;

(b) the factual background;

(c) the current drafting of the trust instrument and its construction;

(d) what the maker's intentions are alleged to have been;

(e) how the current drafting of the trust instrument fails to correctly record the maker's intentions;

(f) how the court is being asked to rectify the trust instrument;

(g) the position of the other interested parties;

(h) the approximate value of the estate or fund in issue.

In cases involving a professionally prepared trust instrument, the key witness evidence is generally likely to be that of the individual or individuals who were involved in taking instructions for, drafting and/or arranging the execution of the instrument. Indeed, in some cases the draftsman may be the only witness.[776] Depending on how involved they were, any attesting witnesses may also be able to shed light on the settlor's intentions and on the process by which the trust instrument was prepared.

If the maker discussed his intentions with family and/or friends (who may or may not be beneficiaries or intended beneficiaries of the trust), these individuals may also be able to give evidence on the issue.

CPR Practice Direction 57AC applies to "*trial witness statements*"[777] in the Business and Property Courts. This appears to include claims for rectification of unilateral trust documents (other than wills).[778] Paragraph 18.28 of the Chancery Guide provides: "*When preparing <u>trial</u> witness statements in a rectification claim, careful thought needs to be given to compliance with (or dispensation from) the requirements of PD 57AC. This is a particularly important consideration in rectification claims where the passage of time or the nature of the rectification sought may mean that there*

776 See e.g. the will case of *Re Bimson* [2010] EWHC 3679 (Ch) at [6].

777 Defined by paragraph 1.2 of CPR Practice Direction 57AC as "*a witness statement that is served pursuant to an order made under rule 32.4(2), or pursuant to rule 8.5 or an order made under rule 8.6(1)(b), or that is prepared for the trial of an unfair prejudice petition or a contributory's just and equitable winding up petition, including supplemental or reply witness statements where allowed by the court*".

778 Paragraph 1.3(6) of CPR Practice Direction 57AC provides that the Practice Direction does not apply to "*proceedings falling within CPR Part 57, which applies to [...] claims for the rectification of wills*", unless the court orders otherwise.

is no witness able to give evidence as to the relevant events and/or where it is necessary for a witness to express a belief as to whether there has been a mistake and/or to explain what happened". In an appropriate case, it may be possible to ask the court to dispense with the requirements of CPR Practice Direction 57AC by making an application without notice and asking that it be determined without a hearing.[779]

Disposal hearing/trial

At the disposal hearing (in CPR Part 8 claims) or trial (in CPR Part 7 claims), the court will hear the argument in favour and against rectification. In CPR Part 8 claims, directions will have previously been given as to whether there should be oral evidence and cross-examination of any of the witnesses (e.g. the draftsman).[780]

Disposal hearings/trials in rectification claims are generally listed in public, i.e. in a court which is open to members of the public.[781] Whilst it may be possible in some cases to persuade a court to list the claim in private pursuant to CPR rule 39.2(3),[782] or to impose some other less

---

779 See paragraphs 4.2 and 4.4 of CPR Practice Direction 57AC.

780 See paragraph 13.33 of the Chancery Guide.

781 Under the general rule in CPR rule 39.2(1).

782 CPR rule 39.2 requires the court to sit in private if it is satisfied (i) that "*it is necessary to sit in private to secure the proper administration of justice*" and (ii) that one or more of the 7 sub-rules of CPR rule 39.2(3) is engaged. Of those sub-rules, those which may be engaged in a rectification claim are likely to be (c), (d), (f) and/or (g), which provide:

(c) [the hearing] involves confidential information (including information relating to personal financial matters) and publicity would damage that confidentiality;

(d) a private hearing is necessary to protect the interests of any child or protected party;

[...]

extensive reporting restriction,[783] a party seeking such an order is likely to have to show compelling reasons why the court should depart from the principle of open justice.[784]

Judgment

The Master or judge will decide how, when and where to deliver judgment. Judgment may be delivered orally immediately at the conclusion of the hearing (a so-called '*ex tempore*' judgment),[785] or may be reserved. A reserved judgment may be delivered orally at a later date or, more commonly, may be circulated in written draft to the parties and then formally handed down at a subsequent date. Sometimes – particularly in urgent cases – the court may announce its decision and make any necessary order at the conclusion of the hearing and provide its reasoned judgment at a later date.[786]

Costs

As indicated at 5.2.3 above, if the trust instrument was professionally prepared and the circumstances indicate that a professional negligence claim against the draftsman is likely, his insurers may have agreed in advance to fund the costs of the rectification claim. Where the claim is unopposed, the court will often be asked to make no order as to costs, on

---

(*f*) *[the hearing] involves uncontentious matters arising in the administration of trusts or in the administration of a deceased person's estate; or*

(*g*) *the court for any other reason considers [a hearing in private] to be necessary to secure the proper administration of justice.*"

783 See e.g. *A v D* [2017] EWHC 2222 (Ch) and *ABC v JKL* [2019] EWHC 2416 (Ch).

784 See in this regard the Court of Appeal's guidance in *MN v OP* [2019] EWCA Civ 679 regarding privacy and reporting restrictions in the context of applications pursuant to the Variation of Trusts Act 1958.

785 See e.g. *Slattery v Jagger* [2015] EWHC 3976 (Ch).

786 See e.g. *Sovereign Trustees Ltd v Lewis* [2016] EWHC 2593 (Ch) at [13] and [43], and *ABC v JKL* [2019] EWHC 2416 (Ch) at [4].

the basis that the parties will recover their costs from the draftsman's insurer as agreed.[787]

On the other hand, if the rectification claim is contested, the general rule (which applies in all civil litigation) is that the unsuccessful party will be ordered to pay the costs of the successful party.[788] However, costs are ultimately in the discretion of the court,[789] and the court may therefore decide to depart from that starting point and make a different costs order. In general terms, in deciding costs the court will try to ensure that the costs are in fact borne by the negligent draftsman and/or (in contested case) by the party who has lost, and not by the successful party. In deciding precisely how this should be achieved in the circumstances of the case, the court will have to take into account the parties' respective interests, and in particular who would in fact bear the costs if the costs are ordered to be paid out of the trust.[790] It may also be possible to seek a non-party costs order against the firm responsible for the negligent drafting.[791]

<u>Order</u>

If the rectification claim succeeds, the order will need to make it clear precisely how the instrument is being rectified. It will usually be sensible for one of the recitals to record that the court was satisfied that the trust instrument fails to record the maker's intentions.

---

787 See e.g. *Re Bimson* [2010] EWHC 3679 (Ch) at [23] and *Gerling v Gerling* [2010] EWHC 3661 (Ch) at [50].

788 CPR rule 44.2.(2)(a).

789 Section 51(1) of the Senior Courts Act 1981.

790 See e.g. *Marley v Rawlings (costs)* [2014] UKSC 51 and *Slattery v Jagger* [2015] EWHC 3976 (Ch) at [103]-[112].

791 See CPR rule 46.2. Such an order was sought e.g. in *Royal Commonwealth Society for the Blind v Beasant* [2021] EWHC 352 (Ch) at [19]-[48] (the costs order was not considered on appeal: [2022] EWHC 1319 (Ch) at [35]).

How the rectification is best recorded in the order is will depend on precisely what the rectification consists of. In general terms, it is suggested that:

(a) if the rectification is straightforward and can be clearly described in few words, this can be done in the body of the order (e.g. "clause 5 is rectified by the insertion of "Brünnhilde," between "daughters" and "Gerhilde"");[792]

(b) however, if the rectification is less straightforward, it is likely to be sensible for the body of the order to refer to a schedule (e.g. by providing: "the Deed is rectified in the manner set out in the Schedule hereto"), and for the schedule to then set out the rectified version of the relevant provisions of the trust instrument.

Paragraphs 16.8 to 16.22 of the Chancery Guide contain guidance in relation to the drafting, filing and sealing of orders following a hearing; paragraph 16.23 contains an example form of order.

Appeals

A party who is dissatisfied with the court's decision must obtain the court's permission in order to appeal it.[793] The court will only grant permission to appeal if it considers that the appeal would have a real prospect of success, or that there is some other compelling reason for the appeal to be heard.[794]

Although this is not strictly required, it is generally sensible for a party who wishes to appeal to first seek permission from the lower court.[795] This is usually done when judgment is delivered or handed down and

792 See Example 10.

793 CPR rule 52.3(1).

794 CPR rule 52.6(1).

795 Pursuant to CPR rule 52.3(2)(a); see e.g. *In re T (A Child)* [2002] EWCA Civ 1736 at [12]-[13].

consequential issues, such as the terms of the order giving effect to the judgment and costs, are decided.[796]

If the lower court refuses permission, or if permission was not sought from it, permission must be sought from the appeal court by filing an Appellant's Notice.[797] Unless the court orders otherwise, the time limit for doing so is "*21 days after the date of the decision of the lower court*".[798] That is a relatively short time limit, which cannot be extended by agreement between the parties,[799] and it must be borne in mind that the period starts to run from the date of the decision of the lower court and not, if later, the date on which consequential matters are decided or the date on which the order giving effect to the decision is approved and sealed.[800] If – as is quite common – the lower court's judgment is circulated to the parties in draft and then formally handed down in the absence of the parties, and a hearing to decide consequential matter is arranged at a later date, the lower court should be asked to direct[801] that the 21-day period will only start to run from the date of the later hearing, rather than from the date on which judgment was handed down.[802]

796 See paragraph 12.91 of the Chancery Guide.

797 CPR rules 52.3(2)(b) and 52.12(1).

798 CPR rule 52.12(2)(b).

799 CPR rule 52.15(2).

800 See e.g. *Sayers v Clarke Walker (A Firm)* [2002] EWCA Civ 645 at [8]-[9] and *Owusu v Jackson* [2002] EWCA Civ 877 at [24]-[27].

801 Pursuant to CPR 52.12(2)(a).

802 See e.g. *Jackson v Marina Homes Ltd* [2007] EWCA Civ 1404 at [8]. This is envisaged by paragraph 12.91 of the Chancery Guide.

Compromise

In some cases it may be possible to compromise a rectification claim after proceedings have been issued.[803] The mechanism by which the compromise should be implemented will inevitably depend on its terms and on the particular circumstances of the case. In most cases, the following will have to be considered:

(a) Whether the compromise has any tax implications and, if so, how these should be addressed.

(b) Whether a court order rectifying the trust instrument is required, and if so whether the court can be asked to make the order by consent without hearing full argument. In *Burford (Fareham) Ltd v Christian Vision*[804] (which involved the rectification of a deed of assignment of warranties) the court held that there is no "*blanket rule that rectification should not be ordered by consent*"[805] and that the question is one of the court's discretion. However, it should be borne in mind that this jurisdiction is exercised sparingly. In this regard, paragraphs 18.23 and 18.24 of the Chancery Guide provide: "*It is not the practice of the court to make an order for rectification by default or by consent or without a hearing save in exceptional cases. In all cases, even if unopposed, the court will not make an order without being satisfied that it is justified by the evidence. The court will therefore wish to scrutinise carefully the changes that are proposed and the reasons for them*".

(c) Whether the court's approval of the compromise is required, which will be the case where one or more of the parties is a minor,[806] an

803 The circumstances in which it may be possible to resolve a rectification issue without the need for court proceedings are considered at 5.2.2 above.

804 [2005] EWHC 2533 (Ch).

805 [2005] EWHC 2533 (Ch) at [7].

806 CPR rule 21.10.

adult who lacks capacity to conduct litigation[807] and/or a party who has been appointed to represent others pursuant to CPR rule 19.9.[808]

Paragraphs 16.36 to 16.41 of the Chancery Guide contain guidance in relation to consent orders.

807 *Ibid.*

808 CPR rule 19.9(5).

CHAPTER SIX

MISTAKE AND HASTINGS-BASS

When dealing with a voluntary lifetime transaction[809] in which something has gone wrong, it is usually worth considering whether the doctrine of mistake and/or the so-called 'rule in *Re Hastings-Bass*' can assist.[810] These doctrines are different from construction and rectification, both in their nature and as regards the remedy they can lead to. This chapter provides a summary overview of the two doctrines and of their interplay with construction and rectification.

6.1 Mistake

The law

The doctrine of equitable mistake has regained popularity following *Pitt v Holt*.[811] In that case the Supreme Court adopted the approach of the Court of Appeal and the House of Lords in *Ogilvie v Littleboy*,[812] a case which was described as having "*emerged from the shadows [...] after a century of obscurity*".[813]

---

809 The doctrine of mistake and *Hastings-Bass* discussed in chapter cannot be invoked to address a drafting problem in a will.

810 Other possible vitiating factors which might also need to be considered include lack of capacity, fraud, misrepresentation, duress and/or undue influence. These are outside the scope of this book.

811 [2013] UKSC 26.

812 (1897) 13 TLR 399 and (1899) 15 TLR 294.

813 *Pitt v Holt* [2013] UKSC 26 at [12].

The applicable principles which emerge from *Pitt v Holt*[814] have been summarised as follows:[815]

> *(1) a donor can rescind a gift by showing that he acted under some mistake of so serious a character as to render it unjust on the part of the donee to retain the gift: [101], quoting Ogilvie v Littleboy (1897) 13 TLR 399 at 400;*
>
> *(2) a mistake is to be distinguished from mere inadvertence or misprediction: [104];*
>
> *(3) forgetfulness, inadvertence or ignorance are not, as such, a mistake but can lead to a false belief or assumption which the law will recognise as a mistake: [105];*
>
> *(4) it does not matter that the mistake was due to carelessness on the part of the person making the voluntary disposition unless the circumstances are such as to show that he deliberately ran the risk, or must be taken to have run the risk, of being wrong: [114];*

814 [2013] UKSC 26.

815 In *Van der Merwe v Goldman* [2016] EWHC 790 (Ch) at [26]. The references in square brackets are to paragraph numbers of the decision in *Pitt v Holt*. This summary was adopted in *Smith v Stanley* [2019] EWHC 2168 (Ch) at [62]-[63], *Re Clarke* [2019] EWHC 1193 and 1194 (Ch) at [103] and *Bhaur v Equity First Trustees (Nevis) Ltd* [2021] EWHC 2581 (Ch) at [104]. See also the similar 4-point summary in *Kennedy v Kennedy* [2014] EWHC 4129 (Ch) at [36], which was adopted in *Freedman v Freedman* [2015] EWHC 1457 (Ch) at [16], *South Downs Trustees Ltd v GH* [2018] EWHC 1064 (Ch) at [33], *Hartogs v Sequent (Schweiz) AG* [2019] EWHC 1915 (Ch) at [19], *Rogge v Rogge* [2019] EWHC 1949 (Ch) at [43], *Mackay v Wesley* [2020] EWHC 1215 (Ch) at [135], *Carroll v Carroll* [2020] EWHC 3924 (Ch) at [48], *Abadir v Credit Suisse Trust Ltd* [2021] EWHC 2573 (Ch) at [10], *Bhaur v Equity First Trustees (Nevis) Ltd* [2021] EWHC 2581 (Ch) at [102], *JCT Employer Ser Trustees Ltd v Khadem* [2021] EWHC 2929 (Ch)at [32] and *Hopes v Burton* [2022] EWHC 2770 (Ch) at [33].

(5) equity requires the gravity of the mistake to be assessed in terms of injustice or unconscionability: [124];

(6) the evaluation of unconscionability is objective: [125];

(7) the gravity of the mistake must be assessed by a close examination of the facts which include the circumstances of the mistake and its consequences for the party making the mistaken disposition: [126];

(8) the court needs to focus intensely on the facts of the particular case: [126];

(9) a mistake about the tax consequences of a transaction can be a relevant mistake: [129]-[132];

(10) where the relevant mistake is a mistake about the tax consequences of a transaction, then:

> *"[i]n some cases of artificial tax avoidance, the court might think it right to refuse relief, either on the ground that such claimants, acting on supposedly expert advice, must be taken to have accepted the risk that the scheme would prove ineffective, or on the ground that discretionary relief should be refused on grounds of public policy." [135];*

(11) it is not pointless, nor is it acting in vain, to set aside a transaction and to remove a liability to pay tax, even where that is the principal, or the only, effect of the setting aside: [136]-[141]."

The remedy

If the court is satisfied that a relevant type of mistake has occurred, this renders the transaction voidable in equity (not void at law).[816] The remedy is usually rescission, i.e. the setting aside or undoing of the

816 *Kennedy v Kennedy* [2014] EWHC 4129 (Ch) at [41].

transaction.[817] The remedy is discretionary and the court has to consider whether it should in fact be granted. In doing so it will take into account factors such as any delay in bringing the claim and any rights any third party may have acquired.[818]

If the court rescinds the transaction, it is treated as never having taken place.[819] In the case of voluntary dispositions, the court may rescind a transaction in part and notwithstanding that restitution is impossible.[820]

The interplay with construction and rectification

As the above outline shows, mistake is fundamentally different from construction and rectification. Construction involves asking the court to clarify the terms of the transaction. Rectification involves asking the court to correct a mistake in the way in which the transaction has been recorded (as opposed to a mistake in the transaction itself).[821] Both can affect the consequences of the transaction, including its tax consequences, but in both the hoped-for outcome is one in which the transaction continues to stand, but its terms (and thus potentially its consequences) are clarified and/or corrected.

On the other hand, mistake involves asking the court to set aside the

817 See e.g. *Pitt v Holt* [2013] UKSC 26 at [130] and *Payne v Tyler* [2019] EWHC 2347 (Ch) at [33].

818 See e.g. *Bainbridge v Bainbridge* [2016] EWHC 898 (Ch) at [20].

819 See e.g. *Pitt v Holt* [2013] UKSC 26 at [130] ("*if a transaction is set aside the Court is in effect deciding that a transaction of the specified description is not to be treated as having occurred*") and *Bainbridge v Bainbridge* [2016] EWHC 898 (Ch) at [37] ("*the effect of an equitable rescission for mistake is to undo the transaction from the beginning. It is thereafter treated for the purposes of the general law as if it never took place*").

820 See e.g. *Kennedy v Kennedy* [2014] EWHC 4129 (Ch) at [46], *Bainbridge v Bainbridge* [2016] EWHC 898 (Ch) at [21]-[22] and *Rogge v Rogge* [2019] EWHC 1949 (Ch) at [167]-[168].

821 See e.g. *Racal Group Services Ltd v Ashmore* [1995] STC 1151 at 1154h.

transaction altogether because it was entered into as a result of the mistake. The hoped-for outcome is one in which the transaction is rescinded, i.e. treated as if it had never happened.

In most situations it is likely that the factual circumstances will mean that it is only desirable to seek either construction/rectification or mistake, but not both. For instance, in general terms where the intention was to carry out a transaction at a particular time, rescinding it is unlikely to be desirable. This is the case for example with transactions which are intended to be potentially exempt transfers ("PET") for inheritance tax purposes, which must be made a sufficient number of years[822] prior to the donor's death to achieve a tax advantage, and with deeds varying the devolution of an estate, which must be made within 2 years of the deceased's death in order to be 'read back' for inheritance tax and capital gains tax purposes.[823] With these sorts of transactions, if a mistake comes to light some time – perhaps several years – after the transaction, then rescinding the transaction altogether is unlikely to be desirable. In the case of the former, the donor's death will now inevitably be some years closer or may even have already happened, so it will be undesirable or impossible to rescind the original transaction and make a new PET.[824] In the case of the latter, the 2-year period may have expired by the time the mistake comes to light, and it will therefore be impossible to rescind the

822 At least 3 and preferably more than 7.

823 See section 142 of the Inheritance Tax Act 1984 and section 62 of the Taxation of Chargeable Gains Act 1992.

824 See e.g. *Allnutt v Wilding* [2007] EWCA Civ 412, in which the Court of Appeal expressly acknowledged this point at [8]: "*The trustees here do not ask this court to set aside the settlement on the grounds that a mistake was made by the settlor in executing a discretionary settlement instead of an interest in possession settlement. This is not surprising. The effect of setting aside this settlement would be that the funds would then form part of the settlor's estate and would be liable to inheritance tax. It is, of course, impossible for any new settlement to be executed, which would have the tax advantages that the settlor and his advisers hoped to achieve*".

original deed of variation and make a new one.[825] In these sorts of cases, the hope will be to remedy the error through construction and/or rectification.

On the other hand, following *Pitt v Holt* the doctrine of mistake is often invoked where the transaction has led to unexpected tax consequences.[826] In such cases, the construction of the relevant instrument will often be clear (so a construction claim will not be necessary or appropriate) and it will not be possible to argue that there is a mistake in the way in which the transaction has been recorded – particularly where the donor/settlor has acted on professional advice and the documentation giving effect to the transaction is clear and accords with the advice (but the problem is the advice is wrong). Instead, in these sorts of cases, the hope will be to remedy the error by setting aside the transaction altogether on the basis of mistake.

In certain particular factual circumstances, it may be desirable to argue construction and/or rectification and mistake in the alternative. This might be, for example, where the argument would run along the following lines: the transaction should be construed in way X; alternatively, the documents recording it should be rectified so as to record X. However, if that is not possible as a matter of construction or rectification, and the court concludes that instead of being X the transaction is in fact Y, then the transaction was entered into as a result of a mistake and should be rescinded.

---

825 See e.g. *Ashcroft v Barnsdale* [2010] EWHC 1948 (Ch), *Vallings v Gibbon* [2013] EWHC 2862 (Ch), *Giles v Royal National Institute for the Blind* [2014] EWHC 1373 (Ch) and *Vaughan-Jones v Vaughan-Jones* [2015] EWHC 1086 (Ch).

826 See e.g. *Pitt v Holt* [2013] UKSC 26 itself, *Freedman v Freedman* [2015] EWHC 1457 (Ch), *Van der Merwe v Goldman* [2016] EWHC 790 (Ch), *Smith v Stanley* [2019] EWHC 2168 (Ch), *Hartogs v Sequent (Schweiz) AG* [2019] EWHC 1915 (Ch) and *Payne v Tyler* [2019] EWHC 2347 (Ch).

6.2 *Hastings-Bass*

The law

Until *Pitt v Holt*[827] it seemed that the so-called 'rule in *Re Hastings-Bass*'[828] had developed into a powerful weapon which allowed trustees and other fiduciaries[829] to unravel a transaction which had unexpected consequences (often fiscal). One of its best-known formulations came from *Sieff v Fox*:[830]

Where trustees act under a discretion given to them by the terms of the trust, in circumstances in which they are free to decide whether or not to exercise that discretion, but the effect of the exercise is different from that which they intended, the court will interfere with their action if it is clear that they would not have acted as they did had they not failed to take into account considerations which they ought to have taken into account, or taken into account consideration which they ought not to have taken into account.

However, in *Pitt v Holt* the Court of Appeal and then the Supreme Court made it clear that the 'rule' had been misunderstood and misapplied, and reformulated it in a much narrower way by requiring that the failure by the trustee to take into account a relevant consideration, or his taking into account an irrelevant consideration, must amount to a breach of fiduciary duty before the rule is engaged.

As a result, all decisions pre-dating *Pitt v Holt* in which the rule in *Re Hastings-Bass* was applied must now be treated with considerable caution. It also seems that in most factual situations in which before *Pitt v Holt*

827 [2013] UKSC 26.

828 The 'rule' derives its name from the Court of Appeal decision in *Re Hastings-Bass* [1975] Ch 25.

829 The 'rule' only applies to trustees or other fiduciaries: see e.g. *Pitt v Holt* [2013] UKSC 26 at [6]. The doctrine of mistake is not restricted in this way.

830 [2005] EWHC 1312 (Ch) at [119].

trustees would have invoked the rule in *Re Hastings-Bass*, the doctrine of mistake is now likely to be invoked instead.[831] The main reason for this is that to rely on mistake it is not necessary to establish that there has been a breach of trust, which is often likely to be difficult where the transaction was entered into following receipt of (incorrect) professional advice.

The remedy

The remedy is similar (if not identical) to that available in relation to mistake. If the court is satisfied that the rule applies, the effect of this is to render the transaction voidable in equity (not void at law).[832] The remedy is usually rescission, i.e. the setting aside or undoing of the transaction.[833] The remedy is discretionary and the court has to consider whether it should in fact be granted. In doing so it will take into account factors such as any delay in bringing the claim and any rights any third party may have acquired.[834]

If the court rescinds the transaction, it is treated as never having taken place.[835] In the case of voluntary dispositions, the court may rescind a transaction in part and notwithstanding that restitution is impossible.[836]

---

831 This is the position in England and Wales. However, several offshore jurisdictions passed legislation to reverse *Pitt v Holt* and enacted what is in effect a statutory rule in *Re Hastings-Bass*.

832 *Pitt v Holt* [2013] UKSC 26 at [93].

833 See e.g. *Pitt v Holt* [2013] UKSC 26 at [130].

834 See e.g. the mistake case of *Bainbridge v Bainbridge* [2016] EWHC 898 (Ch) at [20].

835 See e.g. *Pitt v Holt* [2013] UKSC 26 at [130] ("*if a transaction is set aside the Court is in effect deciding that a transaction of the specified description is not to be treated as having occurred*").

836 See e.g. the mistake cases of *Kennedy v Kennedy* [2014] EWHC 4129 (Ch) at [46], *Bainbridge v Bainbridge* [2016] EWHC 898 (Ch) at [21]-[22] and *Rogge v Rogge* [2019] EWHC 1949 (Ch) at [167]-[168]. The

The interplay with construction and rectification

The interplay between construction and rectification on the one hand and the rule in *Re Hastings-Bass* on the other is very similar (if not identical) to the interplay between construction and rectification and mistake, which is considered at greater length above.

In summary, once again the main point is that the result of a successful construction and/or rectification claim is that the transaction will stand but its terms will be clarified and/or corrected, whereas the result of a successful *Hastings-Bass* claim is that the transaction will be set aside altogether and treated as having never occurred. This is something to be carefully considered when deciding whether to pursue a claim for construction/rectification, or a *Hastings-Bass* claim, or perhaps both.[837]

statements made in those cases appear to be of general application (and not restricted to mistake claims).

837 See e.g. the pre-*Pitt v Holt* case of *Jiggens v Low* [2010] EWHC 1566 (Ch), in which the court set aside a deed of appointment which had had unintended capital gains tax consequences on the basis of *Hastings-Bass*, and therefore considered it unnecessary to decide the alternative claims for construction and/or rectification of the deed (at [19]).

MORE BOOKS BY LAW BRIEF PUBLISHING

A selection of our other titles available now:-

'A Practical Guide to Estate Administration and Crypto Assets' by Richard Marshall
'A Practical Guide to Managing GDPR Data Subject Access Requests – Second Edition' by Patrick O'Kane
'A Practical Guide to Parental Alienation in Private and Public Law Children Cases' by Sam King QC & Frankie Shama
'Contested Heritage – Removing Art from Land and Historic Buildings' by Richard Harwood QC, Catherine Dobson, David Sawtell
'The Limits of Separate Legal Personality: When Those Running a Company Can Be Held Personally Liable for Losses Caused to Third Parties Outside of the Company' by Dr Mike Wilkinson
'A Practical Guide to Transgender Law' by Robin Moira White & Nicola Newbegin
'A Practical Guide to 'Stranded Spouses' in Family Law' by Mani Singh Basi
'A Practical Guide to Residential Freehold Conveyancing' by Lorraine Richardson
'A Practical Guide to Pensions on Divorce for Lawyers' by Bryan Scant
'A Practical Guide to Challenging Sham Marriage Allegations in Immigration Law' by Priya Solanki
'A Practical Guide to Legal Rights in Scotland' by Sarah-Jane Macdonald
'A Practical Guide to New Build Conveyancing' by Paul Sams & Rebecca East
'A Practical Guide to Defending Barristers in Disciplinary Cases' by Marc Beaumont
'A Practical Guide to Inherited Wealth on Divorce' by Hayley Trim
'A Practical Guide to Practice Direction 12J and Domestic Abuse in Private Law Children Proceedings' by Rebecca Cross & Malvika Jaganmohan
'A Practical Guide to Confiscation and Restraint' by Narita Bahra QC, John Carl Townsend, David Winch
'A Practical Guide to the Law of Forests in Scotland' by Philip Buchan
'A Practical Guide to Health and Medical Cases in Immigration Law' by Rebecca Chapman & Miranda Butler

‘A Practical Guide to Bad Character Evidence for Criminal Practitioners by Aparna Rao

‘A Practical Guide to Extradition Law post-Brexit’ by Myles Grandison et al

‘A Practical Guide to Hoarding and Mental Health for Housing Lawyers’ by Rachel Coyle

‘A Practical Guide to Psychiatric Claims in Personal Injury – 2nd Edition’ by Liam Ryan

‘Stephens on Contractual Indemnities’ by Richard Stephens

‘A Practical Guide to the EU Succession Regulation’ by Richard Frimston

‘A Practical Guide to Solicitor and Client Costs – 2nd Edition’ by Robin Dunne

‘Constructive Dismissal – Practice Pointers and Principles’ by Benjimin Burgher

‘A Practical Guide to Religion and Belief Discrimination Claims in the Workplace’ by Kashif Ali

‘A Practical Guide to the Law of Medical Treatment Decisions’ by Ben Troke

‘Fundamental Dishonesty and QOCS in Personal Injury Proceedings: Law and Practice’ by Jake Rowley

‘A Practical Guide to the Law in Relation to School Exclusions’ by Charlotte Hadfield & Alice de Coverley

‘A Practical Guide to Divorce for the Silver Separators’ by Karin Walker

‘The Right to be Forgotten – The Law and Practical Issues’ by Melissa Stock

‘A Practical Guide to Planning Law and Rights of Way in National Parks, the Broads and AONBs’ by James Maurici QC, James Neill et al

‘A Practical Guide to Election Law’ by Tom Tabori

‘A Practical Guide to the Law in Relation to Surrogacy’ by Andrew Powell

‘A Practical Guide to Claims Arising from Fatal Accidents – 2nd Edition’ by James Patience

‘A Practical Guide to the Ownership of Employee Inventions – From Entitlement to Compensation’ by James Tumbridge & Ashley Roughton

‘A Practical Guide to Asbestos Claims’ by Jonathan Owen & Gareth McAloon

‘A Practical Guide to Stamp Duty Land Tax in England and Northern Ireland’ by Suzanne O’Hara

‘A Practical Guide to the Law of Farming Partnerships’ by Philip Whitcomb

‘Covid-19, Homeworking and the Law – The Essential Guide to Employment and GDPR Issues’ by Forbes Solicitors

‘Covid-19 and Criminal Law – The Essential Guide’ by Ramya Nagesh

'Covid-19 and Family Law in England and Wales – The Essential Guide' by Safda Mahmood
'A Practical Guide to the Law of Unlawful Eviction and Harassment – 2nd Edition' by Stephanie Lovegrove
'Covid-19, Brexit and the Law of Commercial Leases – The Essential Guide' by Mark Shelton
'A Practical Guide to Costs in Personal Injury Claims – 2nd Edition' by Matthew Hoe
'A Practical Guide to the General Data Protection Regulation (GDPR) – 2nd Edition' by Keith Markham
'Ellis on Credit Hire – Sixth Edition' by Aidan Ellis & Tim Kevan
'A Practical Guide to Working with Litigants in Person and McKenzie Friends in Family Cases' by Stuart Barlow
'Protecting Unregistered Brands: A Practical Guide to the Law of Passing Off' by Lorna Brazell
'A Practical Guide to Secondary Liability and Joint Enterprise Post-Jogee' by Joanne Cecil & James Mehigan
'A Practical Guide to the Pre-Action RTA Claims Protocol for Personal Injury Lawyers' by Antonia Ford
'A Practical Guide to Neighbour Disputes and the Law' by Alexander Walsh
'A Practical Guide to Forfeiture of Leases' by Mark Shelton
'A Practical Guide to Coercive Control for Legal Practitioners and Victims' by Rachel Horman
'Tackling Disclosure in the Criminal Courts – A Practitioner's Guide' by Narita Bahra QC & Don Ramble
'A Practical Guide to the Law of Driverless Cars – Second Edition' by Alex Glassbrook, Emma Northey & Scarlett Milligan
'A Practical Guide to TOLATA Claims' by Greg Williams
'A Practical Guide to Elderly Law – 2nd Edition' by Justin Patten
'A Practical Guide to Responding to Housing Disrepair and Unfitness Claims' by Iain Wightwick
'A Practical Guide to the Law of Bullying and Harassment in the Workplace' by Philip Hyland
'How to Be a Freelance Solicitor: A Practical Guide to the SRA-Regulated Freelance Solicitor Model' by Paul Bennett
'A Practical Guide to Prison Injury Claims' by Malcolm Johnson

'A Practical Guide to the Small Claims Track – 2nd Edition' by Dominic Bright
'A Practical Guide to Advising Clients at the Police Station' by Colin Stephen McKeown-Beaumont
'A Practical Guide to Antisocial Behaviour Injunctions' by Iain Wightwick
'Practical Mediation: A Guide for Mediators, Advocates, Advisers, Lawyers, and Students in Civil, Commercial, Business, Property, Workplace, and Employment Cases' by Jonathan Dingle with John Sephton
'The Mini-Pupillage Workbook' by David Boyle
'A Practical Guide to Crofting Law' by Brian Inkster
'A Practical Guide to the Law of Domain Names and Cybersquatting' by Andrew Clemson
'A Practical Guide to the Law of Gender Pay Gap Reporting' by Harini Iyengar
'NHS Whistleblowing and the Law' by Joseph England
'Employment Law and the Gig Economy' by Nigel Mackay & Annie Powell
'A Practical Guide to Noise Induced Hearing Loss (NIHL) Claims' by Andrew Mckie, Ian Skeate, Gareth McAloon
'An Introduction to Beauty Negligence Claims – A Practical Guide for the Personal Injury Practitioner' by Greg Almond
'Intercompany Agreements for Transfer Pricing Compliance' by Paul Sutton
'Zen and the Art of Mediation' by Martin Plowman
'A Practical Guide to the SRA Principles, Individual and Law Firm Codes of Conduct 2019 – What Every Law Firm Needs to Know' by Paul Bennett
'A Practical Guide to Adoption for Family Lawyers' by Graham Pegg
'A Practical Guide to Industrial Disease Claims' by Andrew Mckie & Ian Skeate
'A Practical Guide to Redundancy' by Philip Hyland
'A Practical Guide to Vicarious Liability' by Mariel Irvine
'A Practical Guide to Applications for Landlord's Consent and Variation of Leases' by Mark Shelton
'A Practical Guide to Relief from Sanctions Post-Mitchell and Denton' by Peter Causton
'A Practical Guide to Equity Release for Advisors' by Paul Sams
'A Practical Guide to Financial Services Claims' by Chris Hegarty
'The Law of Houses in Multiple Occupation: A Practical Guide to HMO Proceedings' by Julian Hunt

www.ingramcontent.com/pod-product-compliance
Lightning Source LLC
LaVergne TN
LVHW052259200926
848481LV00002B/414
* 9 7 8 1 9 1 6 6 9 8 2 6 0 *